THE SUPERMAN STORY

Written by
MARTIN PASKO
Art by
CURT SWAN · FRANK CHIARAMONTE

TOR

A TOM DOHERTY ASSOCIATES BOOK
NEW YORK

This is a work of fiction. All the characters and events portrayed in this book are fictional, and any resemblance to real people or incidents is purely coincidental.

THE SUPERMAN STORY

Layouts by Bob Rozakis
Edited by Andrew Helfer

A Tor Book
Published by Tom Doherty Associates, LLC
175 Fifth Avenue
New York, NY 10010

www.tor.com

Tor® is a registered trademark of Tom Doherty Associates, LLC.

ISBN 0-812-57742-6
EAN 978-0812-57742-6

First Tor printing: June 1983

Printed in the United States of America

0   9   8   7   6   5

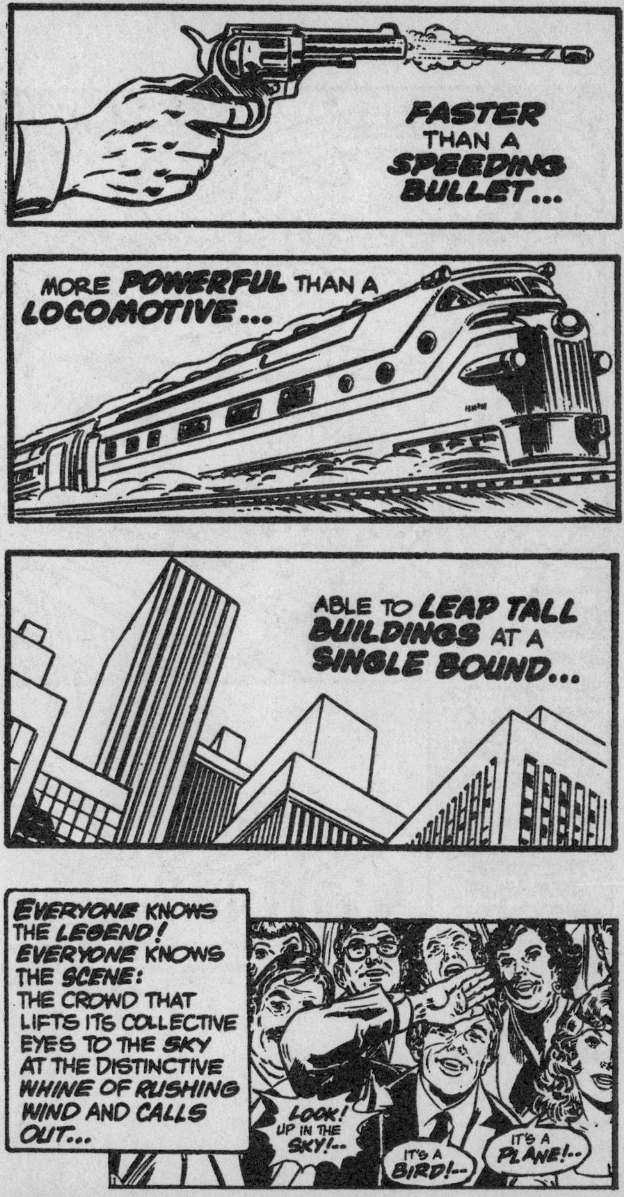
FASTER THAN A SPEEDING BULLET...
MORE POWERFUL THAN A LOCOMOTIVE...
ABLE TO LEAP TALL BUILDINGS AT A SINGLE BOUND...
EVERYONE KNOWS THE LEGEND! EVERYONE KNOWS THE SCENE: THE CROWD THAT LIFTS ITS COLLECTIVE EYES TO THE SKY AT THE DISTINCTIVE WHINE OF RUSHING WIND AND CALLS OUT...
LOOK! UP IN THE SKY!--
IT'S A BIRD!--
IT'S A PLANE!--

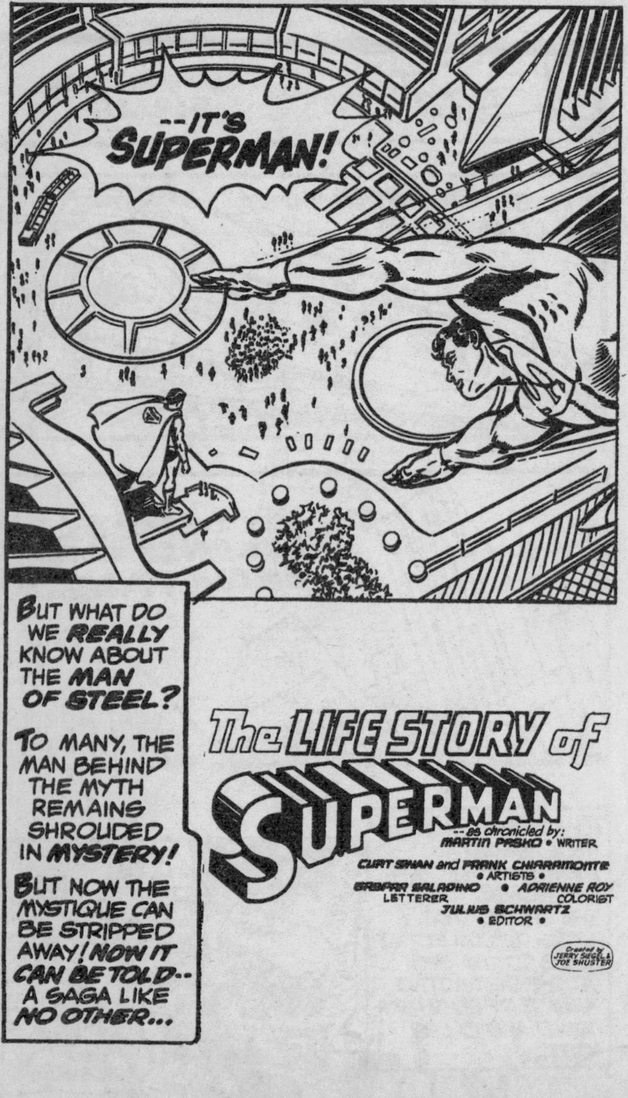
--IT'S SUPERMAN!
BUT WHAT DO WE REALLY KNOW ABOUT THE MAN OF STEEL?
TO MANY, THE MAN BEHIND THE MYTH REMAINS SHROUDED IN MYSTERY!
BUT NOW THE MYSTIQUE CAN BE STRIPPED AWAY! NOW IT CAN BE TOLD-- A SAGA LIKE NO OTHER...
The LIFE STORY of SUPERMAN
--as chronicled by:
MARTIN PASKO • WRITER
CURT SWAN and FRANK CHIARAMONTE
• ARTISTS •
GASPAR SALADINO • ADRIENNE ROY
LETTERER COLORIST
JULIUS SCHWARTZ
• EDITOR •
Created by JERRY SIEGEL & JOE SHUSTER

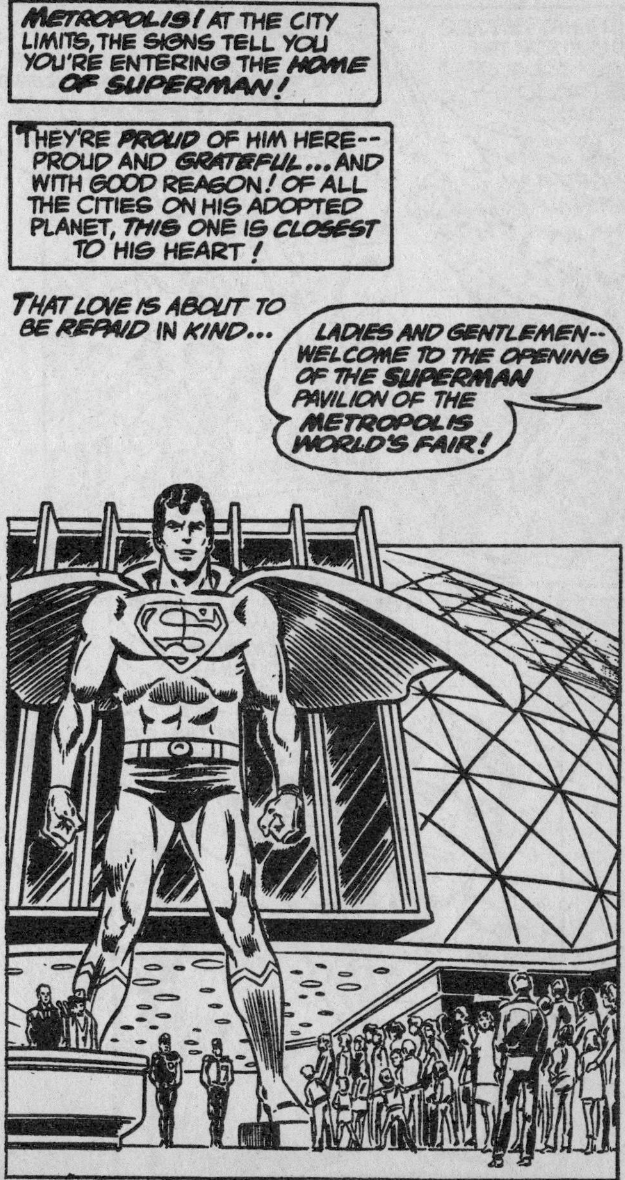
METROPOLIS! AT THE CITY LIMITS, THE SIGNS TELL YOU YOU'RE ENTERING THE HOME OF SUPERMAN!
THEY'RE PROUD OF HIM HERE-- PROUD AND GRATEFUL... AND WITH GOOD REASON! OF ALL THE CITIES ON HIS ADOPTED PLANET, THIS ONE IS CLOSEST TO HIS HEART!
THAT LOVE IS ABOUT TO BE REPAID IN KIND...
LADIES AND GENTLEMEN-- WELCOME TO THE OPENING OF THE SUPERMAN PAVILION OF THE METROPOLIS WORLD'S FAIR!

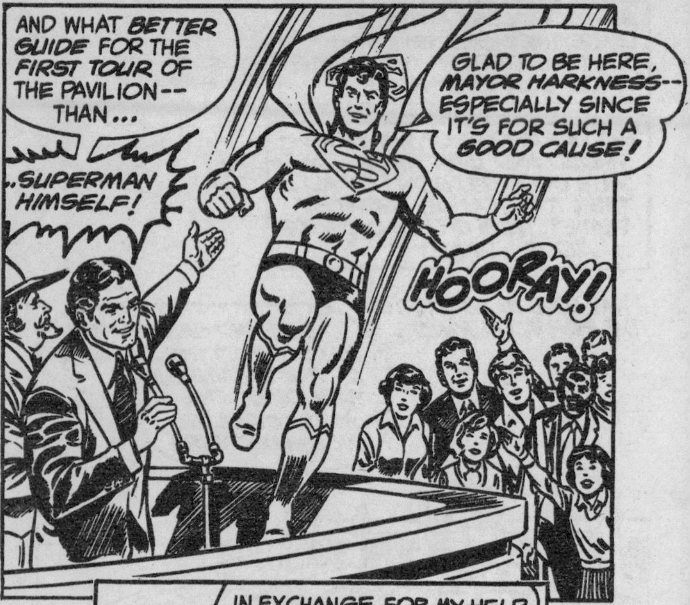
AND WHAT BETTER GUIDE FOR THE FIRST TOUR OF THE PAVILION-- THAN...
...SUPERMAN HIMSELF!
GLAD TO BE HERE, MAYOR HARKNESS-- ESPECIALLY SINCE IT'S FOR SUCH A GOOD CAUSE!
HOORAY!
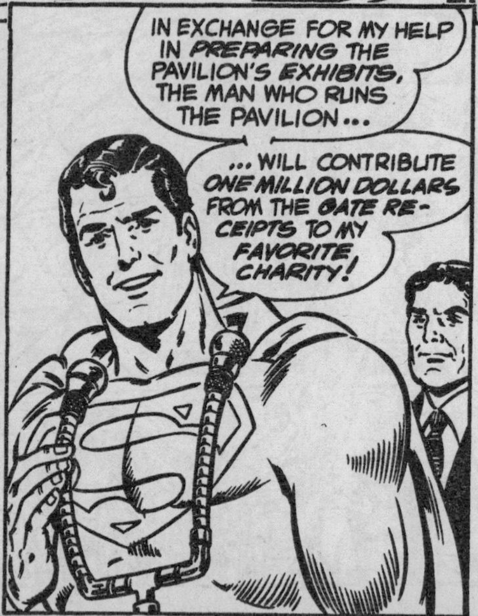
IN EXCHANGE FOR MY HELP IN PREPARING THE PAVILION'S EXHIBITS, THE MAN WHO RUNS THE PAVILION...
...WILL CONTRIBUTE ONE MILLION DOLLARS FROM THE GATE RE-CEIPTS TO MY FAVORITE CHARITY!

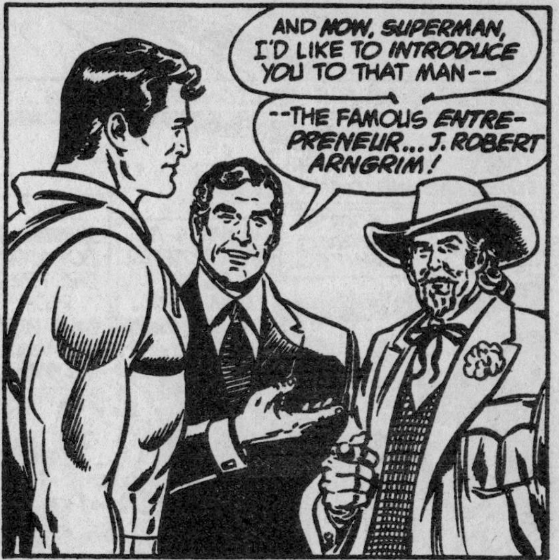
AND NOW, SUPERMAN, I'D LIKE TO INTRODUCE YOU TO THAT MAN--
--THE FAMOUS ENTRE-PRENEUR... J. ROBERT ARNGRIM!

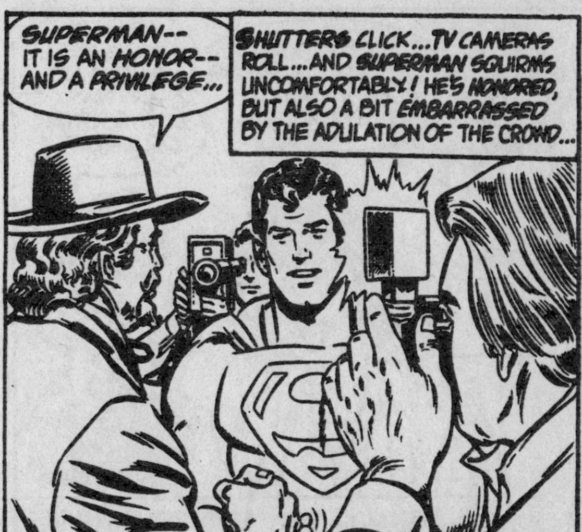
SUPERMAN-- IT IS AN HONOR-- AND A PRIVILEGE...
SHUTTERS CLICK...TV CAMERAS ROLL...AND SUPERMAN SQUIRMS UNCOMFORTABLY! HE'S HONORED, BUT ALSO A BIT EMBARRASSED BY THE ADULATION OF THE CROWD...

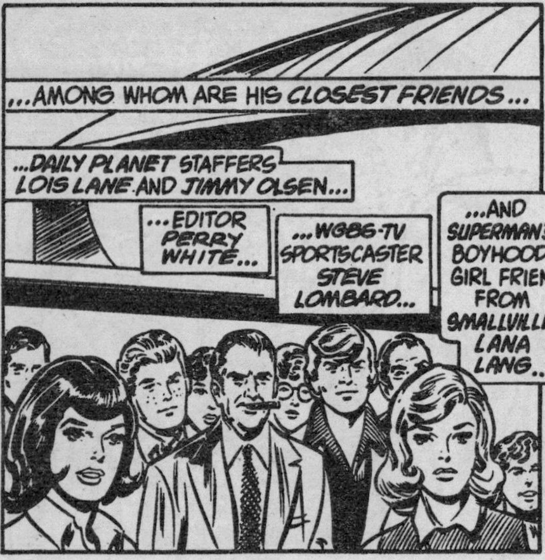
...AMONG WHOM ARE HIS CLOSEST FRIENDS...
...DAILY PLANET STAFFERS LOIS LANE AND JIMMY OLSEN...
...EDITOR PERRY WHITE...
...WGBS-TV SPORTSCASTER STEVE LOMBARD...
...AND SUPERMAN'S BOYHOOD GIRL FRIEND FROM SMALLVILLE--LANA LANG...

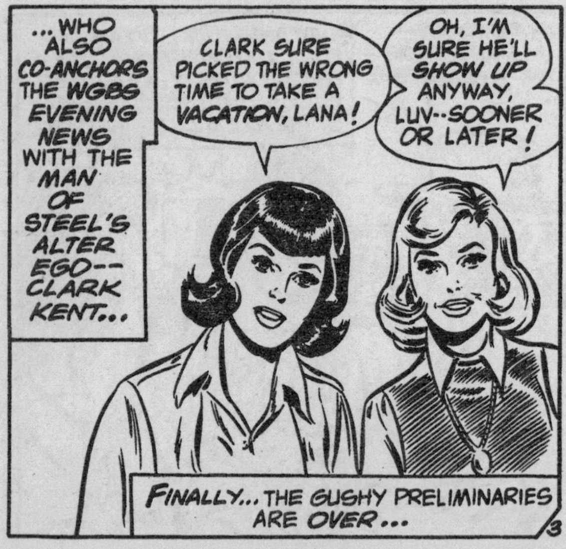
...WHO ALSO CO-ANCHORS THE WGBS EVENING NEWS WITH THE MAN OF STEEL'S ALTER EGO--CLARK KENT...
CLARK SURE PICKED THE WRONG TIME TO TAKE A VACATION, LANA!
OH, I'M SURE HE'LL SHOW UP ANYWAY, LUV--SOONER OR LATER!
FINALLY... THE GUSHY PRELIMINARIES ARE OVER...
3

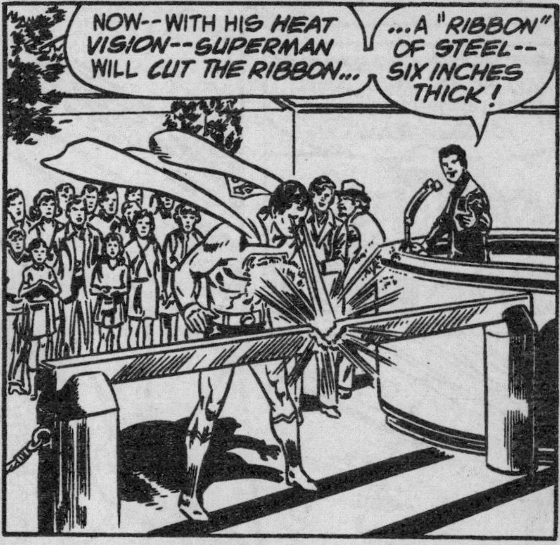
NOW--WITH HIS HEAT VISION--SUPERMAN WILL CUT THE RIBBON...
...A "RIBBON" OF STEEL--SIX INCHES THICK!

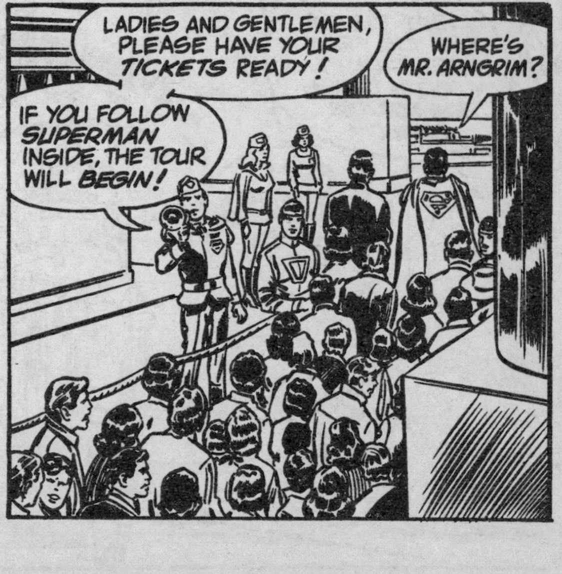
LADIES AND GENTLEMEN, PLEASE HAVE YOUR TICKETS READY!
IF YOU FOLLOW SUPERMAN INSIDE, THE TOUR WILL BEGIN!
WHERE'S MR. ARNGRIM?

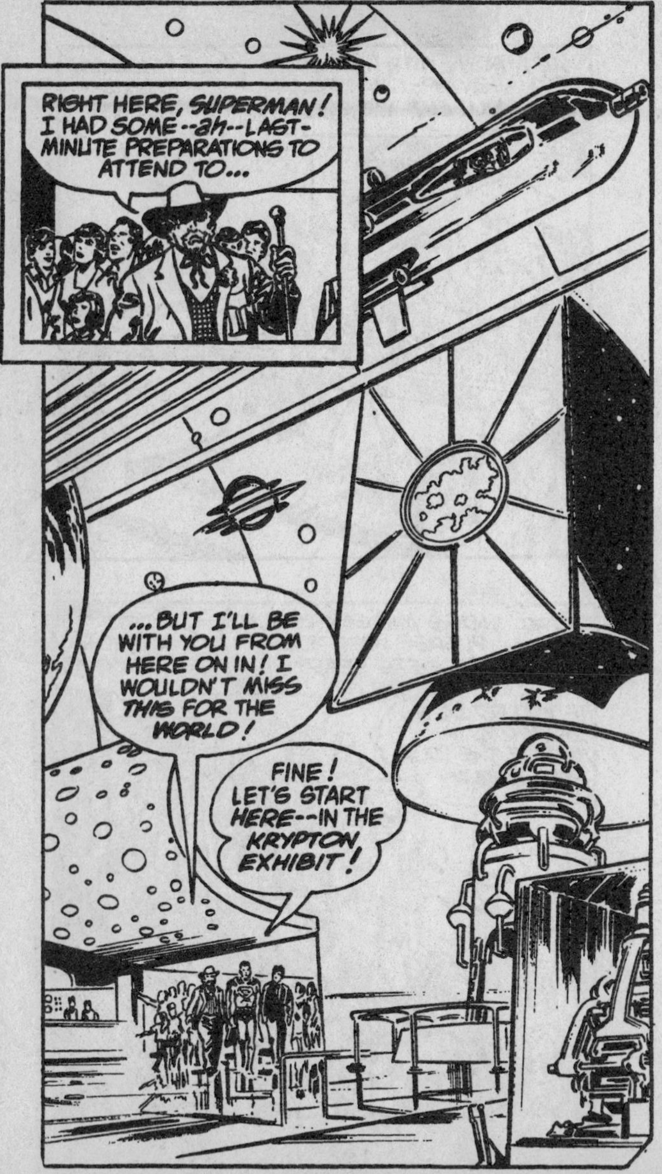
RIGHT HERE, SUPERMAN! I HAD SOME--ah--LAST-MINUTE PREPARATIONS TO ATTEND TO...
...BUT I'LL BE WITH YOU FROM HERE ON IN! I WOULDN'T MISS THIS FOR THE WORLD!
FINE! LET'S START HERE--IN THE KRYPTON EXHIBIT!

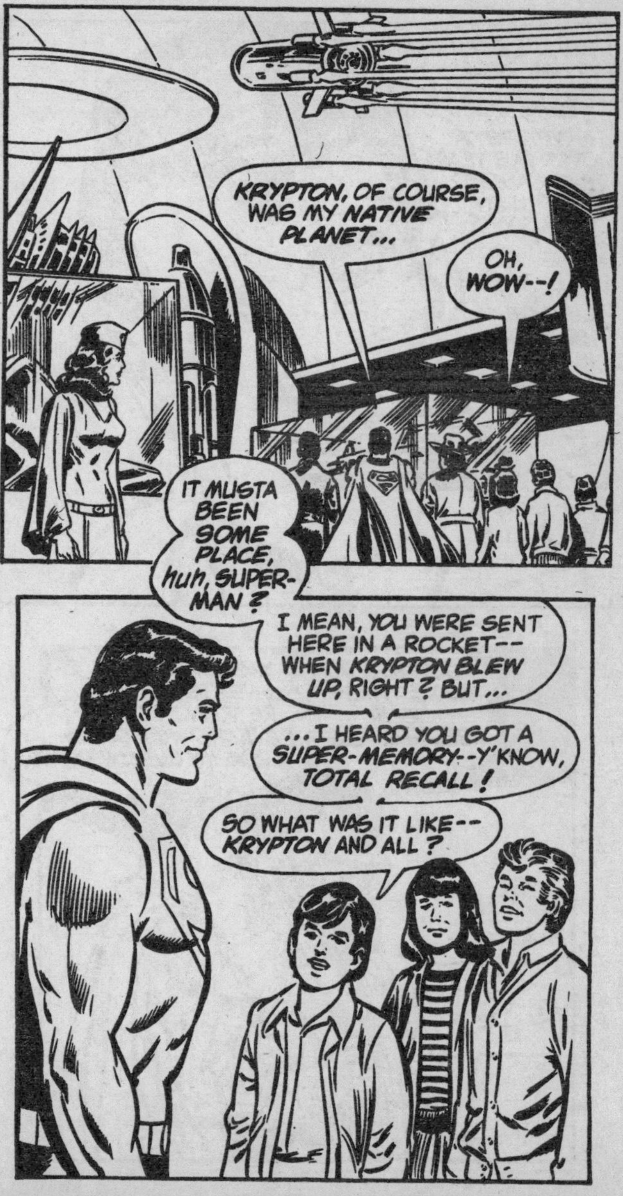
KRYPTON, OF COURSE, WAS MY NATIVE PLANET...
OH, WOW--!
IT MUSTA BEEN SOME PLACE, huh, SUPER-MAN?
I MEAN, YOU WERE SENT HERE IN A ROCKET-- WHEN KRYPTON BLEW UP, RIGHT? BUT...
...I HEARD YOU GOT A SUPER-MEMORY--Y'KNOW, TOTAL RECALL!
SO WHAT WAS IT LIKE-- KRYPTON AND ALL?

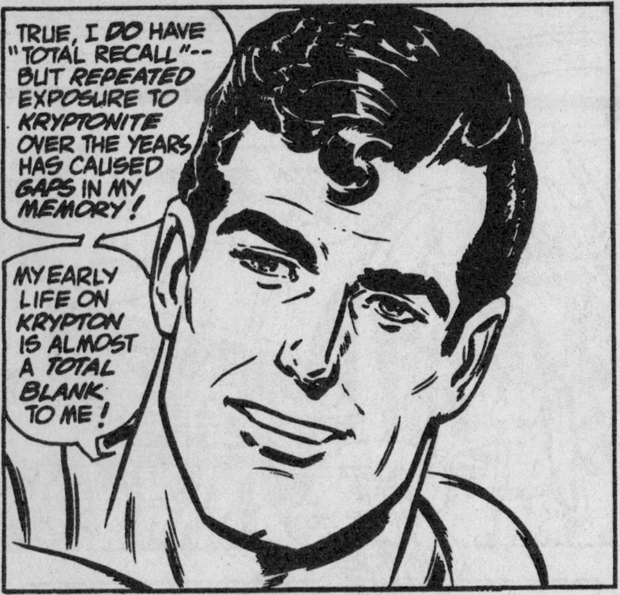
TRUE, I DO HAVE "TOTAL RECALL"-- BUT REPEATED EXPOSURE TO KRYPTONITE OVER THE YEARS HAS CAUSED GAPS IN MY MEMORY!
MY EARLY LIFE ON KRYPTON IS ALMOST A TOTAL BLANK TO ME!

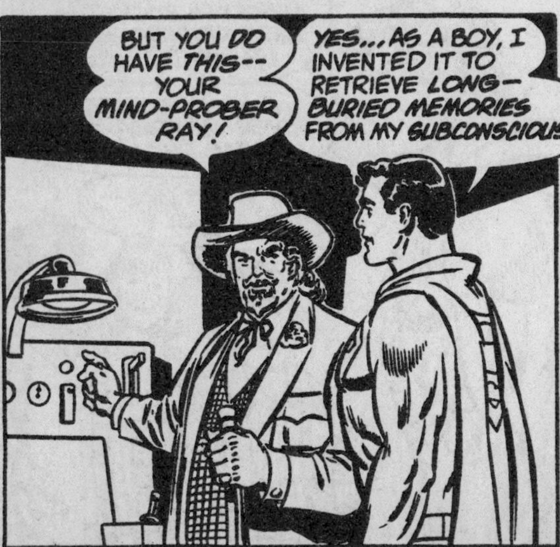
BUT YOU DO HAVE THIS-- YOUR MIND-PROBER RAY!
YES...AS A BOY, I INVENTED IT TO RETRIEVE LONG-BURIED MEMORIES FROM MY SUBCONSCIOUS!

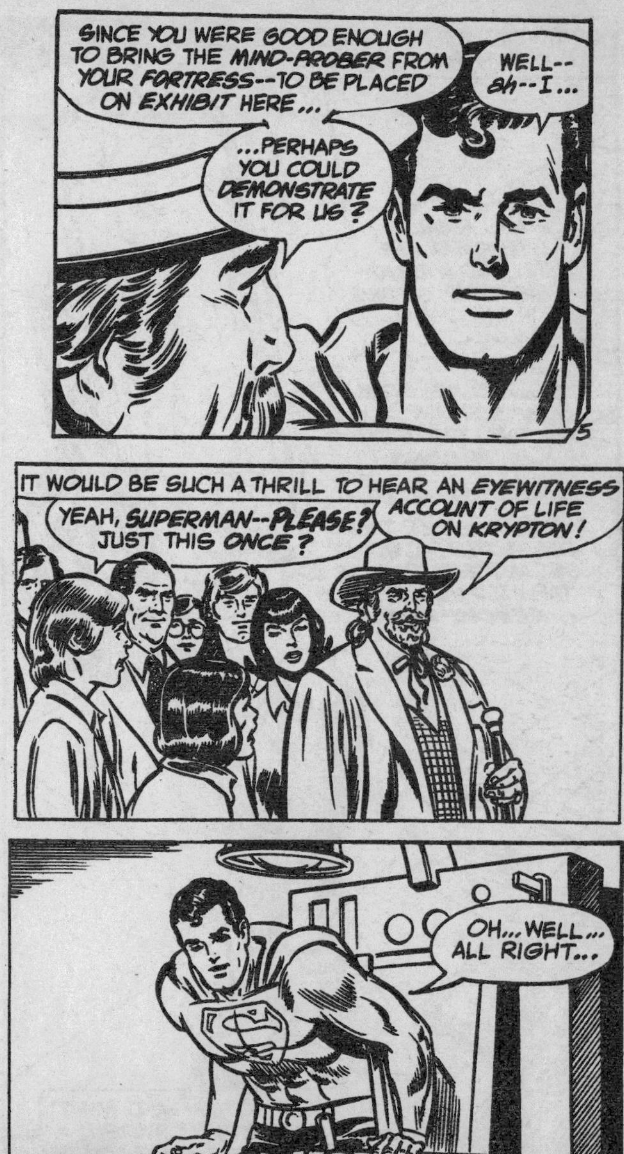
SINCE YOU WERE GOOD ENOUGH TO BRING THE MIND-PROBER FROM YOUR FORTRESS--TO BE PLACED ON EXHIBIT HERE...
...PERHAPS YOU COULD DEMONSTRATE IT FOR US?
WELL--ah--I...
IT WOULD BE SUCH A THRILL TO HEAR AN EYEWITNESS ACCOUNT OF LIFE ON KRYPTON!
YEAH, SUPERMAN--PLEASE? JUST THIS ONCE?
OH... WELL... ALL RIGHT...

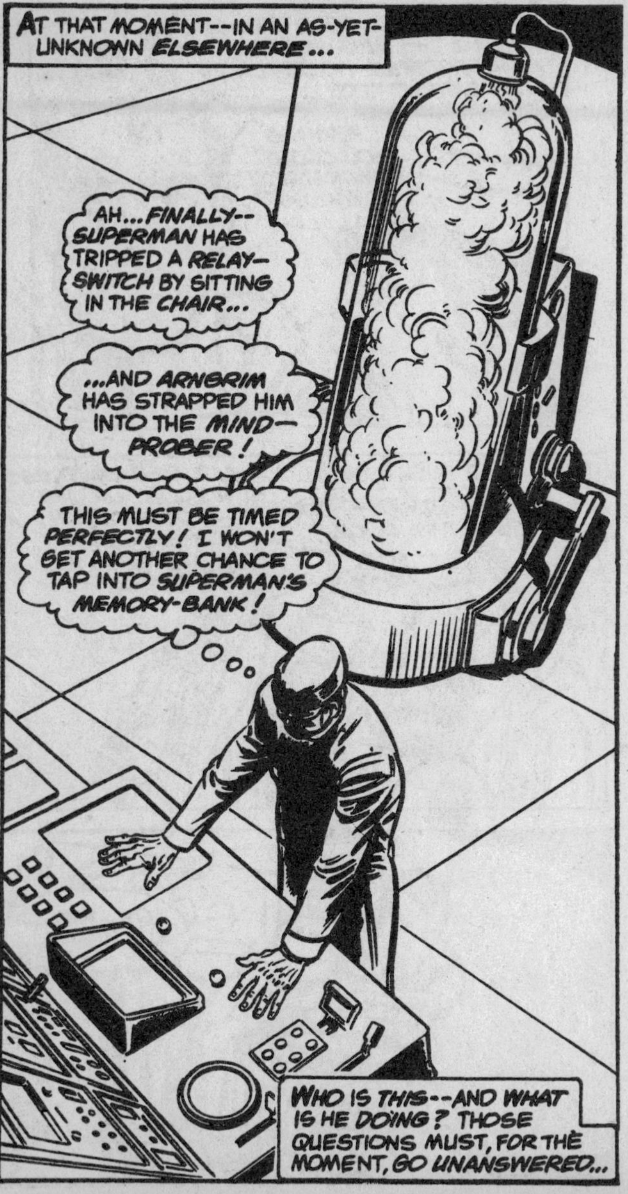
AT THAT MOMENT--IN AN AS-YET-UNKNOWN ELSEWHERE...
AH...FINALLY--SUPERMAN HAS TRIPPED A RELAY-SWITCH BY SITTING IN THE CHAIR...
...AND ARNGRIM HAS STRAPPED HIM INTO THE MIND-PROBER!
THIS MUST BE TIMED PERFECTLY! I WON'T GET ANOTHER CHANCE TO TAP INTO SUPERMAN'S MEMORY-BANK!
WHO IS THIS--AND WHAT IS HE DOING? THOSE QUESTIONS MUST, FOR THE MOMENT, GO UNANSWERED...

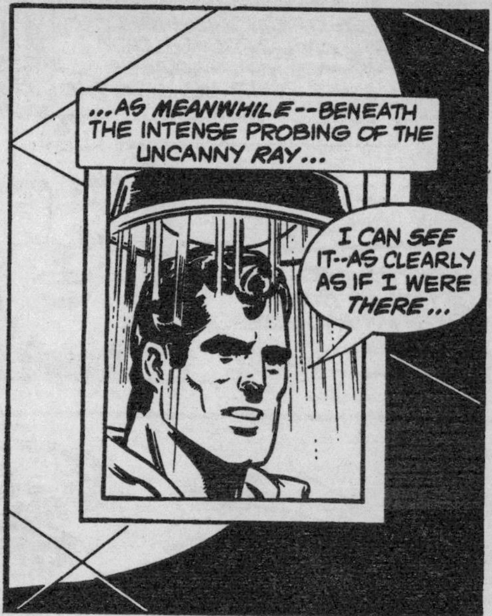
...AS MEANWHILE--BENEATH THE INTENSE PROBING OF THE UNCANNY RAY...
I CAN SEE IT--AS CLEARLY AS IF I WERE THERE...

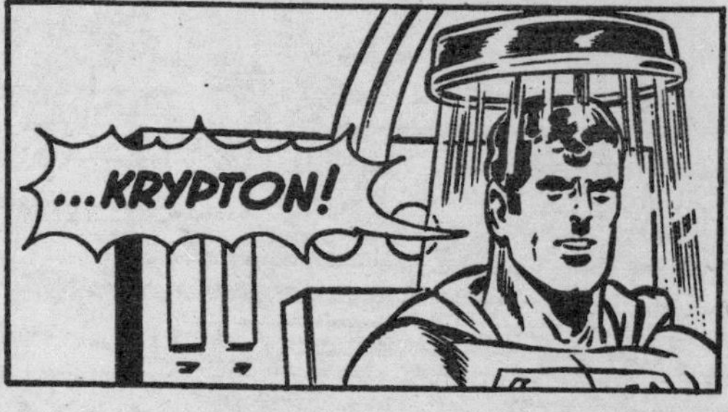
...KRYPTON!

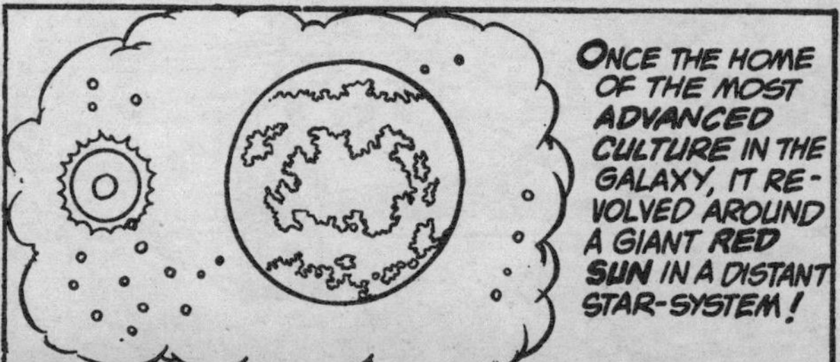
ONCE THE HOME OF THE MOST ADVANCED CULTURE IN THE GALAXY, IT RE-VOLVED AROUND A GIANT RED SUN IN A DISTANT STAR-SYSTEM!

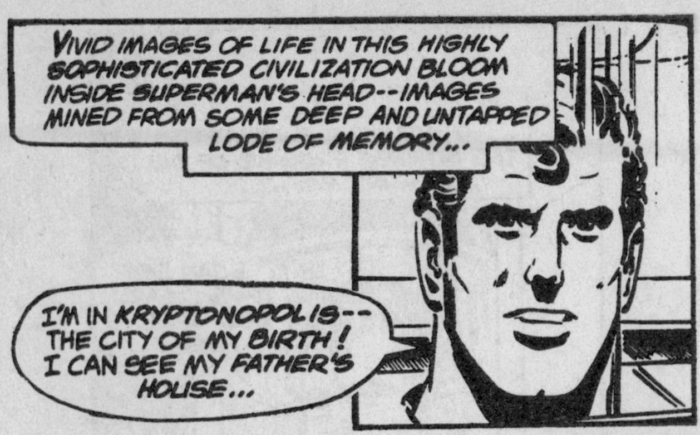
VIVID IMAGES OF LIFE IN THIS HIGHLY SOPHISTICATED CIVILIZATION BLOOM INSIDE SUPERMAN'S HEAD--IMAGES MINED FROM SOME DEEP AND UNTAPPED LODE OF MEMORY...
I'M IN KRYPTONOPOLIS-- THE CITY OF MY BIRTH! I CAN SEE MY FATHER'S HOUSE...

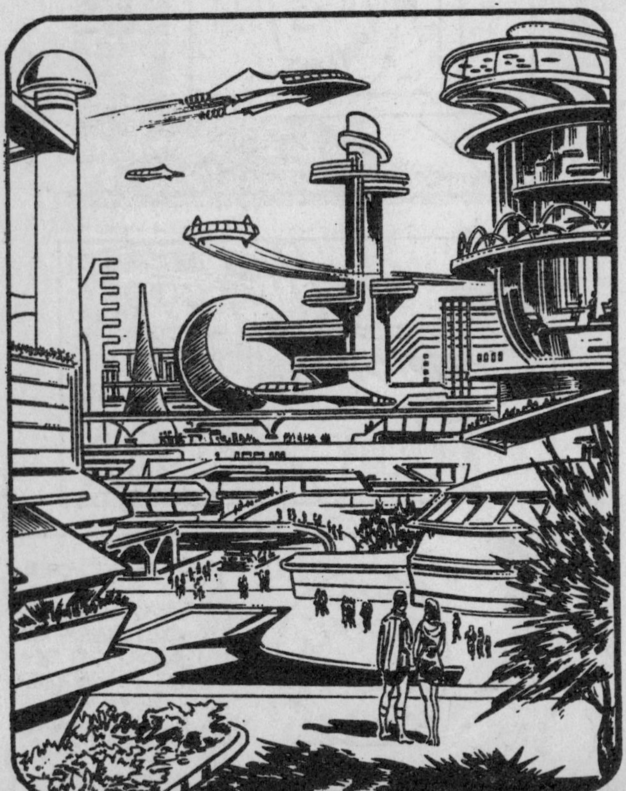

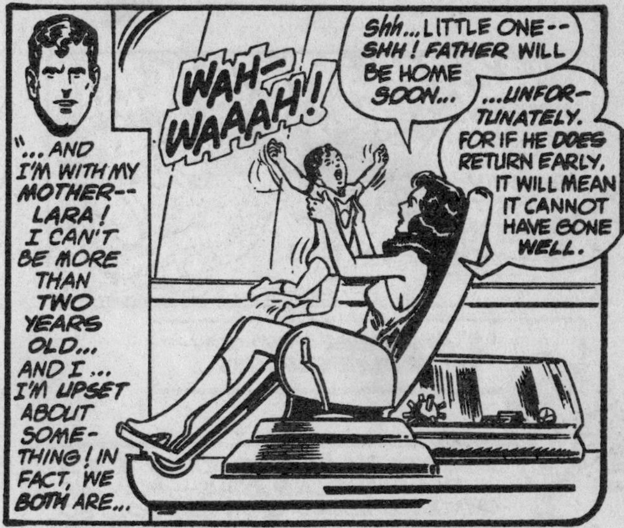
"...AND I'M WITH MY MOTHER-- LARA! I CAN'T BE MORE THAN TWO YEARS OLD... AND I... I'M UPSET ABOUT SOMETHING! IN FACT, WE BOTH ARE...
WAH-WAAAH!
Shh... LITTLE ONE-- SHH! FATHER WILL BE HOME SOON...
...UNFORTUNATELY. FOR IF HE DOES RETURN EARLY, IT WILL MEAN IT CANNOT HAVE GONE WELL.

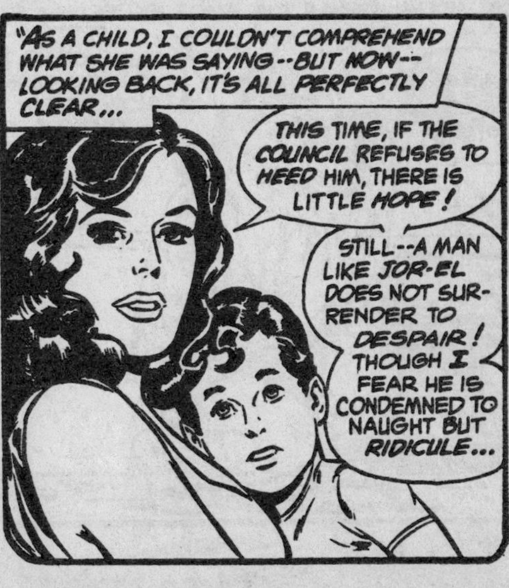
"AS A CHILD, I COULDN'T COMPREHEND WHAT SHE WAS SAYING--BUT NOW-- LOOKING BACK, IT'S ALL PERFECTLY CLEAR...
THIS TIME, IF THE COUNCIL REFUSES TO HEED HIM, THERE IS LITTLE HOPE!
STILL--A MAN LIKE JOR-EL DOES NOT SURRENDER TO DESPAIR! THOUGH I FEAR HE IS CONDEMNED TO NAUGHT BUT RIDICULE...

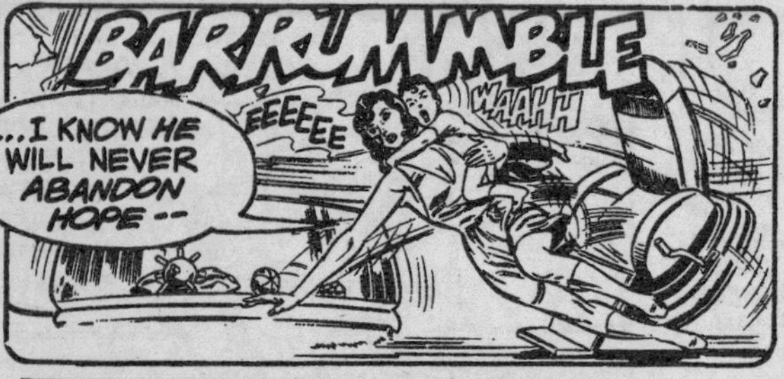
BARRUMMBLE
...I KNOW HE WILL NEVER ABANDON HOPE --
EEEEEEE
WAAHH

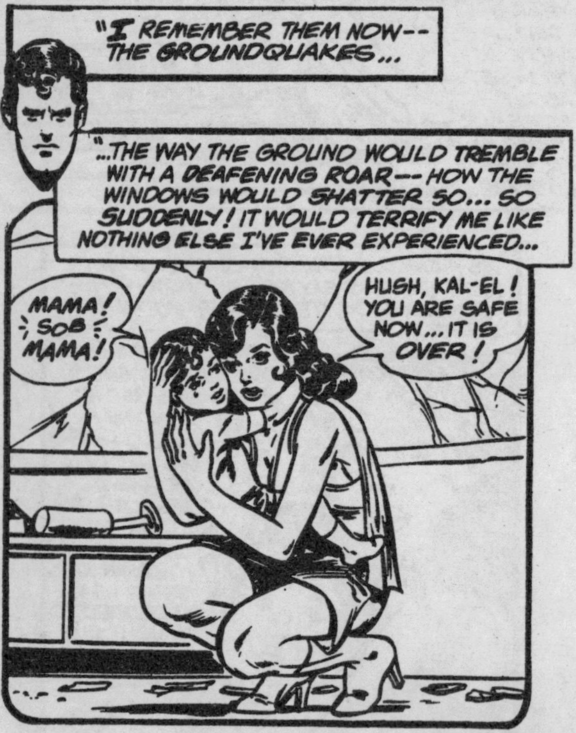
"I REMEMBER THEM NOW-- THE GROUNDQUAKES...
"...THE WAY THE GROUND WOULD TREMBLE WITH A DEAFENING ROAR-- HOW THE WINDOWS WOULD SHATTER SO... SO SUDDENLY! IT WOULD TERRIFY ME LIKE NOTHING ELSE I'VE EVER EXPERIENCED...
MAMA! SOB MAMA!
HUSH, KAL-EL! YOU ARE SAFE NOW... IT IS OVER!

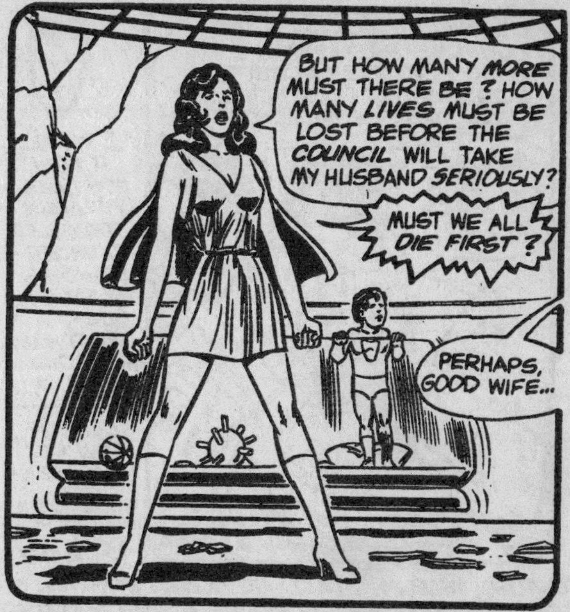
BUT HOW MANY MORE MUST THERE BE ? HOW MANY LIVES MUST BE LOST BEFORE THE COUNCIL WILL TAKE MY HUSBAND SERIOUSLY?
MUST WE ALL DIE FIRST ?
PERHAPS, GOOD WIFE...

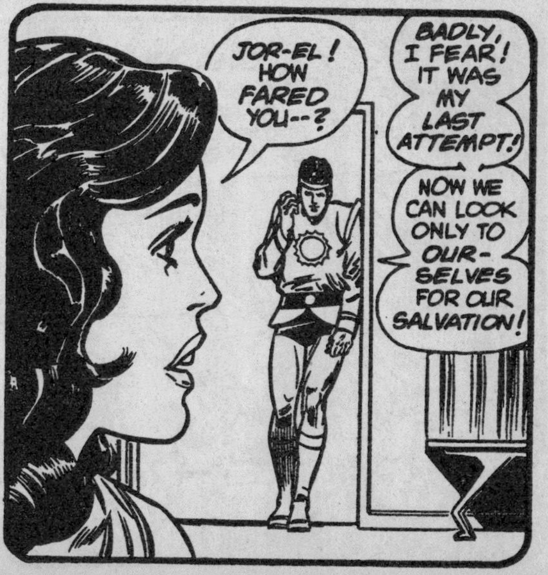
JOR-EL! HOW FARED YOU--?
BADLY, I FEAR! IT WAS MY LAST ATTEMPT!
NOW WE CAN LOOK ONLY TO OUR-SELVES FOR OUR SALVATION!

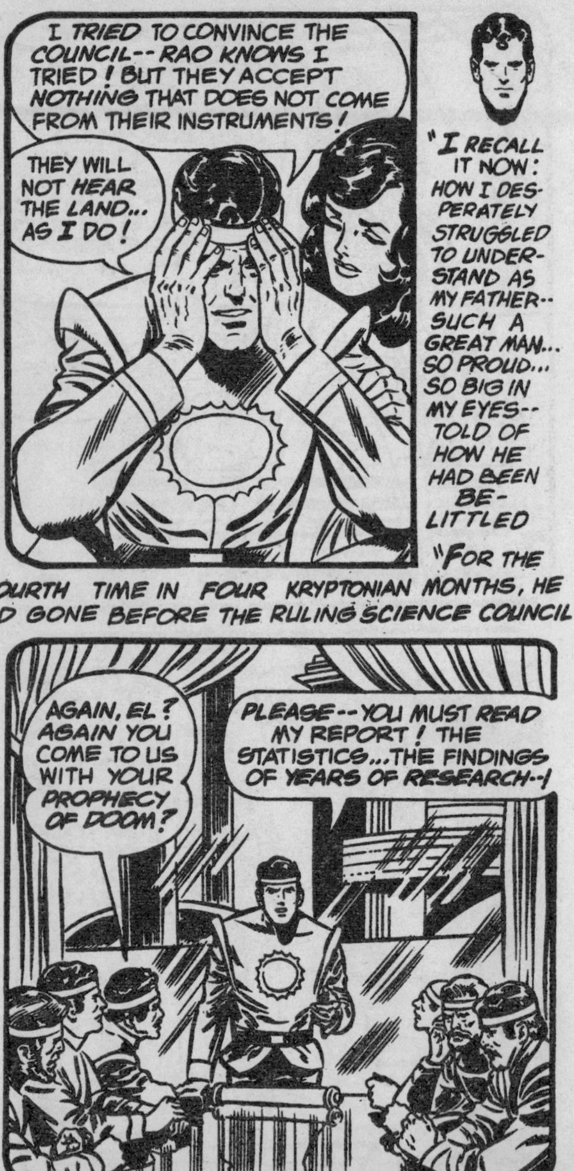
I TRIED TO CONVINCE THE COUNCIL--RAO KNOWS I TRIED! BUT THEY ACCEPT NOTHING THAT DOES NOT COME FROM THEIR INSTRUMENTS!
THEY WILL NOT HEAR THE LAND... AS I DO!
"I RECALL IT NOW: HOW I DESPERATELY STRUGGLED TO UNDERSTAND AS MY FATHER-- SUCH A GREAT MAN... SO PROUD... SO BIG IN MY EYES-- TOLD OF HOW HE HAD BEEN BELITTLED
"FOR THE FOURTH TIME IN FOUR KRYPTONIAN MONTHS, HE HAD GONE BEFORE THE RULING SCIENCE COUNCIL..."
AGAIN, EL? AGAIN YOU COME TO US WITH YOUR PROPHECY OF DOOM?
PLEASE--YOU MUST READ MY REPORT! THE STATISTICS...THE FINDINGS OF YEARS OF RESEARCH--!

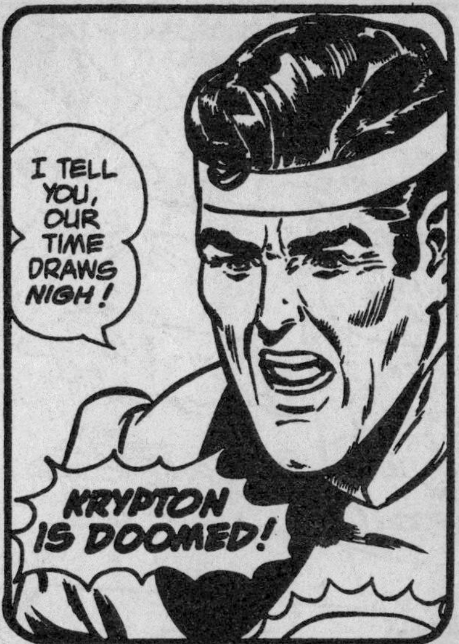
I TELL YOU, OUR TIME DRAWS NIGH!
KRYPTON IS DOOMED!

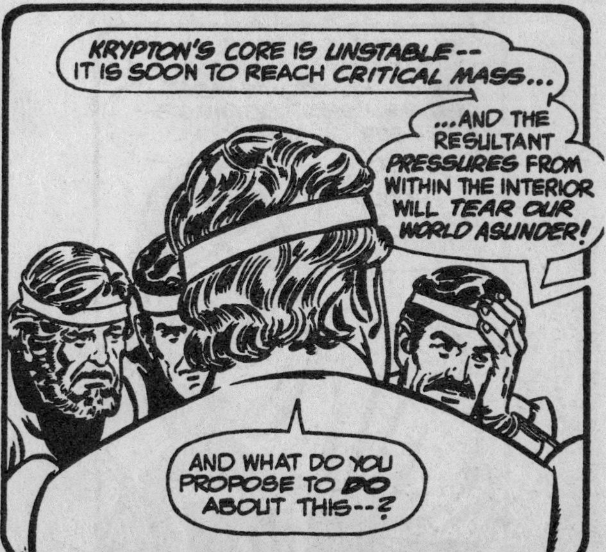
KRYPTON'S CORE IS UNSTABLE-- IT IS SOON TO REACH CRITICAL MASS...
...AND THE RESULTANT PRESSURES FROM WITHIN THE INTERIOR WILL TEAR OUR WORLD ASUNDER!
AND WHAT DO YOU PROPOSE TO DO ABOUT THIS--?

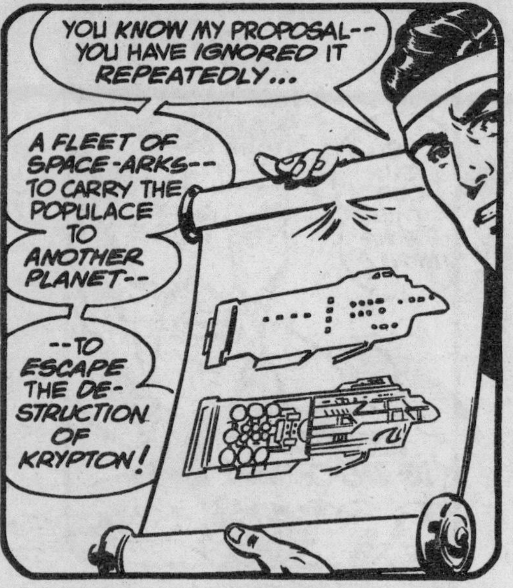
YOU KNOW MY PROPOSAL-- YOU HAVE IGNORED IT REPEATEDLY...
A FLEET OF SPACE-ARKS-- TO CARRY THE POPULACE TO ANOTHER PLANET--
--TO ESCAPE THE DE-STRUCTION OF KRYPTON!

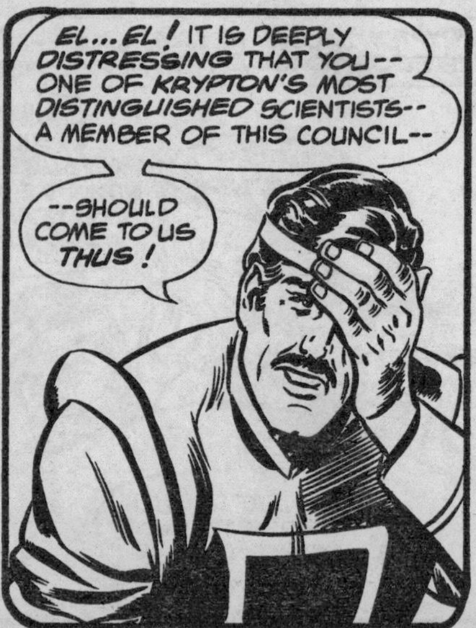
EL...EL! IT IS DEEPLY DISTRESSING THAT YOU-- ONE OF KRYPTON'S MOST DISTINGUISHED SCIENTISTS-- A MEMBER OF THIS COUNCIL--
--SHOULD COME TO US THUS!

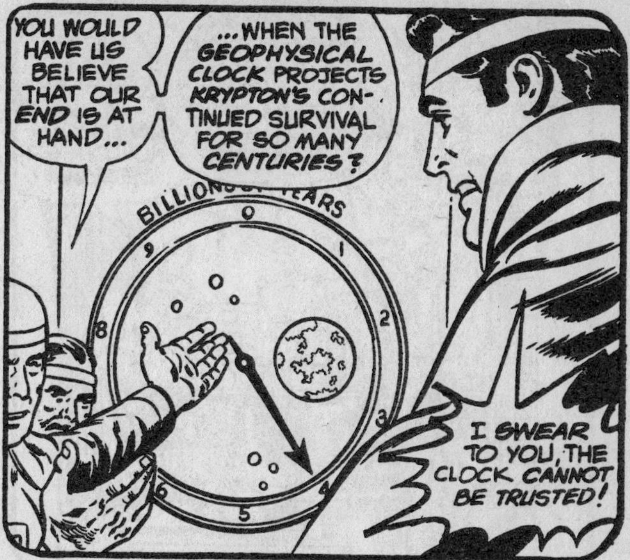
YOU WOULD HAVE US BELIEVE THAT OUR END IS AT HAND...
...WHEN THE GEOPHYSICAL CLOCK PROJECTS KRYPTON'S CONTINUED SURVIVAL FOR SO MANY CENTURIES?
I SWEAR TO YOU, THE CLOCK CANNOT BE TRUSTED!

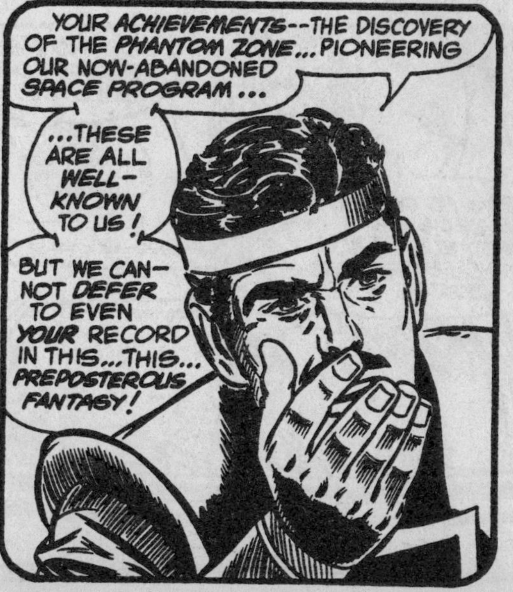
YOUR ACHIEVEMENTS--THE DISCOVERY OF THE PHANTOM ZONE... PIONEERING OUR NOW-ABANDONED SPACE PROGRAM...
...THESE ARE ALL WELL-KNOWN TO US!
BUT WE CANNOT DEFER TO EVEN YOUR RECORD IN THIS... THIS... PREPOSTEROUS FANTASY!

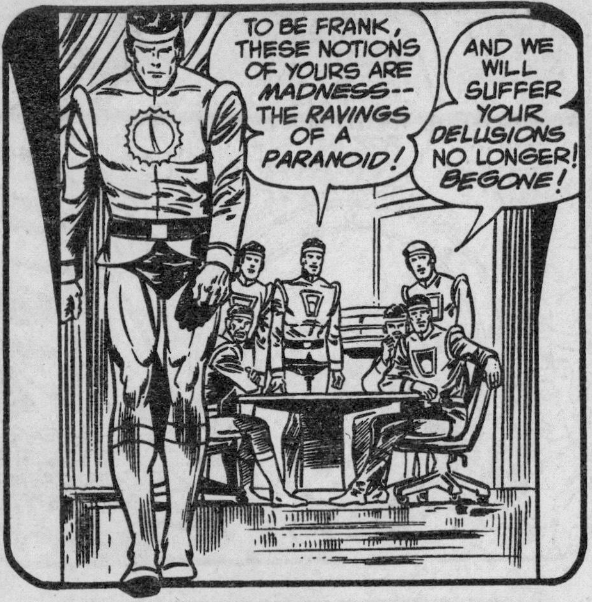
TO BE FRANK, THESE NOTIONS OF YOURS ARE MADNESS-- THE RAVINGS OF A PARANOID!
AND WE WILL SUFFER YOUR DELUSIONS NO LONGER! BEGONE!

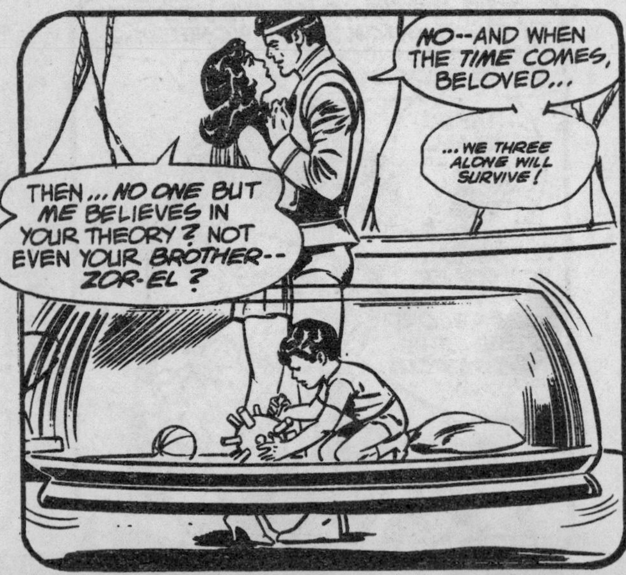
THEN... NO ONE BUT ME BELIEVES IN YOUR THEORY? NOT EVEN YOUR BROTHER-- ZOR-EL?
NO--AND WHEN THE TIME COMES, BELOVED...
...WE THREE ALONE WILL SURVIVE!

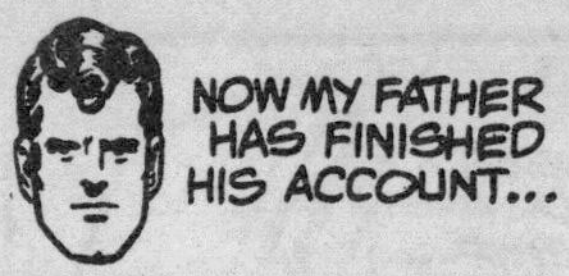
NOW MY FATHER HAS FINISHED HIS ACCOUNT...

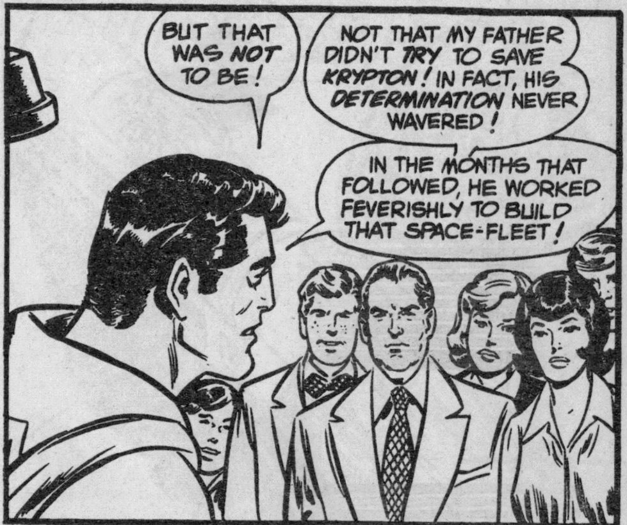
BUT THAT WAS NOT TO BE!
NOT THAT MY FATHER DIDN'T TRY TO SAVE KRYPTON! IN FACT, HIS DETERMINATION NEVER WAVERED!
IN THE MONTHS THAT FOLLOWED, HE WORKED FEVERISHLY TO BUILD THAT SPACE-FLEET!

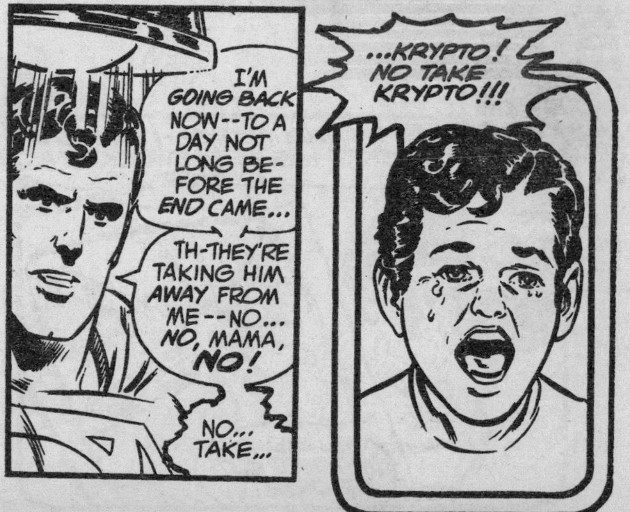
I'M GOING BACK NOW--TO A DAY NOT LONG BEFORE THE END CAME...
TH-THEY'RE TAKING HIM AWAY FROM ME--NO... NO, MAMA, NO!
NO... TAKE...
...KRYPTO! NO TAKE KRYPTO!!!

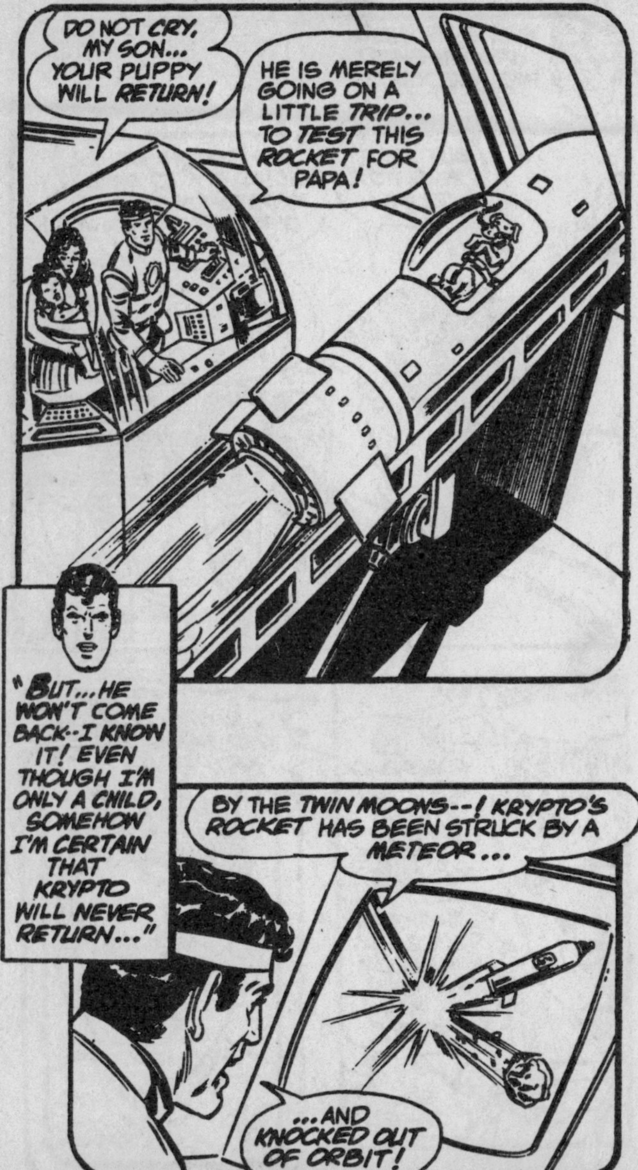
DO NOT CRY, MY SON... YOUR PUPPY WILL RETURN!
HE IS MERELY GOING ON A LITTLE TRIP... TO TEST THIS ROCKET FOR PAPA!
"BUT... HE WON'T COME BACK--I KNOW IT! EVEN THOUGH I'M ONLY A CHILD, SOMEHOW I'M CERTAIN THAT KRYPTO WILL NEVER RETURN..."
BY THE TWIN MOONS--! KRYPTO'S ROCKET HAS BEEN STRUCK BY A METEOR...
...AND KNOCKED OUT OF ORBIT!

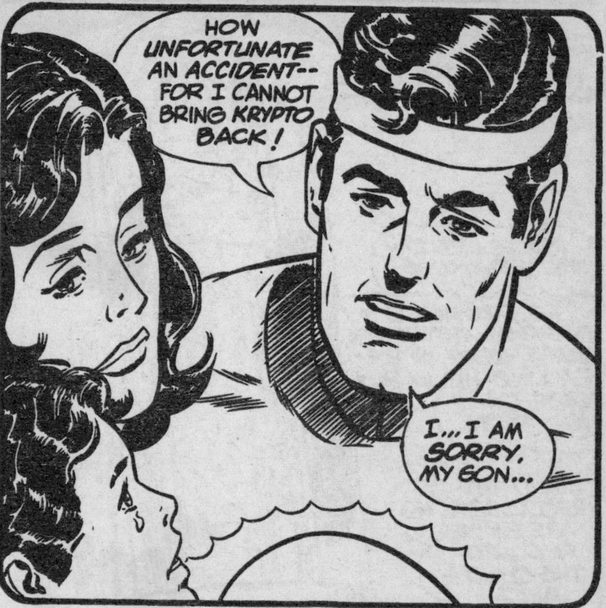
HOW UNFORTUNATE AN ACCIDENT-- FOR I CANNOT BRING KRYPTO BACK!
I... I AM SORRY, MY SON...

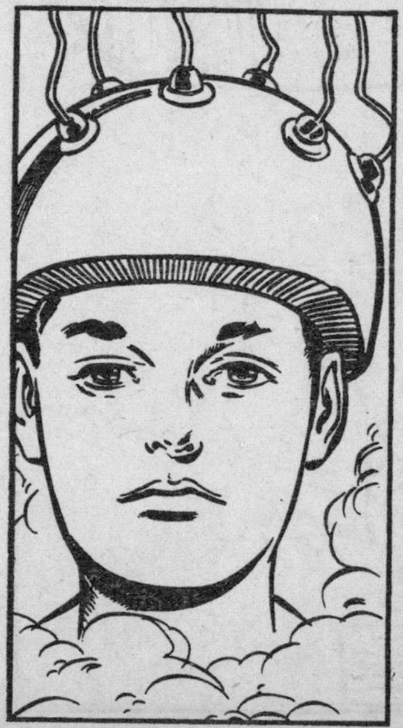

AND AS THE SCENE IS RELIVED IN SUPERMAN'S MIND--AS HE EXPERIENCES THE MOMENT EXACTLY AS HE LIVED IT--A BABY WHO LOOKS ASTONISHINGLY LIKE THE BABY KAL-EL SEEMS TO SHARE THE EXPERIENCE...

...IN THIS UNDERGROUND LABORATORY!

HERE, THE SCENES FROM SUPERMAN'S PAST ARE ALSO RELIVED... BY A CHILD WHO--JUDGING FROM HIS LOOKS--COULD BE SUPERMAN'S YOUNGER BROTHER...

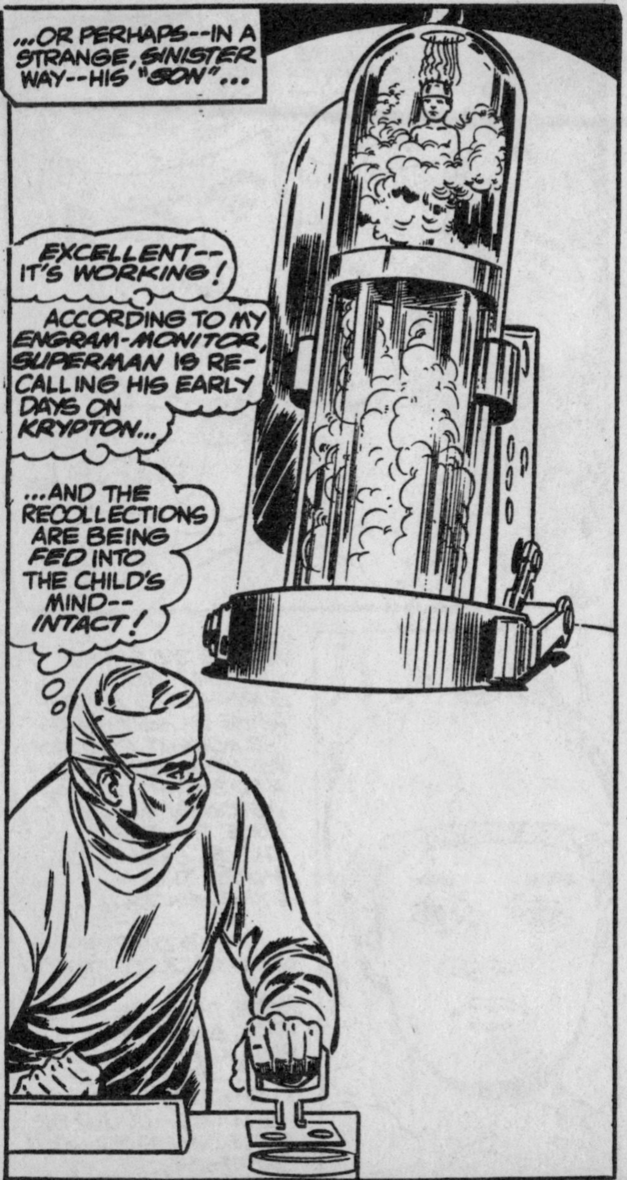
...OR PERHAPS--IN A STRANGE, SINISTER WAY--HIS "SON"...
EXCELLENT--IT'S WORKING!
ACCORDING TO MY ENGRAM-MONITOR, SUPERMAN IS RE-CALLING HIS EARLY DAYS ON KRYPTON...
...AND THE RECOLLECTIONS ARE BEING FED INTO THE CHILD'S MIND--INTACT!

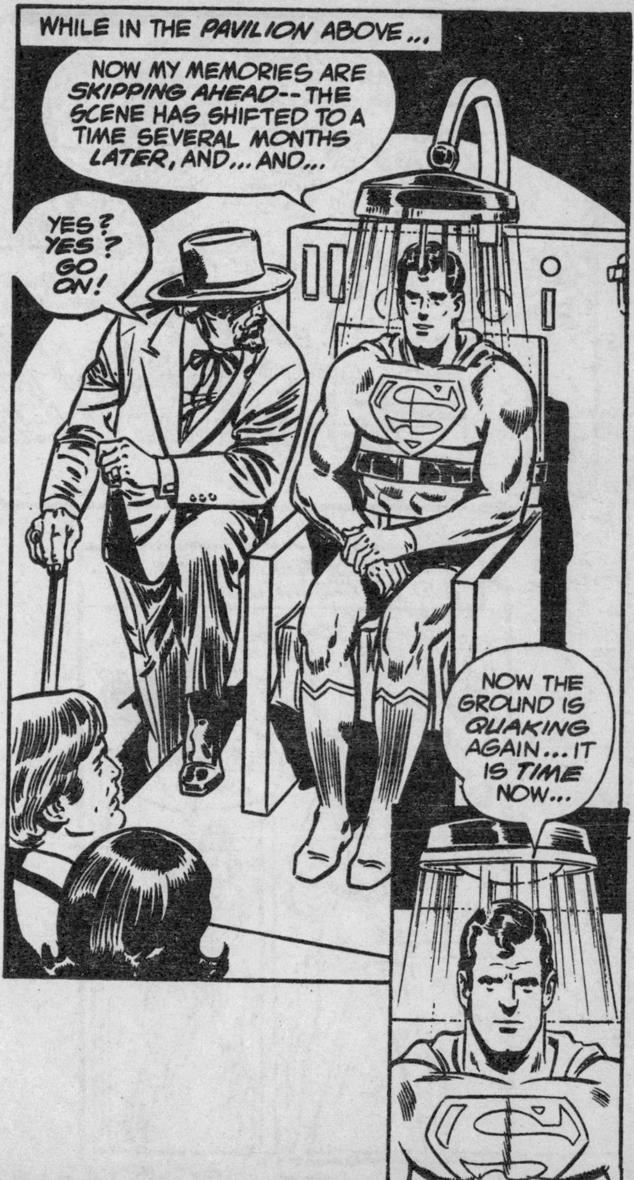
WHILE IN THE PAVILION ABOVE...
NOW MY MEMORIES ARE SKIPPING AHEAD-- THE SCENE HAS SHIFTED TO A TIME SEVERAL MONTHS LATER, AND... AND...
YES? YES? GO ON!
NOW THE GROUND IS QUAKING AGAIN... IT IS TIME NOW...

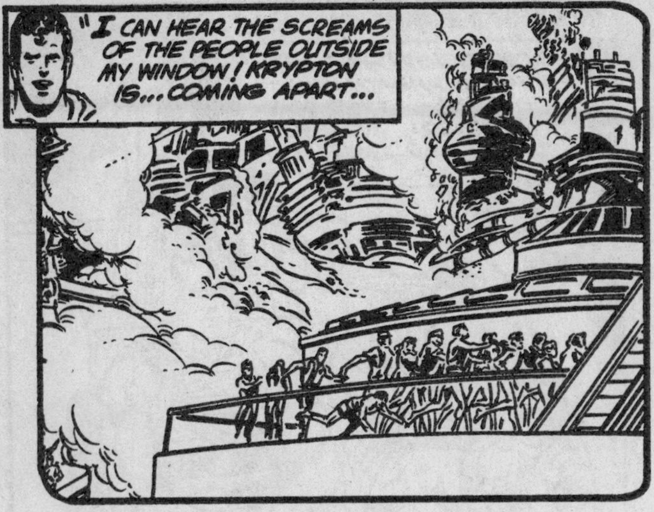
"I CAN HEAR THE SCREAMS OF THE PEOPLE OUTSIDE MY WINDOW! KRYPTON IS...COMING APART...

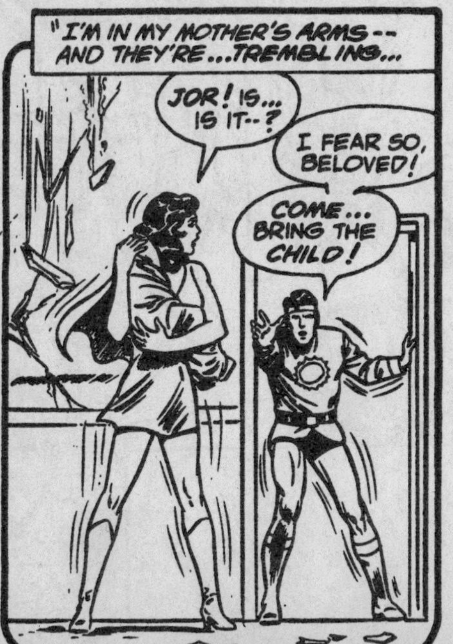
"I'M IN MY MOTHER'S ARMS--AND THEY'RE...TREMBLING...
JOR! IS... IS IT--?
I FEAR SO, BELOVED!
COME... BRING THE CHILD!

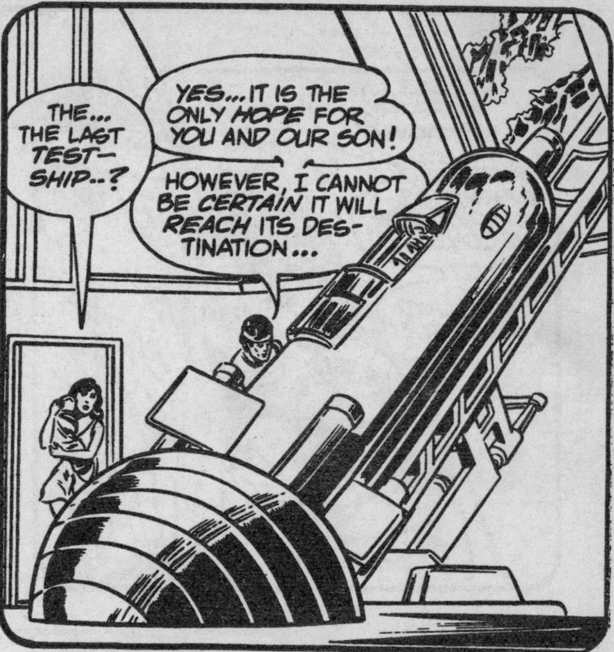
THE... THE LAST TEST-SHIP..?
YES... IT IS THE ONLY HOPE FOR YOU AND OUR SON!
HOWEVER, I CANNOT BE CERTAIN IT WILL REACH ITS DESTINATION...

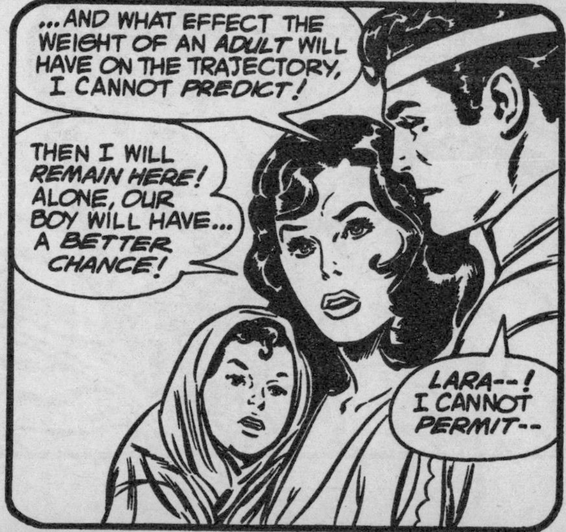
...AND WHAT EFFECT THE WEIGHT OF AN ADULT WILL HAVE ON THE TRAJECTORY, I CANNOT PREDICT!
THEN I WILL REMAIN HERE! ALONE, OUR BOY WILL HAVE... A BETTER CHANCE!
LARA--! I CANNOT PERMIT--

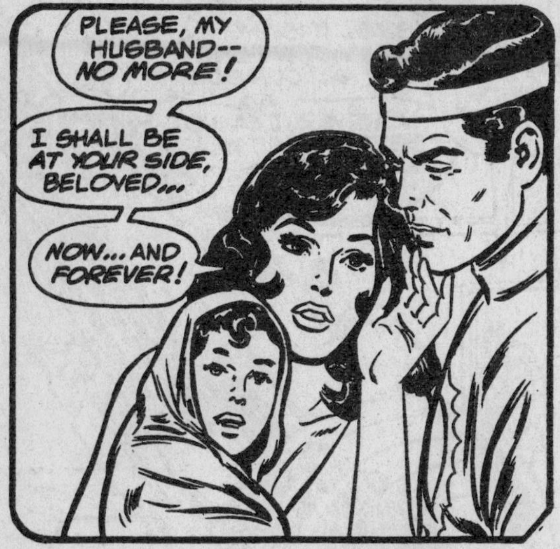
PLEASE, MY HUSBAND-- NO MORE!
I SHALL BE AT YOUR SIDE, BELOVED...
NOW... AND FOREVER!

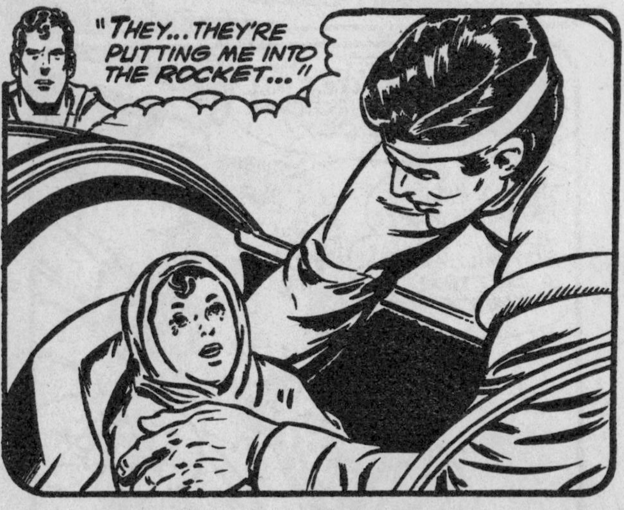
"THEY... THEY'RE PUTTING ME INTO THE ROCKET..."

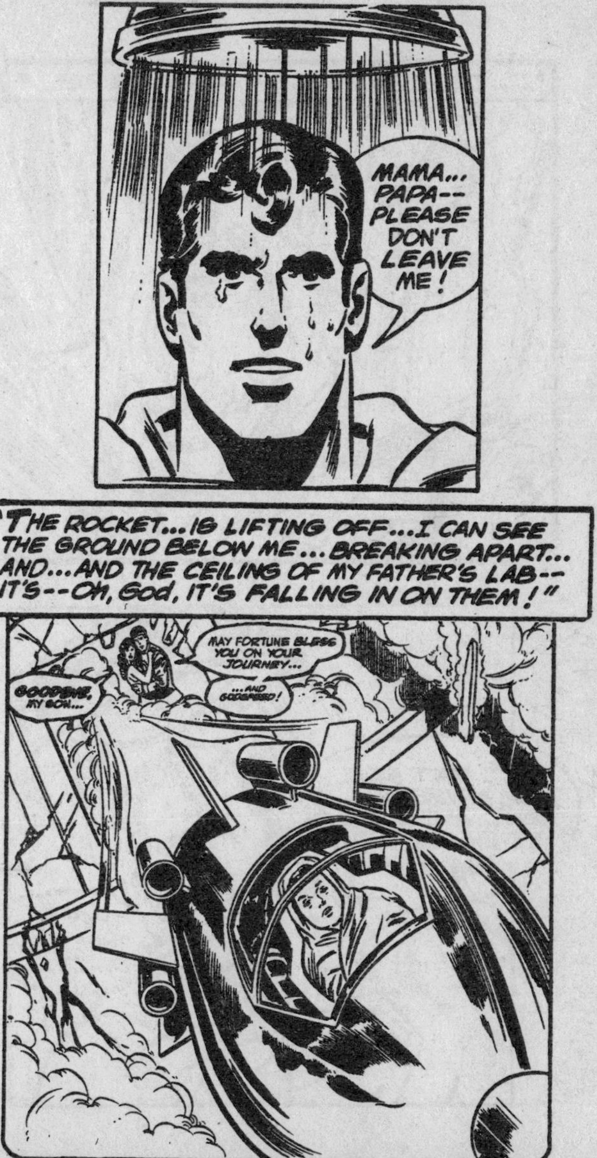
MAMA... PAPA-- PLEASE DON'T LEAVE ME!
"THE ROCKET... IS LIFTING OFF... I CAN SEE THE GROUND BELOW ME... BREAKING APART... AND... AND THE CEILING OF MY FATHER'S LAB-- IT'S--Oh, God, IT'S FALLING IN ON THEM!"
GOODBYE, MY SON...
MAY FORTUNE BLESS YOU ON YOUR JOURNEY...
...AND GODSPEED!

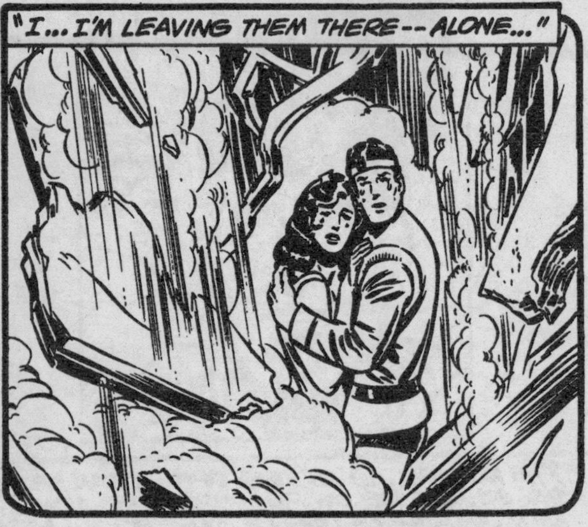
"I... I'M LEAVING THEM THERE--ALONE..."

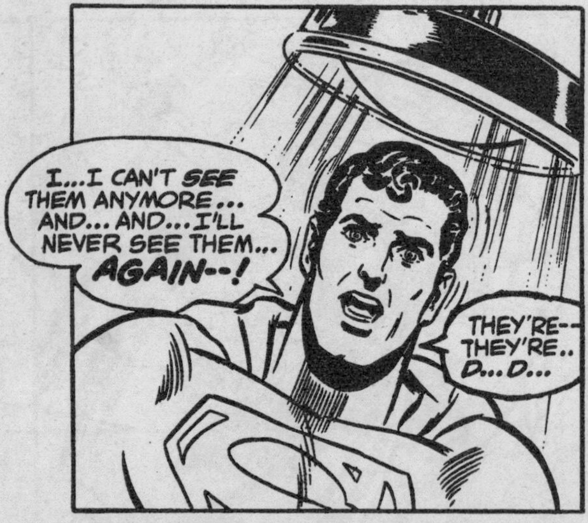
I...I CAN'T SEE THEM ANYMORE... AND... AND... I'LL NEVER SEE THEM... AGAIN--!
THEY'RE--THEY'RE.. D...D...

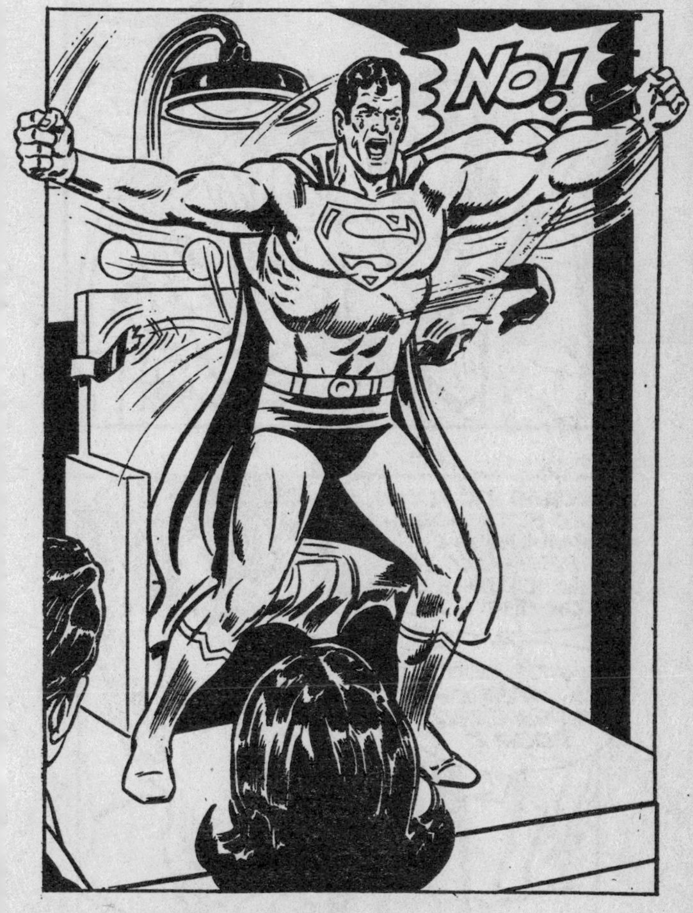
NO!

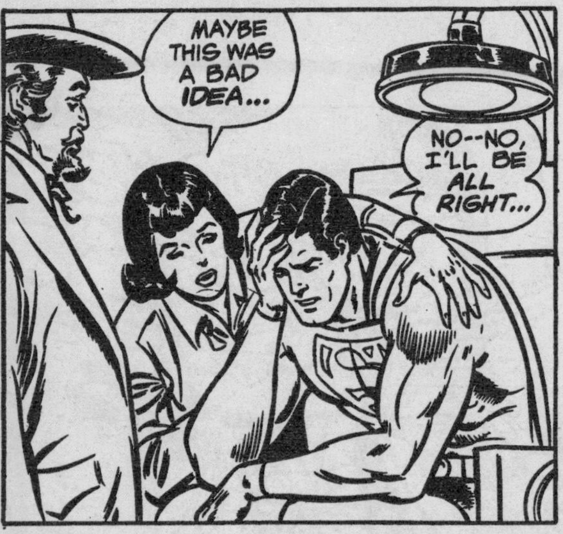
MAYBE THIS WAS A BAD IDEA...
NO--NO, I'LL BE ALL RIGHT...

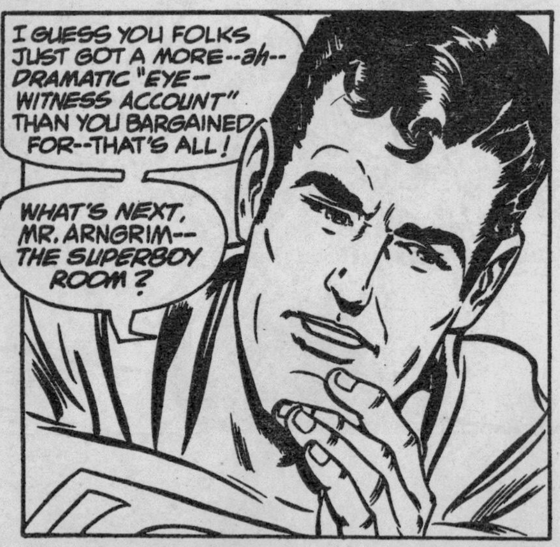
I GUESS YOU FOLKS JUST GOT A MORE--ah--DRAMATIC "EYE-WITNESS ACCOUNT" THAN YOU BARGAINED FOR--THAT'S ALL!
WHAT'S NEXT, MR. ARNGRIM--THE SUPERBOY ROOM?

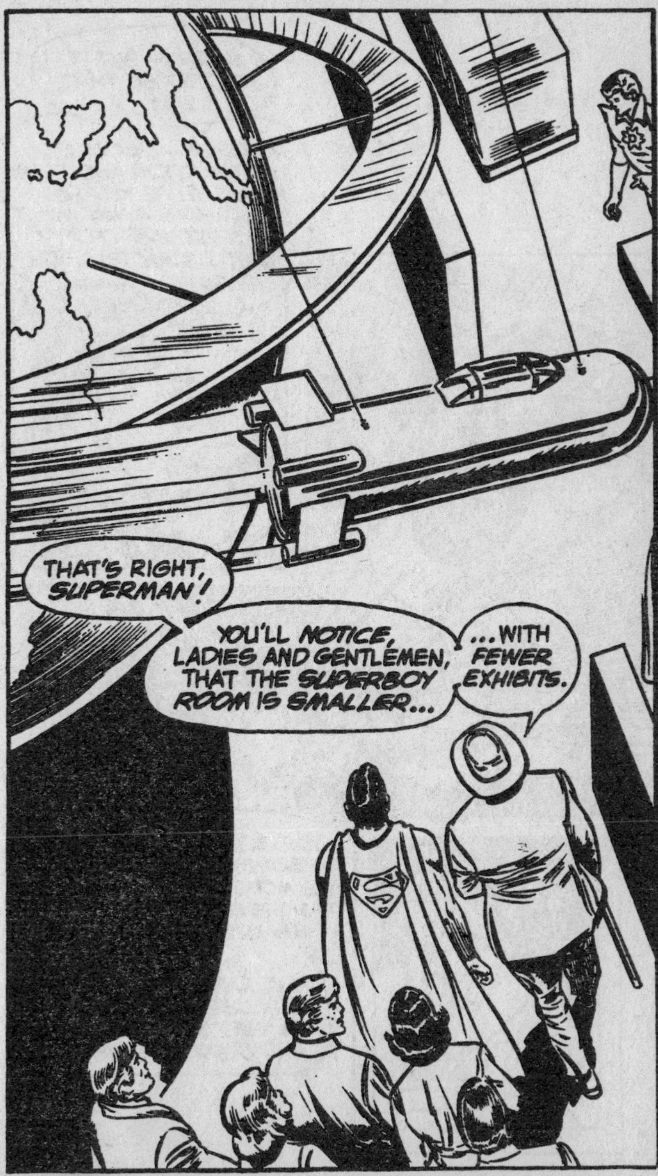
THAT'S RIGHT, SUPERMAN!
YOU'LL NOTICE, LADIES AND GENTLEMEN, THAT THE SUPERBOY ROOM IS SMALLER...
...WITH FEWER EXHIBITS.

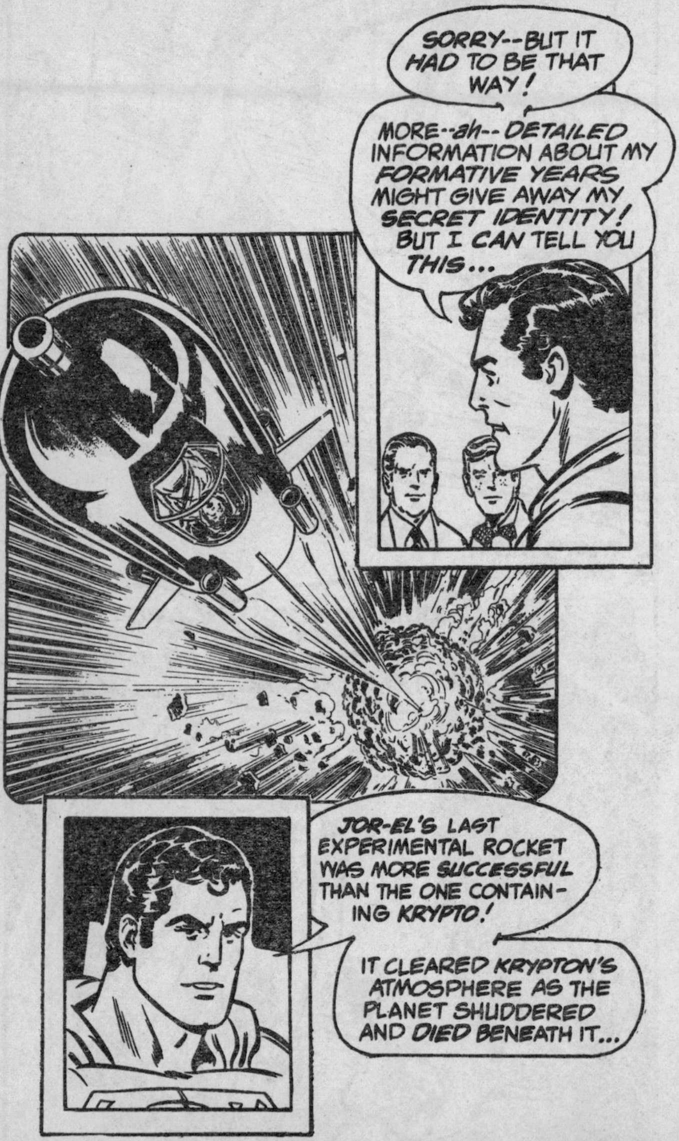
SORRY--BUT IT HAD TO BE THAT WAY!
MORE--ah--DETAILED INFORMATION ABOUT MY FORMATIVE YEARS MIGHT GIVE AWAY MY SECRET IDENTITY! BUT I CAN TELL YOU THIS...
JOR-EL'S LAST EXPERIMENTAL ROCKET WAS MORE SUCCESSFUL THAN THE ONE CONTAIN-ING KRYPTO!
IT CLEARED KRYPTON'S ATMOSPHERE AS THE PLANET SHUDDERED AND DIED BENEATH IT...

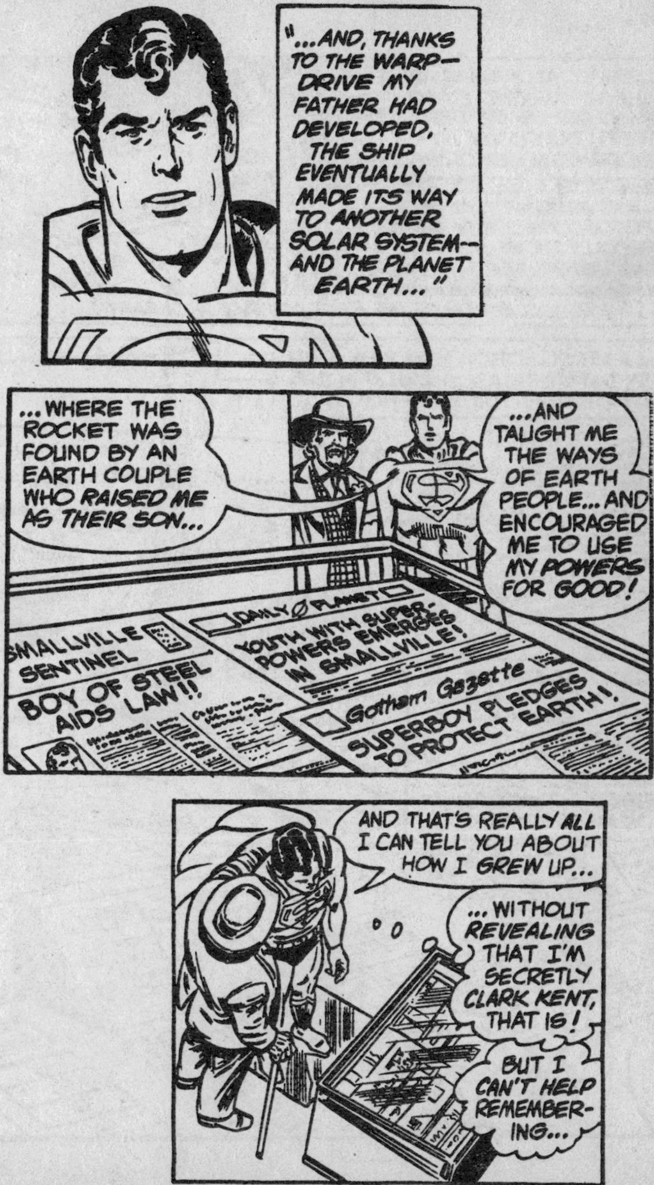
"...AND, THANKS TO THE WARP-DRIVE MY FATHER HAD DEVELOPED, THE SHIP EVENTUALLY MADE ITS WAY TO ANOTHER SOLAR SYSTEM--AND THE PLANET EARTH..."
...WHERE THE ROCKET WAS FOUND BY AN EARTH COUPLE WHO RAISED ME AS THEIR SON...
...AND TAUGHT ME THE WAYS OF EARTH PEOPLE...AND ENCOURAGED ME TO USE MY POWERS FOR GOOD!
DAILY PLANET
YOUTH WITH SUPER-POWERS EMERGES IN SMALLVILLE!
SMALLVILLE SENTINEL
BOY OF STEEL AIDS LAW!!
Gotham Gazette
SUPERBOY PLEDGES TO PROTECT EARTH!
AND THAT'S REALLY ALL I CAN TELL YOU ABOUT HOW I GREW UP...
...WITHOUT REVEALING THAT I'M SECRETLY CLARK KENT, THAT IS!
BUT I CAN'T HELP REMEMBER-ING...

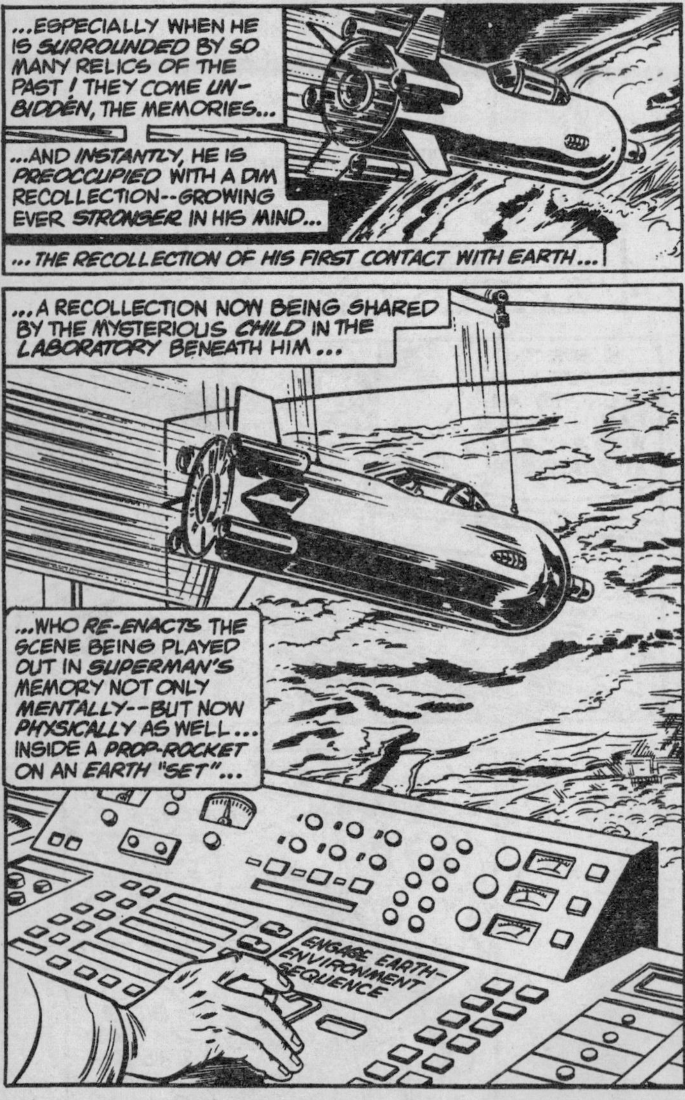
...ESPECIALLY WHEN HE IS SURROUNDED BY SO MANY RELICS OF THE PAST! THEY COME UN-BIDDEN, THE MEMORIES...
...AND INSTANTLY, HE IS PREOCCUPIED WITH A DIM RECOLLECTION--GROWING EVER STRONGER IN HIS MIND...
...THE RECOLLECTION OF HIS FIRST CONTACT WITH EARTH...
...A RECOLLECTION NOW BEING SHARED BY THE MYSTERIOUS CHILD IN THE LABORATORY BENEATH HIM...
...WHO RE-ENACTS THE SCENE BEING PLAYED OUT IN SUPERMAN'S MEMORY NOT ONLY MENTALLY--BUT NOW PHYSICALLY AS WELL... INSIDE A PROP-ROCKET ON AN EARTH "SET"...
ENGAGE EARTH-ENVIRONMENT SEQUENCE

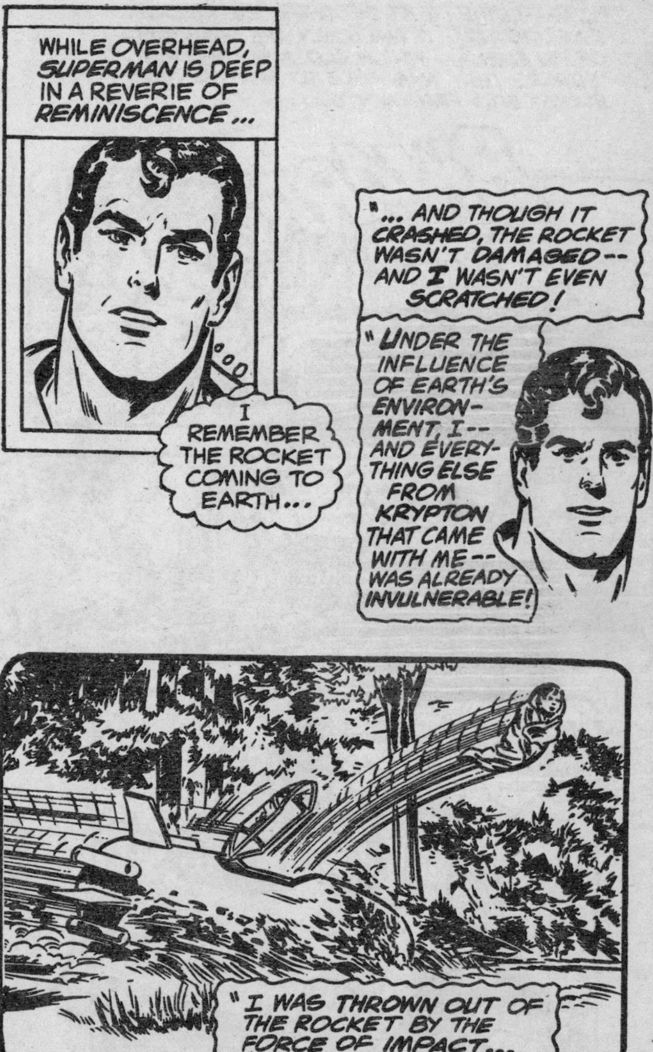
WHILE OVERHEAD, SUPERMAN IS DEEP IN A REVERIE OF REMINISCENCE...
I REMEMBER THE ROCKET COMING TO EARTH...
"... AND THOUGH IT CRASHED, THE ROCKET WASN'T DAMAGED-- AND I WASN'T EVEN SCRATCHED!
"UNDER THE INFLUENCE OF EARTH'S ENVIRONMENT, I-- AND EVERYTHING ELSE FROM KRYPTON THAT CAME WITH ME-- WAS ALREADY INVULNERABLE!
"I WAS THROWN OUT OF THE ROCKET BY THE FORCE OF IMPACT...

"...AS--IN THE NEXT SECOND-- THE ROCKET EXPLODED! IT WAS ONLY THE COMBUSTION OF ITS FUEL-- WHICH HAD ALSO BECOME 'SUPER'--THAT WAS ABLE TO SHATTER THE ROCKET INTO FRAGMENTS...

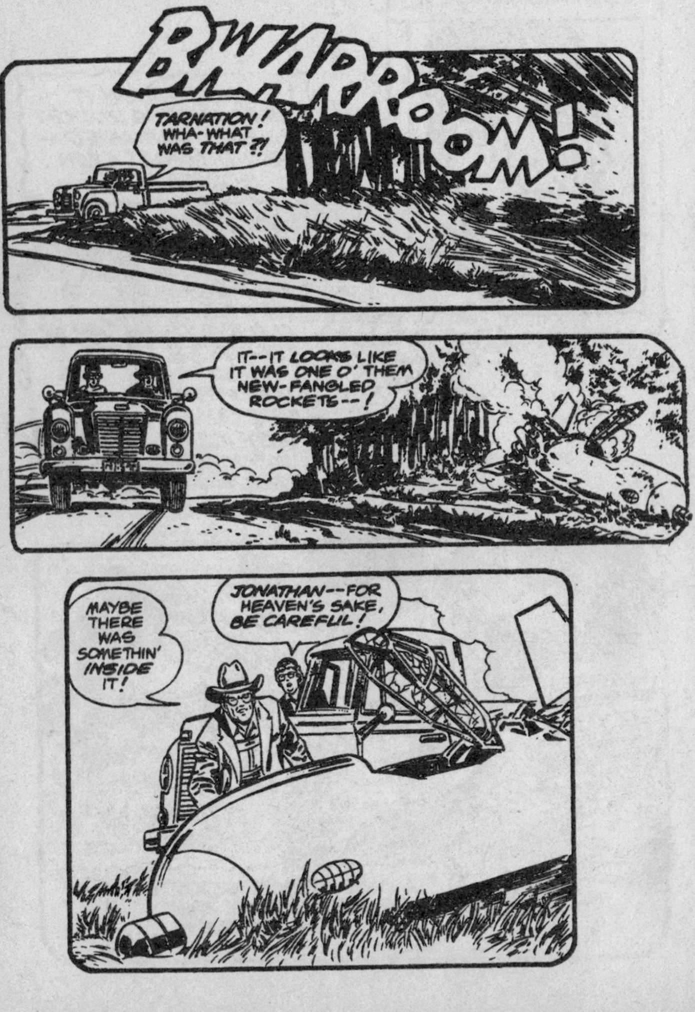
BWAROOM!
TARNATION! WHA-WHAT WAS THAT ?!
IT--IT LOOKS LIKE IT WAS ONE O' THEM NEW-FANGLED ROCKETS--!
MAYBE THERE WAS SOMETHIN' INSIDE IT!
JONATHAN--FOR HEAVEN'S SAKE, BE CAREFUL!

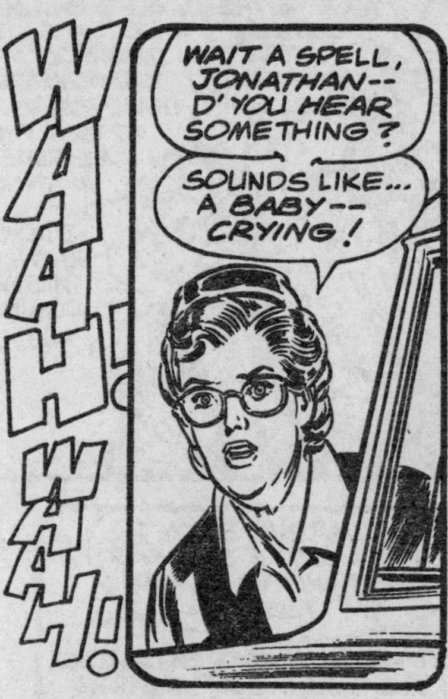
WAAAH! WAAAH!
WAIT A SPELL, JONATHAN-- D' YOU HEAR SOMETHING?
SOUNDS LIKE... A BABY-- CRYING!

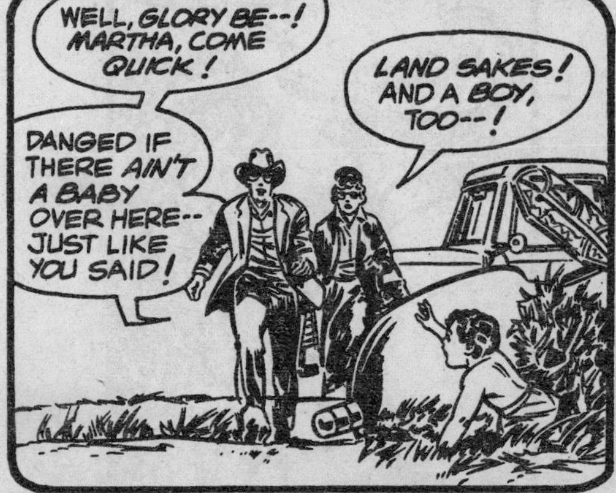
WELL, GLORY BE--! MARTHA, COME QUICK!
DANGED IF THERE AIN'T A BABY OVER HERE-- JUST LIKE YOU SAID!
LAND SAKES! AND A BOY, TOO--!

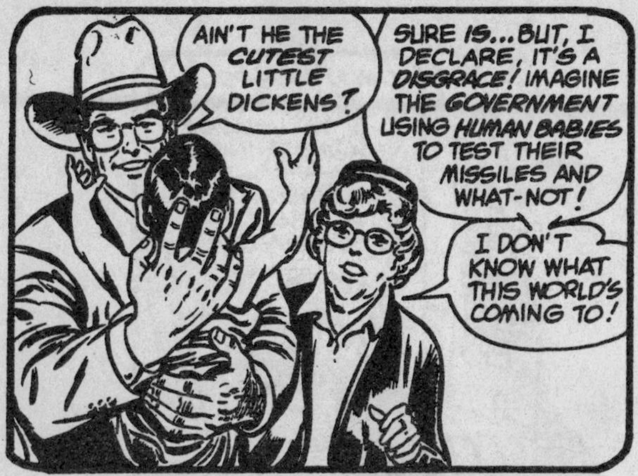
AIN'T HE THE CUTEST LITTLE DICKENS?
SURE IS...BUT, I DECLARE, IT'S A DISGRACE! IMAGINE THE GOVERNMENT USING HUMAN BABIES TO TEST THEIR MISSILES AND WHAT-NOT!
I DON'T KNOW WHAT THIS WORLD'S COMING TO!

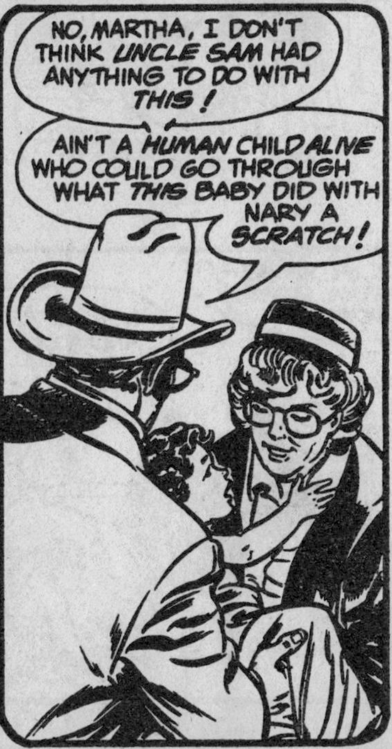
NO, MARTHA, I DON'T THINK UNCLE SAM HAD ANYTHING TO DO WITH THIS!
AIN'T A HUMAN CHILD ALIVE WHO COULD GO THROUGH WHAT THIS BABY DID WITH NARY A SCRATCH!

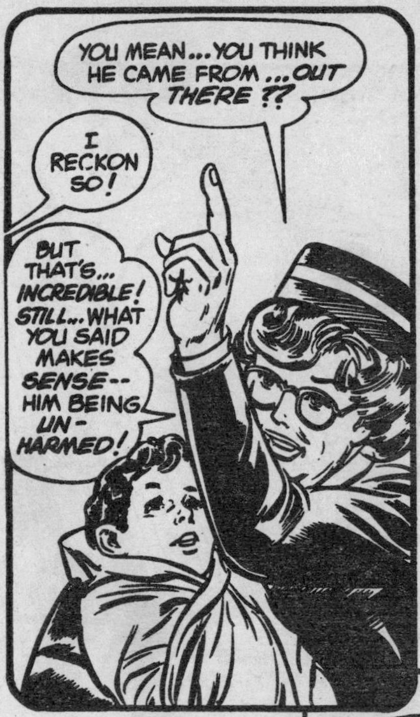
YOU MEAN...YOU THINK HE CAME FROM...OUT THERE??
I RECKON SO!
BUT THAT'S... INCREDIBLE! STILL...WHAT YOU SAID MAKES SENSE-- HIM BEING UN-HARMED!

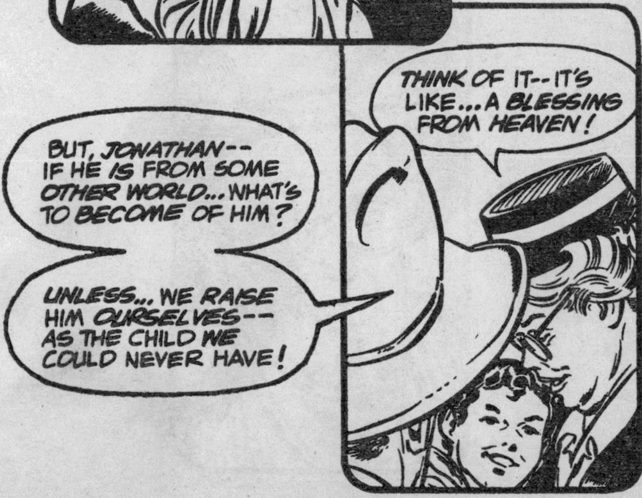
THINK OF IT--IT'S LIKE...A BLESSING FROM HEAVEN!
BUT, JONATHAN-- IF HE IS FROM SOME OTHER WORLD...WHAT'S TO BECOME OF HIM?
UNLESS... WE RAISE HIM OURSELVES-- AS THE CHILD WE COULD NEVER HAVE!

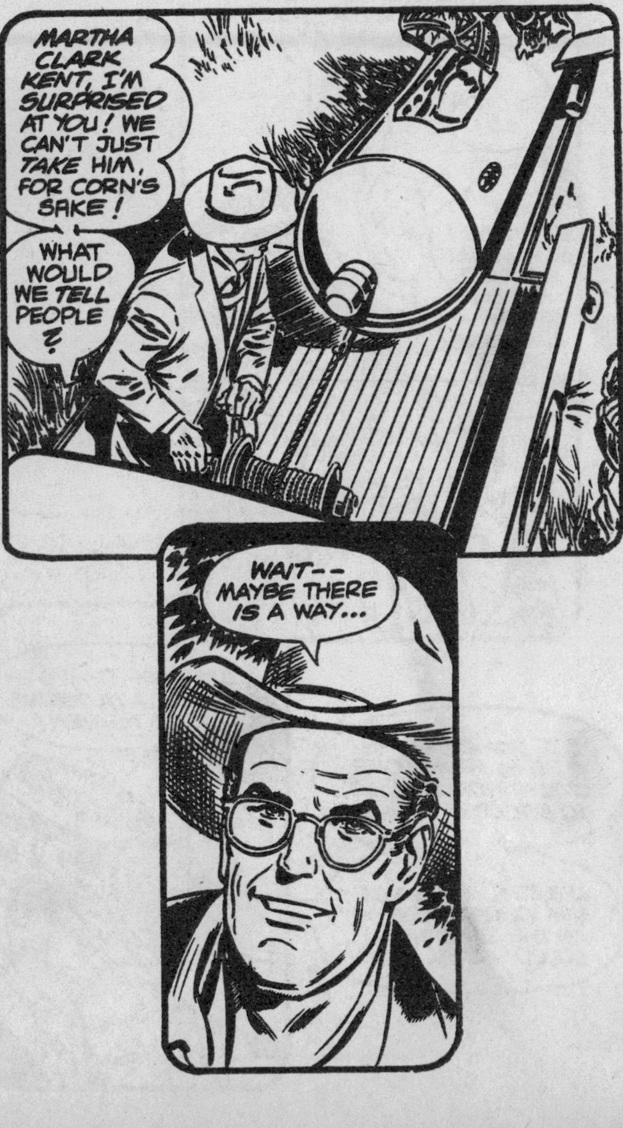
MARTHA CLARK KENT, I'M SURPRISED AT YOU! WE CAN'T JUST TAKE HIM, FOR CORN'S SAKE!
WHAT WOULD WE TELL PEOPLE?
WAIT-- MAYBE THERE IS A WAY...

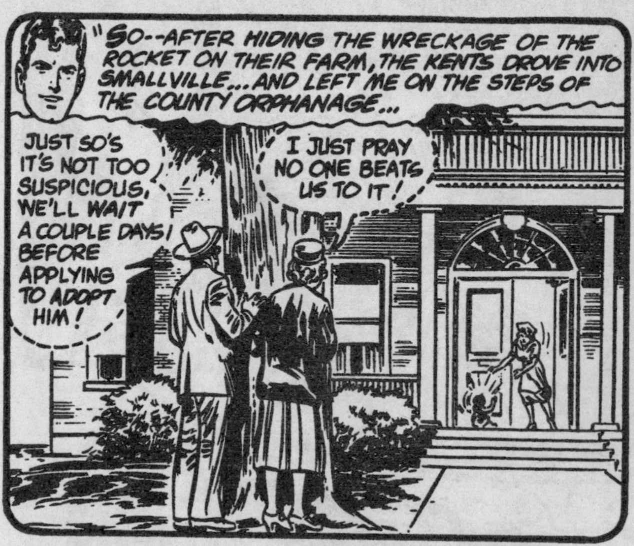
"SO--AFTER HIDING THE WRECKAGE OF THE ROCKET ON THEIR FARM, THE KENTS DROVE INTO SMALLVILLE...AND LEFT ME ON THE STEPS OF THE COUNTY ORPHANAGE...
JUST SO'S IT'S NOT TOO SUSPICIOUS, WE'LL WAIT A COUPLE DAYS BEFORE APPLYING TO ADOPT HIM!
I JUST PRAY NO ONE BEATS US TO IT!

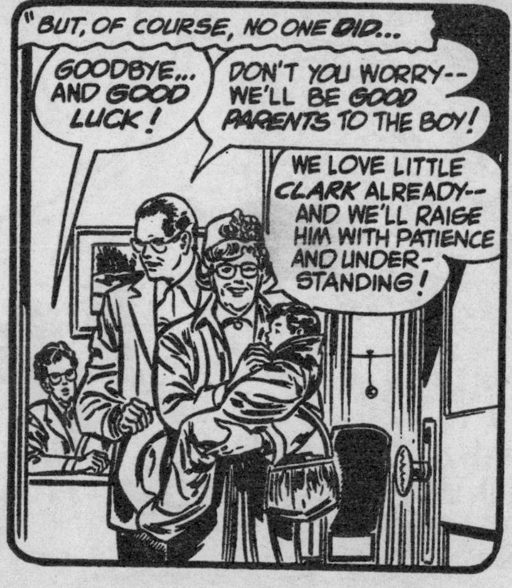
"BUT, OF COURSE, NO ONE DID...
GOODBYE... AND GOOD LUCK!
DON'T YOU WORRY-- WE'LL BE GOOD PARENTS TO THE BOY!
WE LOVE LITTLE CLARK ALREADY-- AND WE'LL RAISE HIM WITH PATIENCE AND UNDER-STANDING!

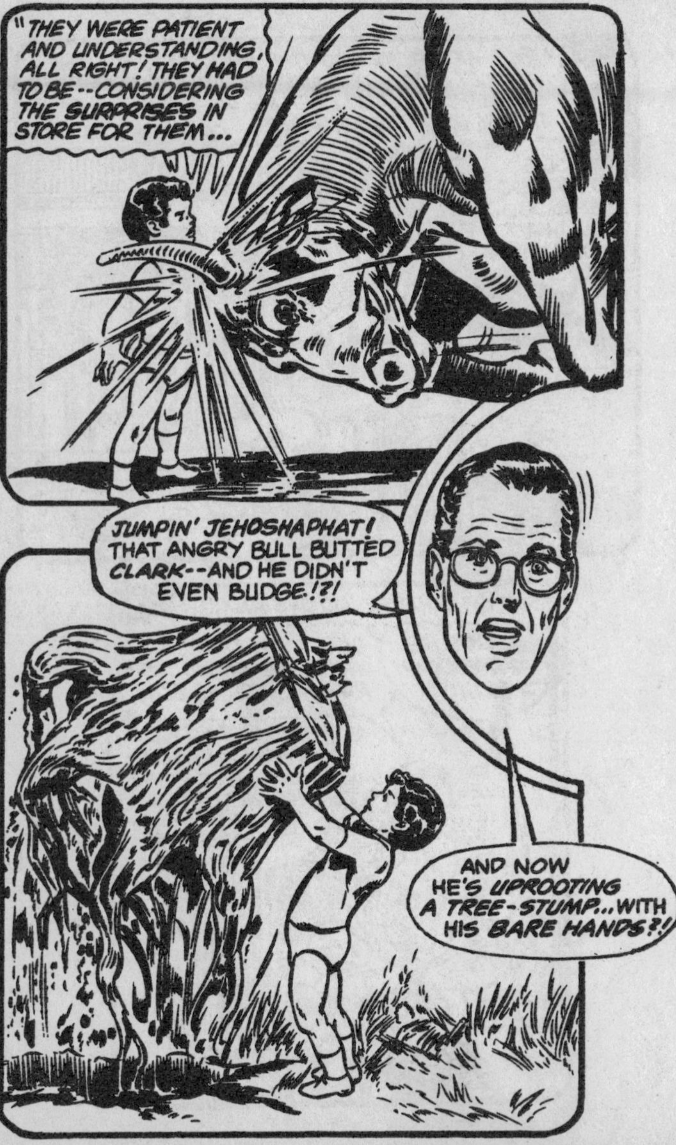
"THEY WERE PATIENT AND UNDERSTANDING, ALL RIGHT! THEY HAD TO BE--CONSIDERING THE SURPRISES IN STORE FOR THEM...
JUMPIN' JEHOSHAPHAT! THAT ANGRY BULL BUTTED CLARK--AND HE DIDN'T EVEN BUDGE.!?!
AND NOW HE'S UPROOTING A TREE-STUMP...WITH HIS BARE HANDS?!

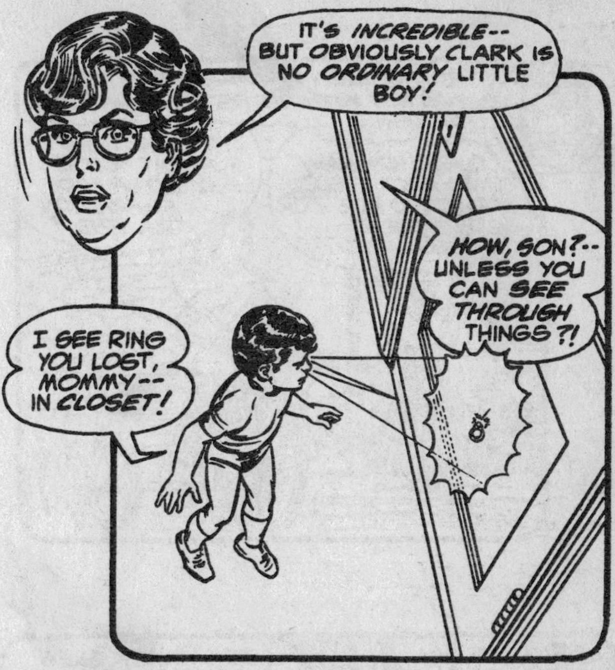
IT'S INCREDIBLE-- BUT OBVIOUSLY CLARK IS NO ORDINARY LITTLE BOY!
HOW, SON?-- UNLESS YOU CAN SEE THROUGH THINGS?!
I SEE RING YOU LOST, MOMMY-- IN CLOSET!

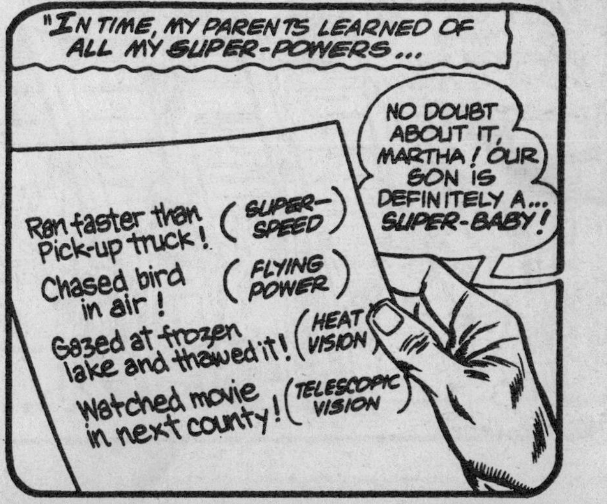
"IN TIME, MY PARENTS LEARNED OF ALL MY SUPER-POWERS...
NO DOUBT ABOUT IT, MARTHA! OUR SON IS DEFINITELY A... SUPER-BABY!
Ran faster than Pick-up truck! (SUPER-SPEED)
Chased bird in air! (FLYING POWER)
Gazed at frozen lake and thawed it! (HEAT VISION)
Watched movie in next county! (TELESCOPIC VISION)

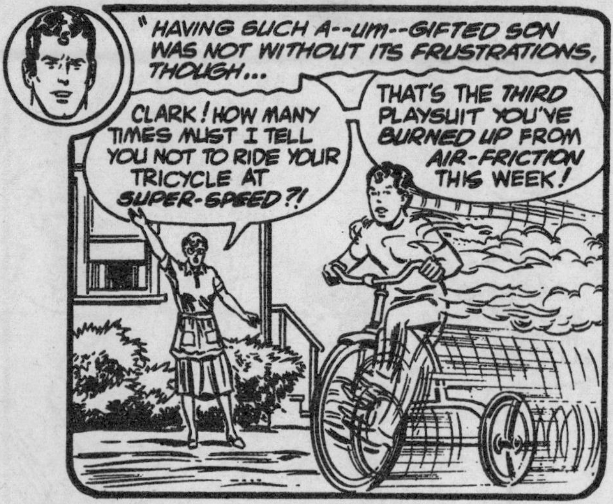
"HAVING SUCH A--UM--GIFTED SON WAS NOT WITHOUT ITS FRUSTRATIONS, THOUGH...
CLARK! HOW MANY TIMES MUST I TELL YOU NOT TO RIDE YOUR TRICYCLE AT SUPER-SPEED?!
THAT'S THE THIRD PLAYSUIT YOU'VE BURNED UP FROM AIR-FRICTION THIS WEEK!

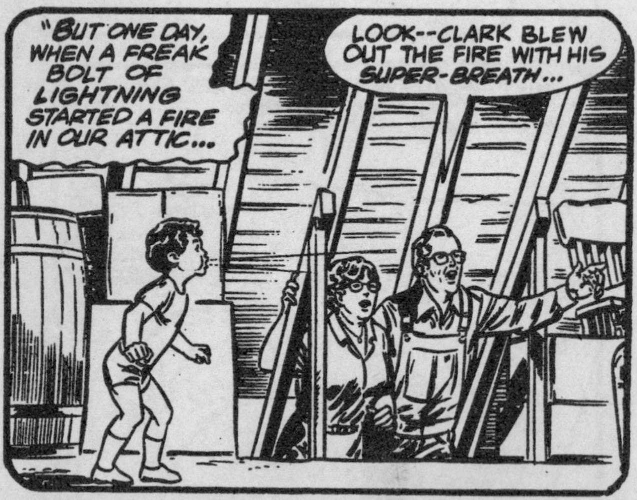
"BUT ONE DAY, WHEN A FREAK BOLT OF LIGHTNING STARTED A FIRE IN OUR ATTIC...
LOOK--CLARK BLEW OUT THE FIRE WITH HIS SUPER-BREATH...

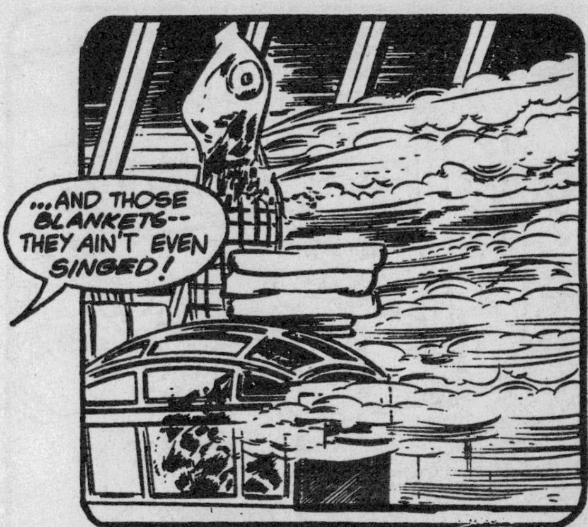
...AND THOSE BLANKETS-- THEY AIN'T EVEN SINGED!

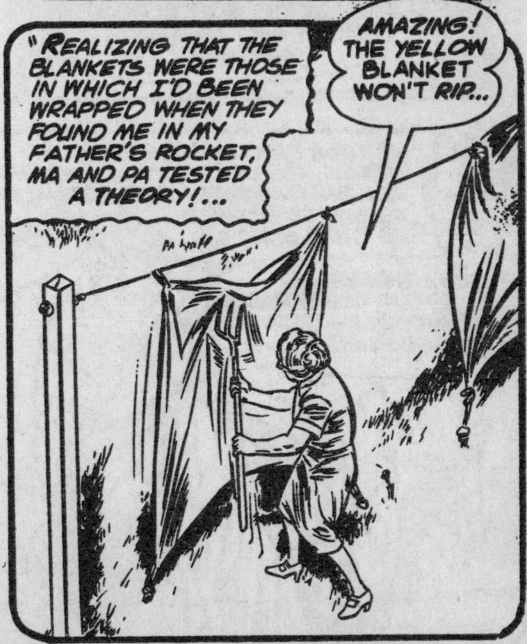
"REALIZING THAT THE BLANKETS WERE THOSE IN WHICH I'D BEEN WRAPPED WHEN THEY FOUND ME IN MY FATHER'S ROCKET, MA AND PA TESTED A THEORY!...
AMAZING! THE YELLOW BLANKET WON'T RIP...

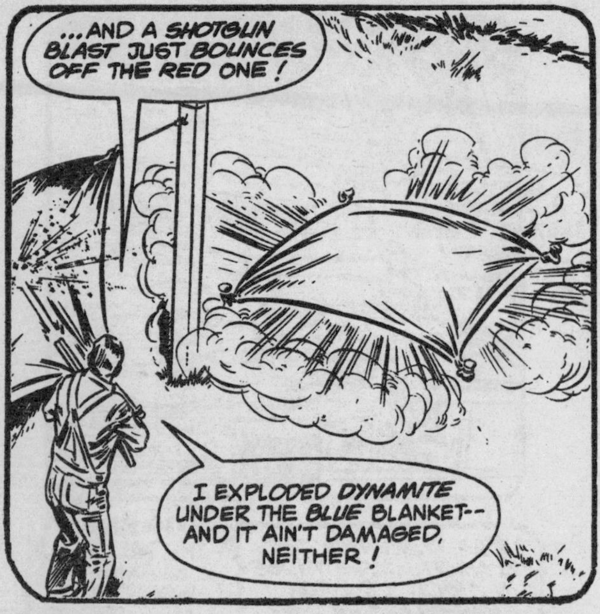
...AND A SHOTGUN BLAST JUST BOUNCES OFF THE RED ONE!
I EXPLODED DYNAMITE UNDER THE BLUE BLANKET-- AND IT AIN'T DAMAGED, NEITHER!

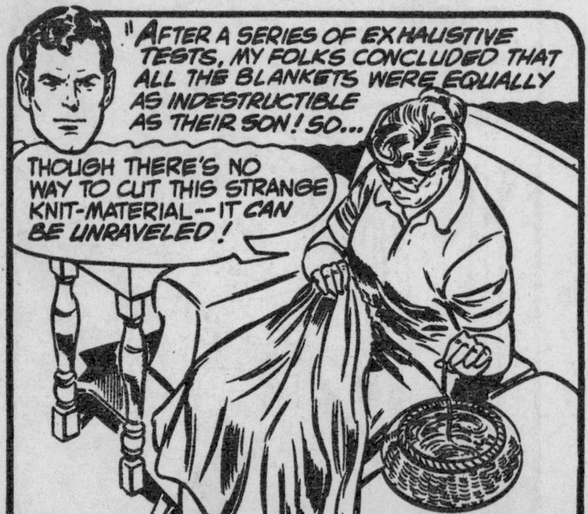
"AFTER A SERIES OF EXHAUSTIVE TESTS, MY FOLKS CONCLUDED THAT ALL THE BLANKETS WERE EQUALLY AS INDESTRUCTIBLE AS THEIR SON! SO...
THOUGH THERE'S NO WAY TO CUT THIS STRANGE KNIT-MATERIAL--IT CAN BE UNRAVELED!

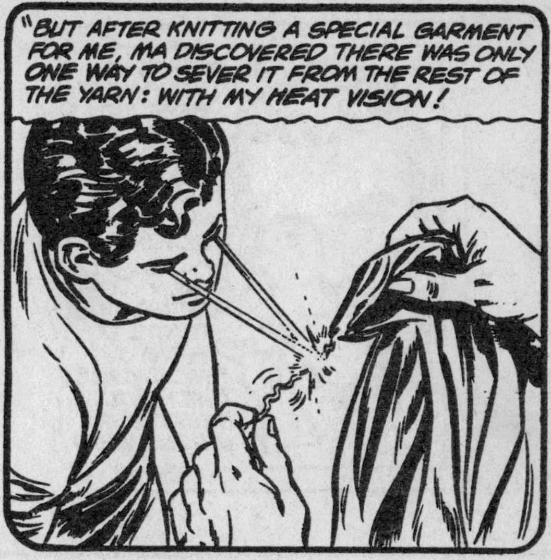
"BUT AFTER KNITTING A SPECIAL GARMENT FOR ME, MA DISCOVERED THERE WAS ONLY ONE WAY TO SEVER IT FROM THE REST OF THE YARN: WITH MY HEAT VISION!

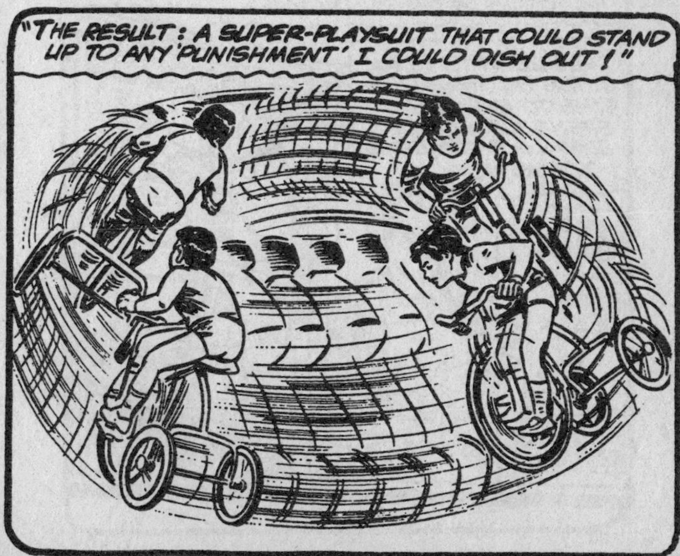
"THE RESULT: A SUPER-PLAYSUIT THAT COULD STAND UP TO ANY 'PUNISHMENT' I COULD DISH OUT!"

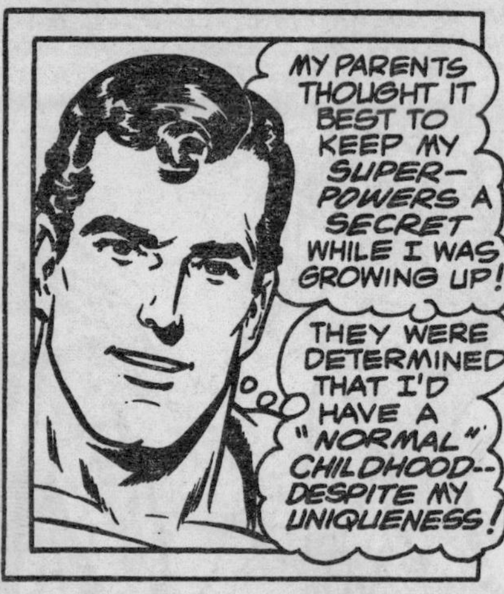
MY PARENTS THOUGHT IT BEST TO KEEP MY SUPER-POWERS A SECRET WHILE I WAS GROWING UP!
THEY WERE DETERMINED THAT I'D HAVE A "NORMAL" CHILDHOOD--DESPITE MY UNIQUENESS!

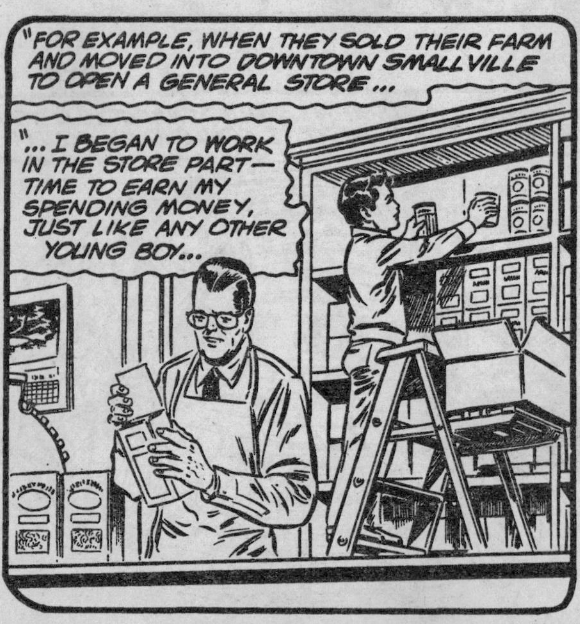
"FOR EXAMPLE, WHEN THEY SOLD THEIR FARM AND MOVED INTO DOWNTOWN SMALLVILLE TO OPEN A GENERAL STORE...
"... I BEGAN TO WORK IN THE STORE PART-TIME TO EARN MY SPENDING MONEY, JUST LIKE ANY OTHER YOUNG BOY...

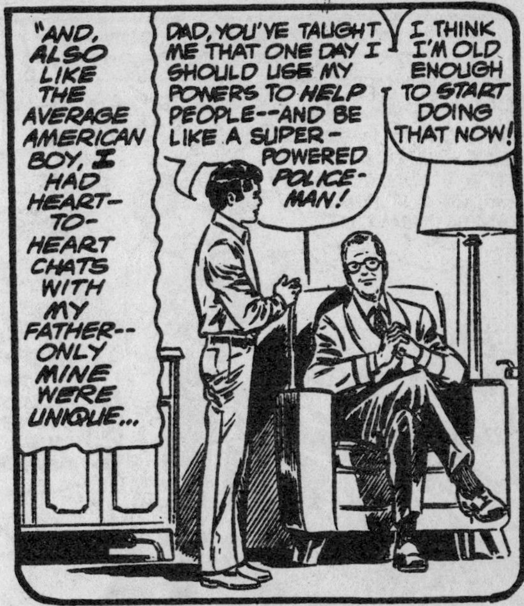
"AND, ALSO LIKE THE AVERAGE AMERICAN BOY, I HAD HEART-TO-HEART CHATS WITH MY FATHER--ONLY MINE WERE UNIQUE...
DAD, YOU'VE TAUGHT ME THAT ONE DAY I SHOULD USE MY POWERS TO HELP PEOPLE--AND BE LIKE A SUPER-POWERED POLICE-MAN!
I THINK I'M OLD ENOUGH TO START DOING THAT NOW!

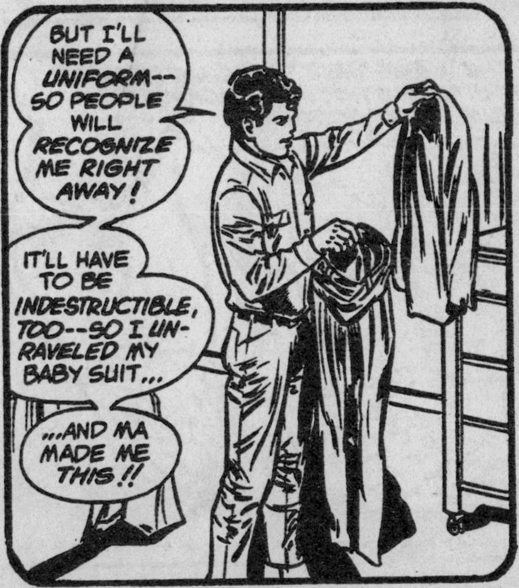
BUT I'LL NEED A UNIFORM--SO PEOPLE WILL RECOGNIZE ME RIGHT AWAY!
IT'LL HAVE TO BE INDESTRUCTIBLE, TOO--SO I UN-RAVELED MY BABY SUIT...
...AND MA MADE ME THIS!!

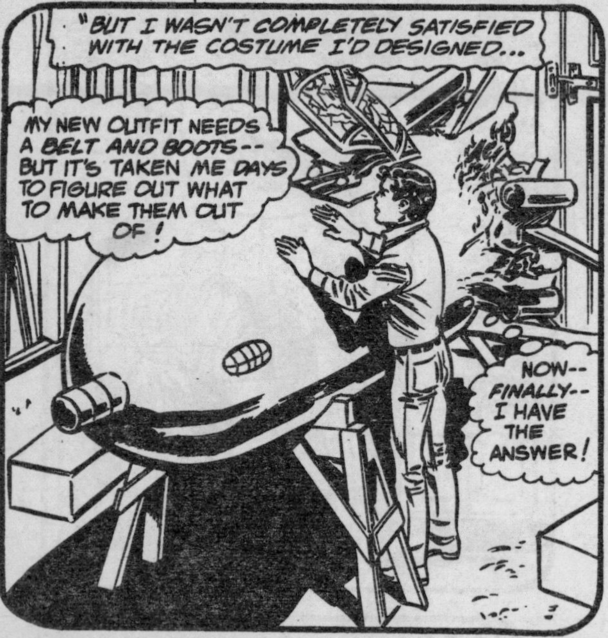
"BUT I WASN'T COMPLETELY SATISFIED WITH THE COSTUME I'D DESIGNED...
MY NEW OUTFIT NEEDS A BELT AND BOOTS-- BUT IT'S TAKEN ME DAYS TO FIGURE OUT WHAT TO MAKE THEM OUT OF!
NOW-- FINALLY-- I HAVE THE ANSWER!

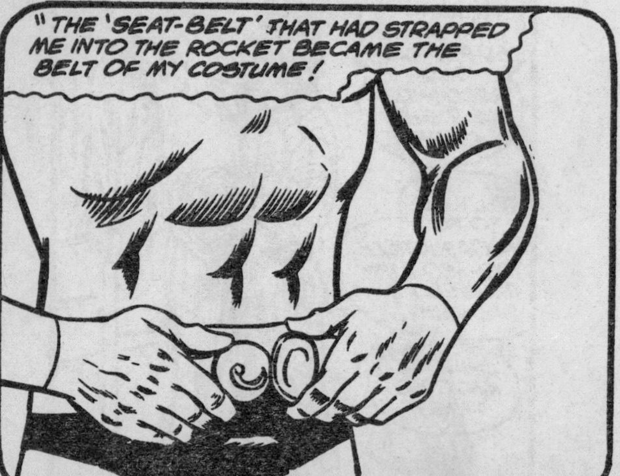
"THE 'SEAT-BELT' THAT HAD STRAPPED ME INTO THE ROCKET BECAME THE BELT OF MY COSTUME!

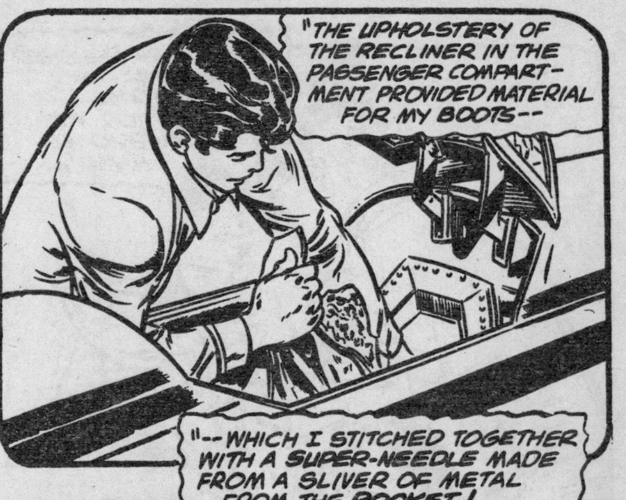
"THE UPHOLSTERY OF THE RECLINER IN THE PASSENGER COMPART-MENT PROVIDED MATERIAL FOR MY BOOTS--

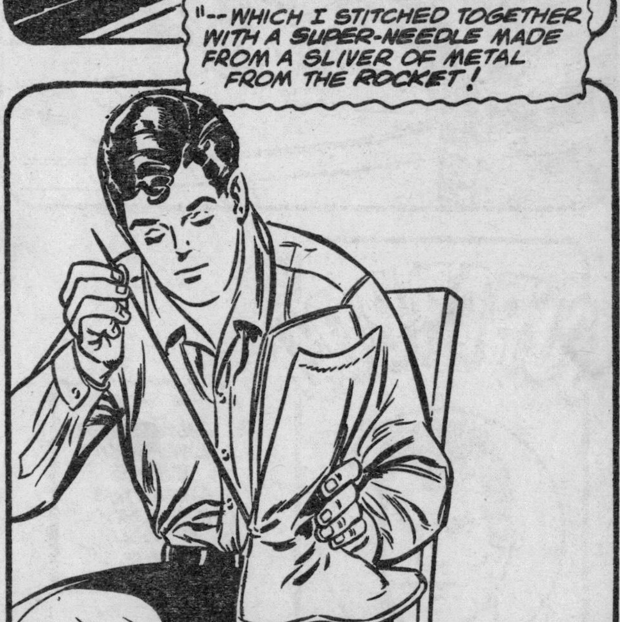
"--WHICH I STITCHED TOGETHER WITH A SUPER-NEEDLE MADE FROM A SLIVER OF METAL FROM THE ROCKET!

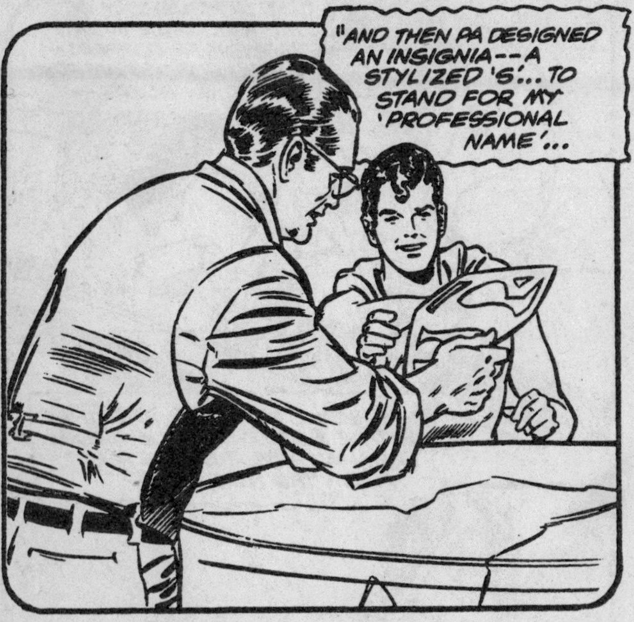
"AND THEN PA DESIGNED AN INSIGNIA--A STYLIZED 'S'...TO STAND FOR MY 'PROFESSIONAL NAME'...

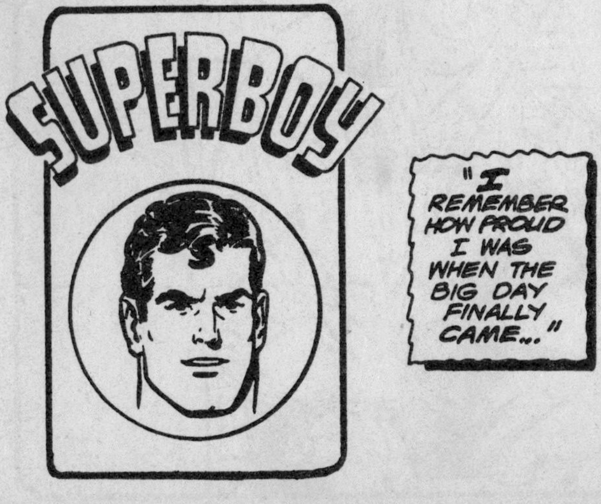
SUPERBOY
"I REMEMBER HOW PROUD I WAS WHEN THE BIG DAY FINALLY CAME..."

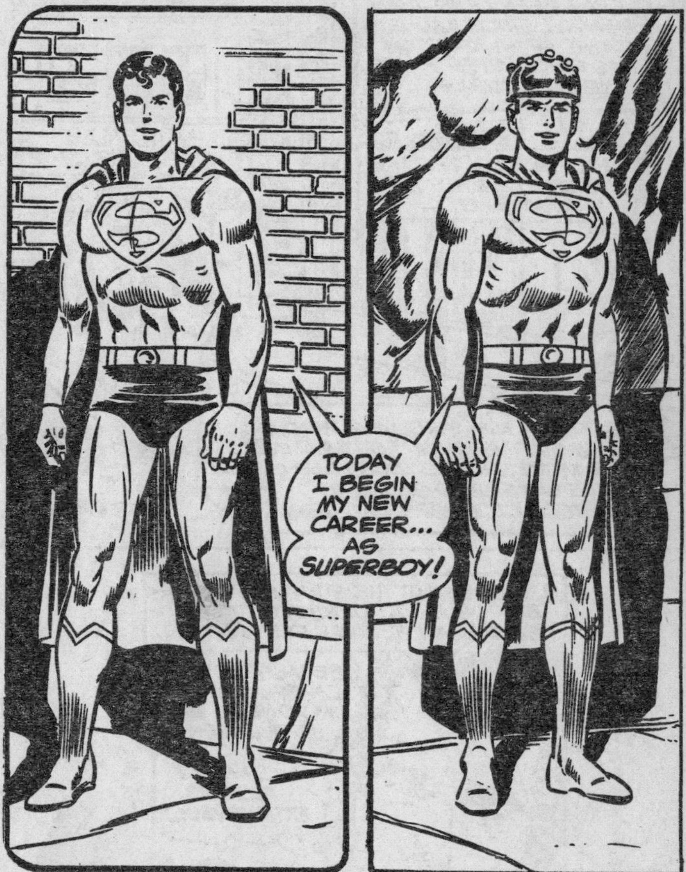
TODAY I BEGIN MY NEW CAREER... AS SUPERBOY!

AND--LIKE ALL OF SUPERMAN'S RECOLLECTIONS--
THIS ONE, TOO, IS SHARED BY A MYSTERIOUS
DOUBLE IN AN UNDERGROUND LABORATORY...

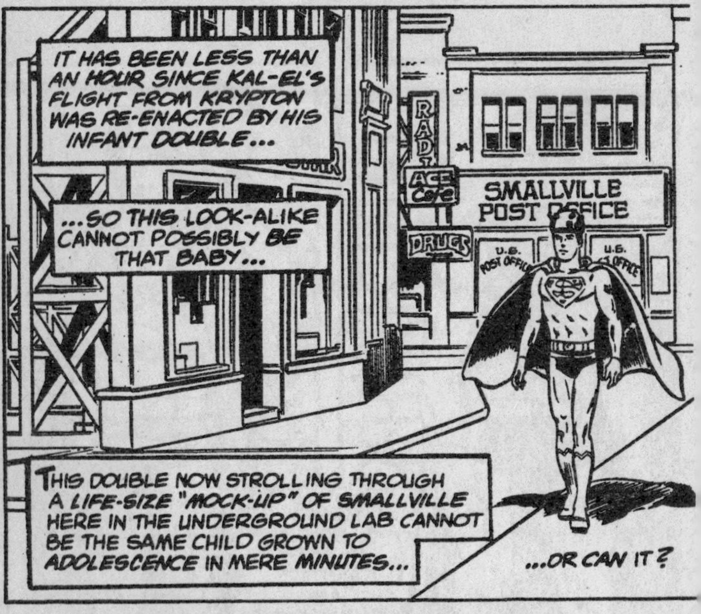
IT HAS BEEN LESS THAN AN HOUR SINCE KAL-EL'S FLIGHT FROM KRYPTON WAS RE-ENACTED BY HIS INFANT DOUBLE...
...SO THIS LOOK-ALIKE CANNOT POSSIBLY BE THAT BABY...
THIS DOUBLE NOW STROLLING THROUGH A LIFE-SIZE "MOCK-UP" OF SMALLVILLE HERE IN THE UNDERGROUND LAB CANNOT BE THE SAME CHILD GROWN TO ADOLESCENCE IN MERE MINUTES...
...OR CAN IT?
SMALLVILLE POST OFFICE
U.S. POST OFFICE
ACE Cafe
DRUGS

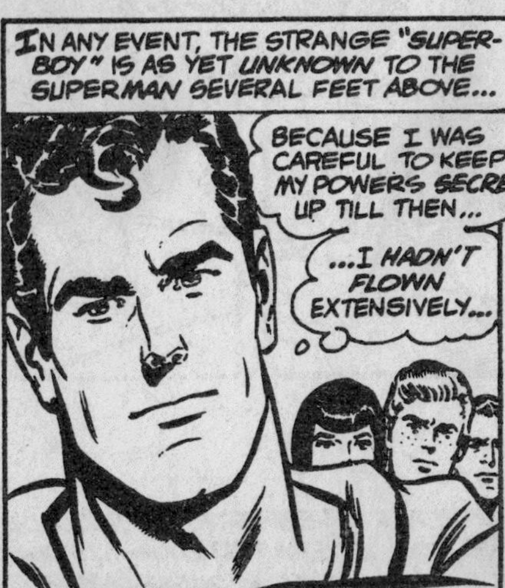
IN ANY EVENT, THE STRANGE "SUPER-BOY" IS AS YET UNKNOWN TO THE SUPERMAN SEVERAL FEET ABOVE...
BECAUSE I WAS CAREFUL TO KEEP MY POWERS SECRET UP TILL THEN...
...I HADN'T FLOWN EXTENSIVELY...

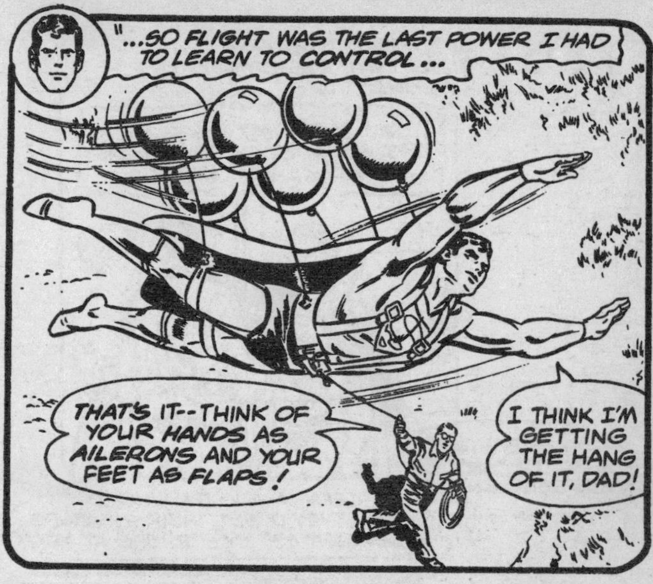
"...SO FLIGHT WAS THE LAST POWER I HAD TO LEARN TO CONTROL...
THAT'S IT--THINK OF YOUR HANDS AS AILERONS AND YOUR FEET AS FLAPS!
I THINK I'M GETTING THE HANG OF IT, DAD!

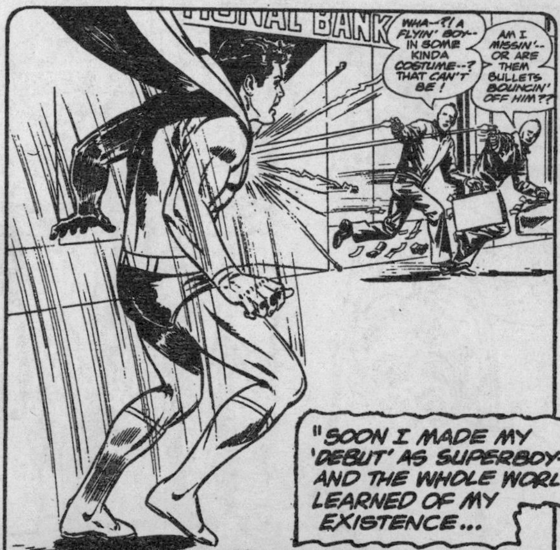
BANK
WHA--?! A FLYIN' BOY--IN SOME KINDA COSTUME--? THAT CAN'T BE!
AM I MISSIN'--OR ARE THEM BULLETS BOUNCIN' OFF HIM??
"SOON I MADE MY 'DEBUT' AS SUPERBOY--AND THE WHOLE WORLD LEARNED OF MY EXISTENCE...

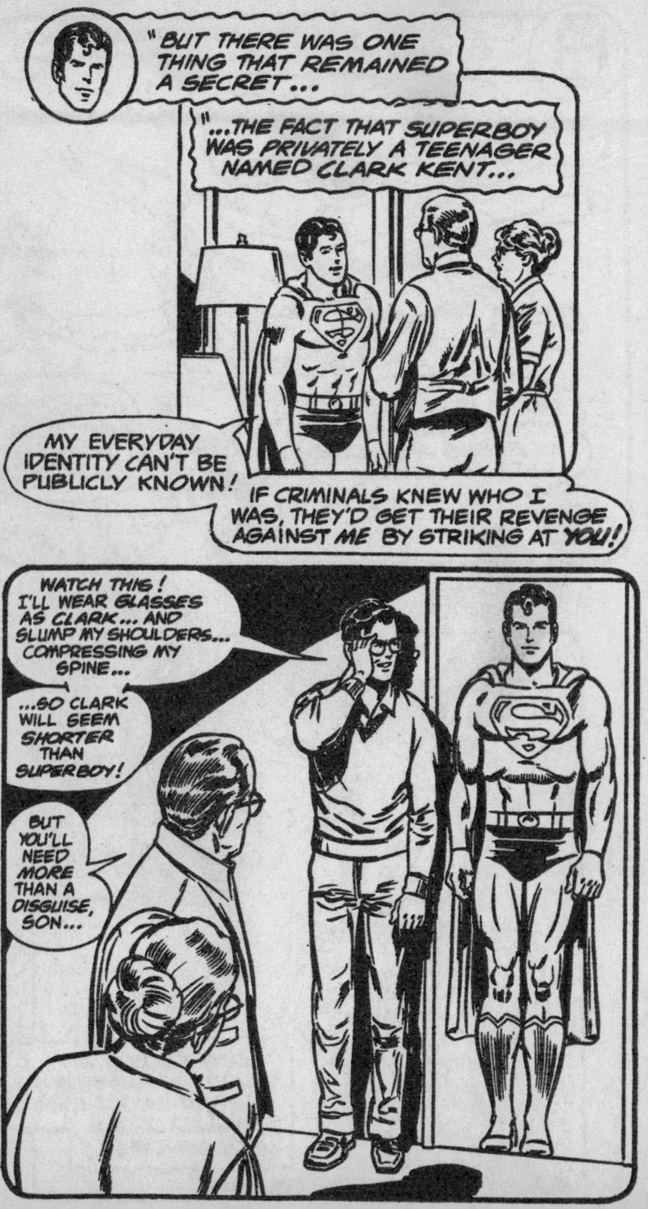
"BUT THERE WAS ONE THING THAT REMAINED A SECRET...
"...THE FACT THAT SUPERBOY WAS PRIVATELY A TEENAGER NAMED CLARK KENT...
MY EVERYDAY IDENTITY CAN'T BE PUBLICLY KNOWN!
IF CRIMINALS KNEW WHO I WAS, THEY'D GET THEIR REVENGE AGAINST ME BY STRIKING AT YOU!
WATCH THIS! I'LL WEAR GLASSES AS CLARK... AND SLUMP MY SHOULDERS... COMPRESSING MY SPINE...
...SO CLARK WILL SEEM SHORTER THAN SUPERBOY!
BUT YOU'LL NEED MORE THAN A DISGUISE, SON...

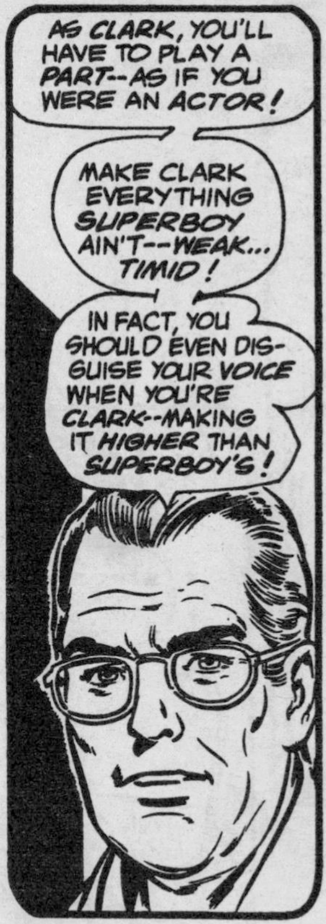
AS CLARK, YOU'LL HAVE TO PLAY A PART--AS IF YOU WERE AN ACTOR!
MAKE CLARK EVERYTHING SUPERBOY AIN'T--WEAK... TIMID!
IN FACT, YOU SHOULD EVEN DIS-GUISE YOUR VOICE WHEN YOU'RE CLARK--MAKING IT HIGHER THAN SUPERBOY'S!

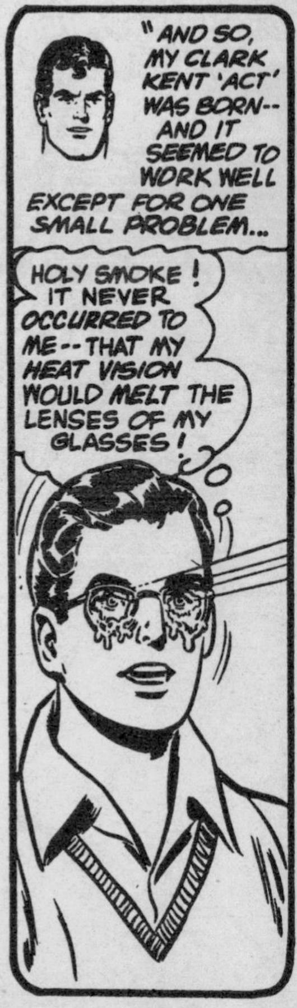
"AND SO, MY CLARK KENT 'ACT' WAS BORN--AND IT SEEMED TO WORK WELL EXCEPT FOR ONE SMALL PROBLEM...
HOLY SMOKE! IT NEVER OCCURRED TO ME--THAT MY HEAT VISION WOULD MELT THE LENSES OF MY GLASSES!

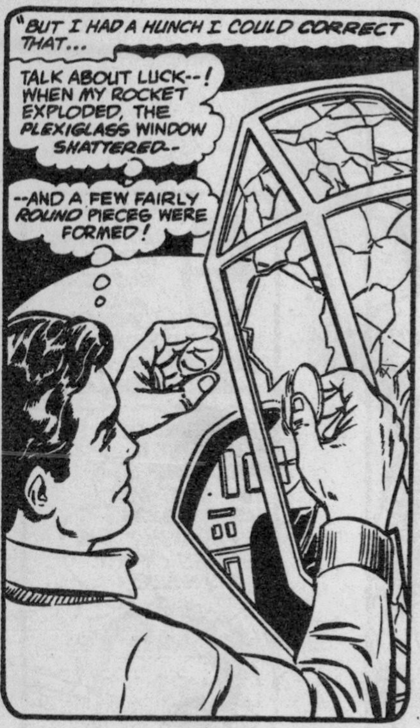
"BUT I HAD A HUNCH I COULD CORRECT THAT...
TALK ABOUT LUCK--! WHEN MY ROCKET EXPLODED, THE PLEXIGLASS WINDOW SHATTERED--
--AND A FEW FAIRLY ROUND PIECES WERE FORMED!

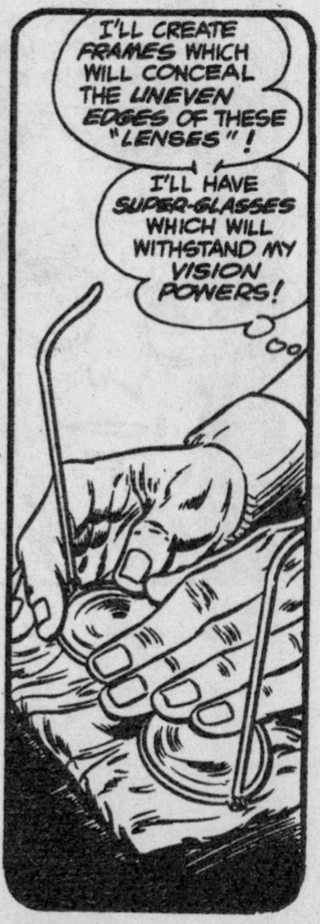
I'LL CREATE FRAMES WHICH WILL CONCEAL THE UNEVEN EDGES OF THESE "LENSES"!
I'LL HAVE SUPER-GLASSES WHICH WILL WITHSTAND MY VISION POWERS!

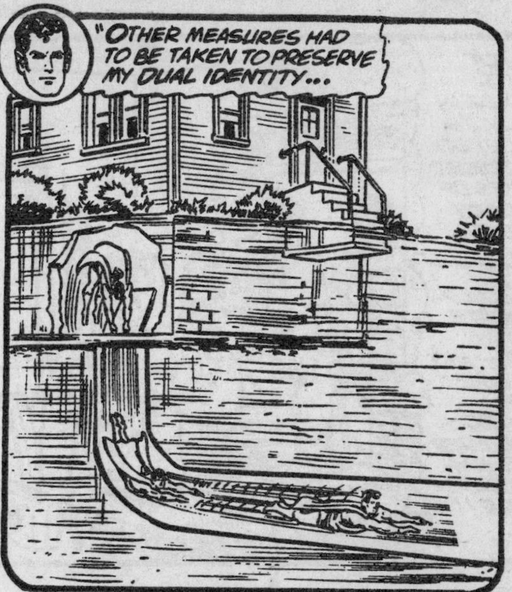
"OTHER MEASURES HAD TO BE TAKEN TO PRESERVE MY DUAL IDENTITY...

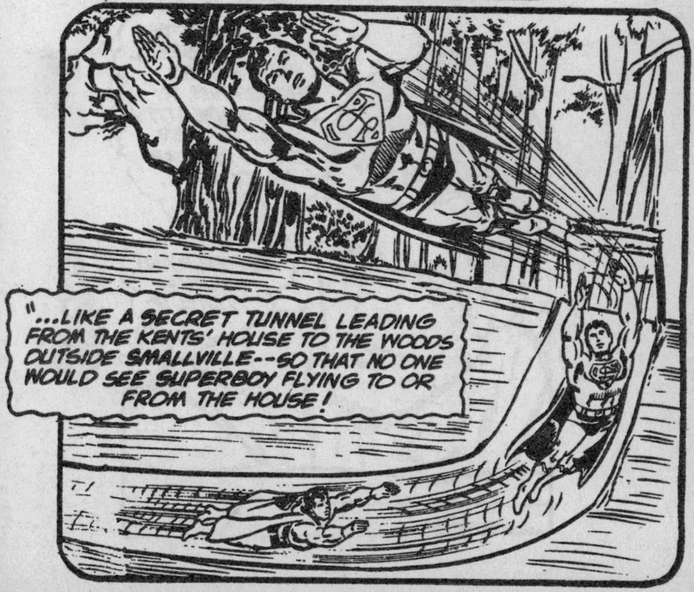
"...LIKE A SECRET TUNNEL LEADING FROM THE KENTS' HOUSE TO THE WOODS OUTSIDE SMALLVILLE--SO THAT NO ONE WOULD SEE SUPERBOY FLYING TO OR FROM THE HOUSE!

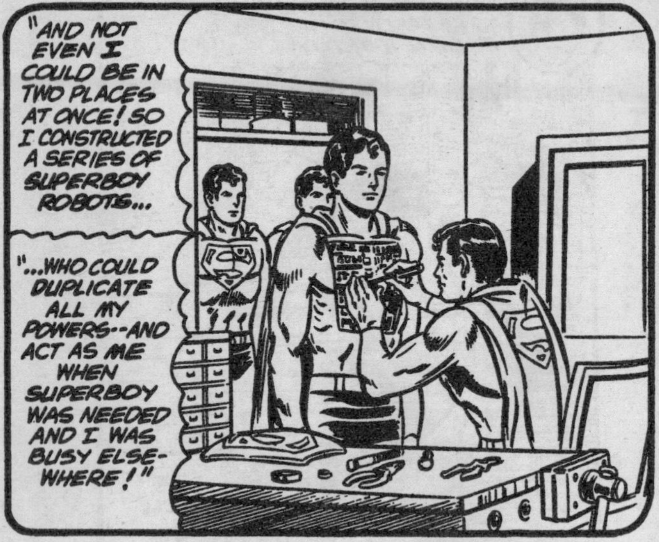
"AND NOT EVEN I COULD BE IN TWO PLACES AT ONCE! SO I CONSTRUCTED A SERIES OF SUPERBOY ROBOTS...
"...WHO COULD DUPLICATE ALL MY POWERS--AND ACT AS ME WHEN SUPERBOY WAS NEEDED AND I WAS BUSY ELSE-WHERE!"

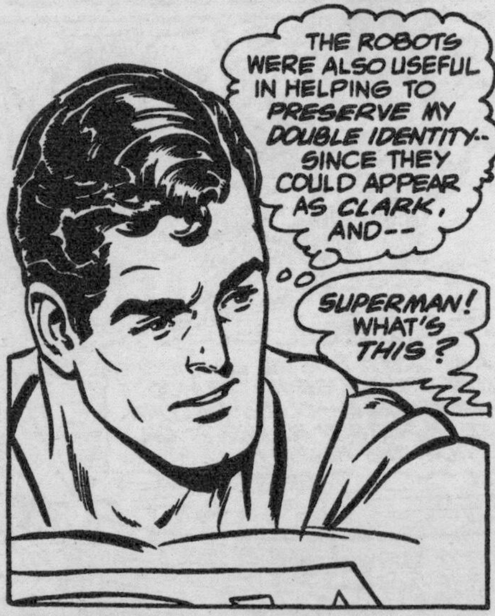
THE ROBOTS WERE ALSO USEFUL IN HELPING TO PRESERVE MY DOUBLE IDENTITY--SINCE THEY COULD APPEAR AS CLARK, AND--
SUPERMAN! WHAT'S THIS?

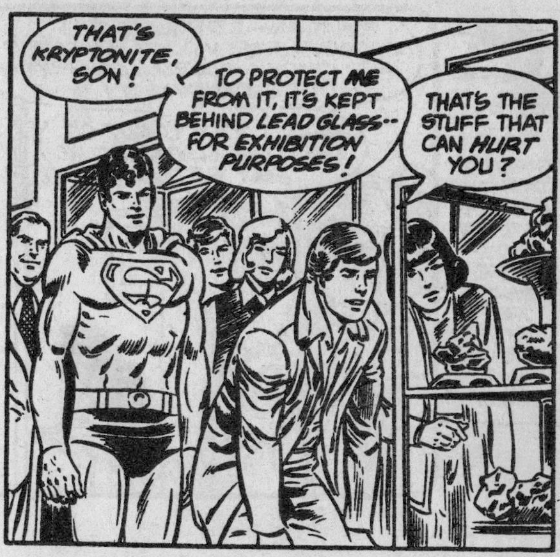
THAT'S KRYPTONITE, SON!
TO PROTECT ME FROM IT, IT'S KEPT BEHIND LEAD GLASS-- FOR EXHIBITION PURPOSES!
THAT'S THE STUFF THAT CAN HURT YOU?

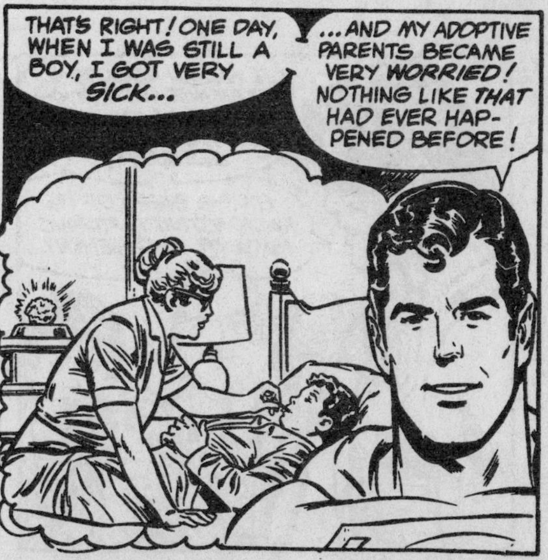
THAT'S RIGHT! ONE DAY, WHEN I WAS STILL A BOY, I GOT VERY SICK...
...AND MY ADOPTIVE PARENTS BECAME VERY WORRIED! NOTHING LIKE THAT HAD EVER HAP-PENED BEFORE!

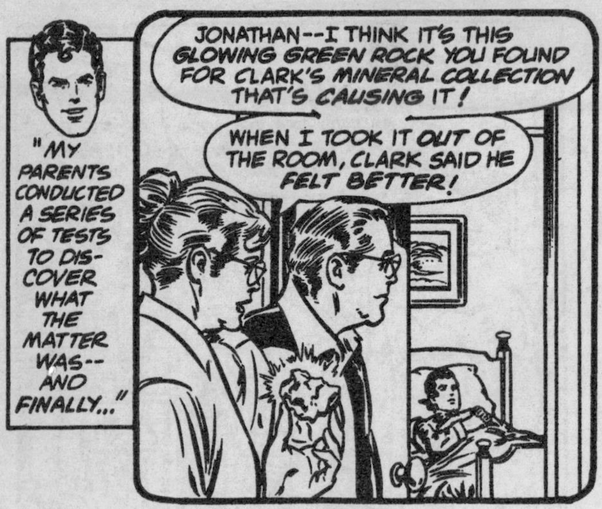
"MY PARENTS CONDUCTED A SERIES OF TESTS TO DIS-COVER WHAT THE MATTER WAS--AND FINALLY..."
JONATHAN--I THINK IT'S THIS GLOWING GREEN ROCK YOU FOUND FOR CLARK'S MINERAL COLLECTION THAT'S CAUSING IT!
WHEN I TOOK IT OUT OF THE ROOM, CLARK SAID HE FELT BETTER!

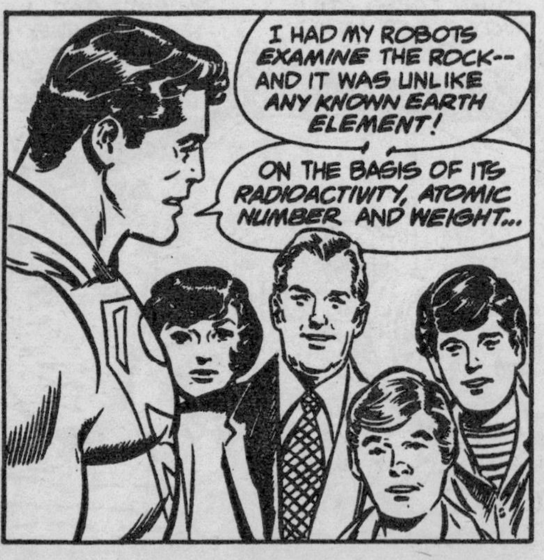
I HAD MY ROBOTS EXAMINE THE ROCK--AND IT WAS UNLIKE ANY KNOWN EARTH ELEMENT!
ON THE BASIS OF ITS RADIOACTIVITY, ATOMIC NUMBER AND WEIGHT...

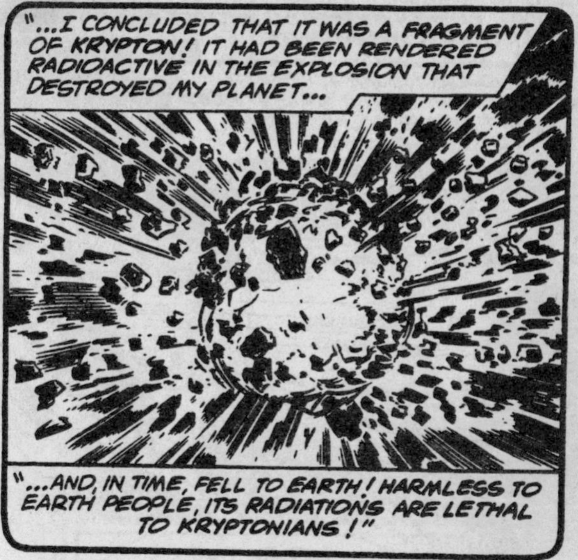
"...I CONCLUDED THAT IT WAS A FRAGMENT OF KRYPTON! IT HAD BEEN RENDERED RADIOACTIVE IN THE EXPLOSION THAT DESTROYED MY PLANET...
"...AND, IN TIME, FELL TO EARTH! HARMLESS TO EARTH PEOPLE, ITS RADIATIONS ARE LETHAL TO KRYPTONIANS!"

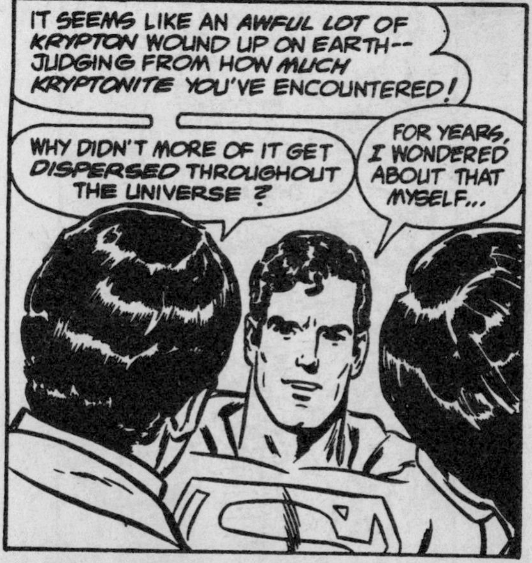
IT SEEMS LIKE AN AWFUL LOT OF KRYPTON WOUND UP ON EARTH-- JUDGING FROM HOW MUCH KRYPTONITE YOU'VE ENCOUNTERED!
WHY DIDN'T MORE OF IT GET DISPERSED THROUGHOUT THE UNIVERSE?
FOR YEARS, I WONDERED ABOUT THAT MYSELF...

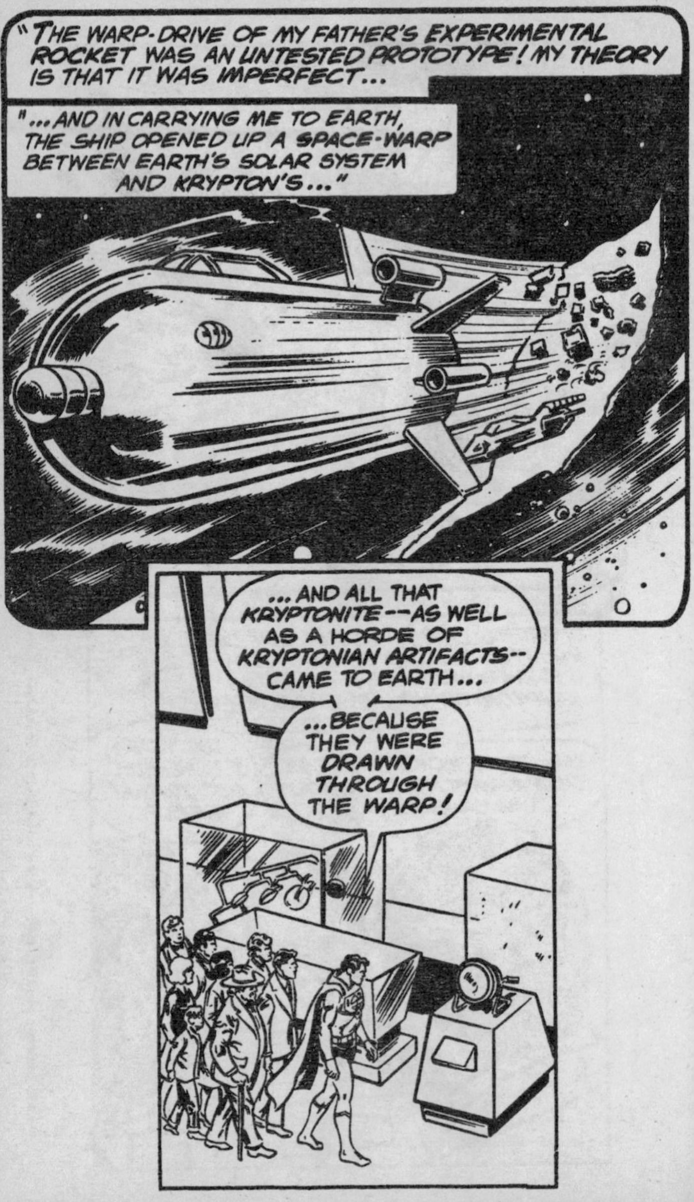
"THE WARP-DRIVE OF MY FATHER'S EXPERIMENTAL ROCKET WAS AN UNTESTED PROTOTYPE! MY THEORY IS THAT IT WAS IMPERFECT...
"...AND IN CARRYING ME TO EARTH, THE SHIP OPENED UP A SPACE-WARP BETWEEN EARTH'S SOLAR SYSTEM AND KRYPTON'S..."
...AND ALL THAT KRYPTONITE--AS WELL AS A HORDE OF KRYPTONIAN ARTIFACTS--CAME TO EARTH...
...BECAUSE THEY WERE DRAWN THROUGH THE WARP!

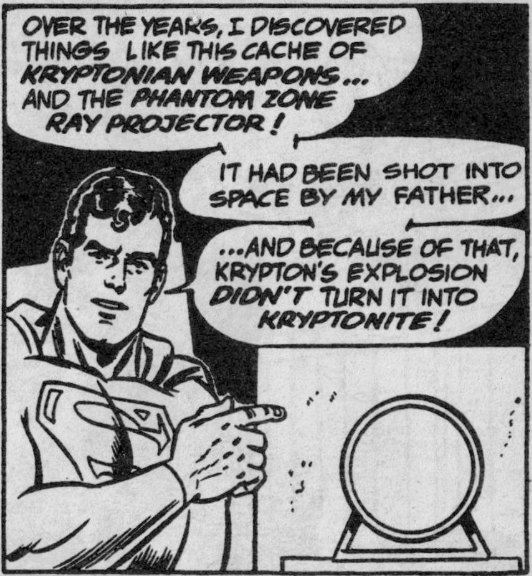
OVER THE YEARS, I DISCOVERED THINGS LIKE THIS CACHE OF KRYPTONIAN WEAPONS... AND THE PHANTOM ZONE RAY PROJECTOR!
IT HAD BEEN SHOT INTO SPACE BY MY FATHER...
...AND BECAUSE OF THAT, KRYPTON'S EXPLOSION DIDN'T TURN IT INTO KRYPTONITE!

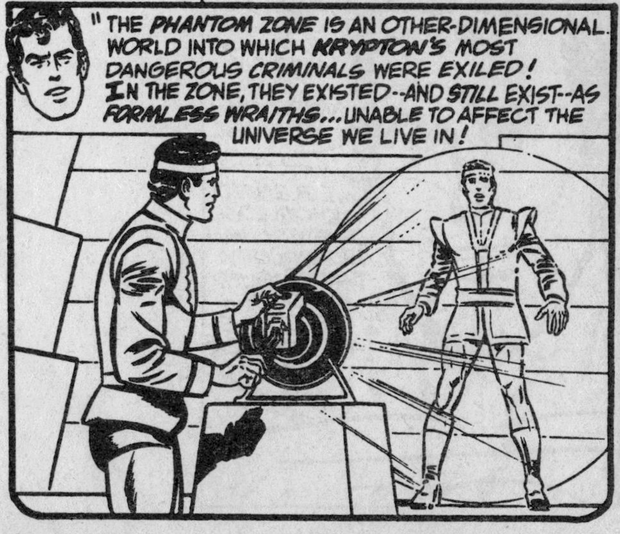
"THE PHANTOM ZONE IS AN OTHER-DIMENSIONAL WORLD INTO WHICH KRYPTON'S MOST DANGEROUS CRIMINALS WERE EXILED! IN THE ZONE, THEY EXISTED--AND STILL EXIST--AS FORMLESS WRAITHS...UNABLE TO AFFECT THE UNIVERSE WE LIVE IN!

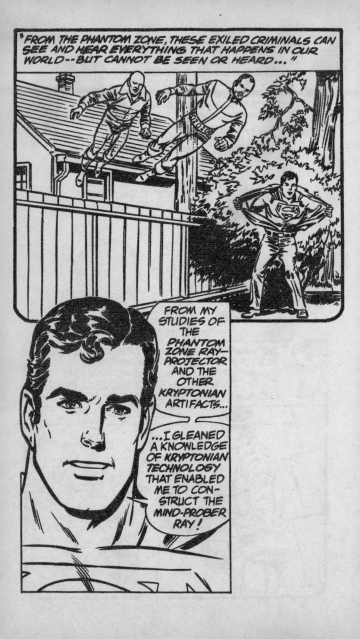

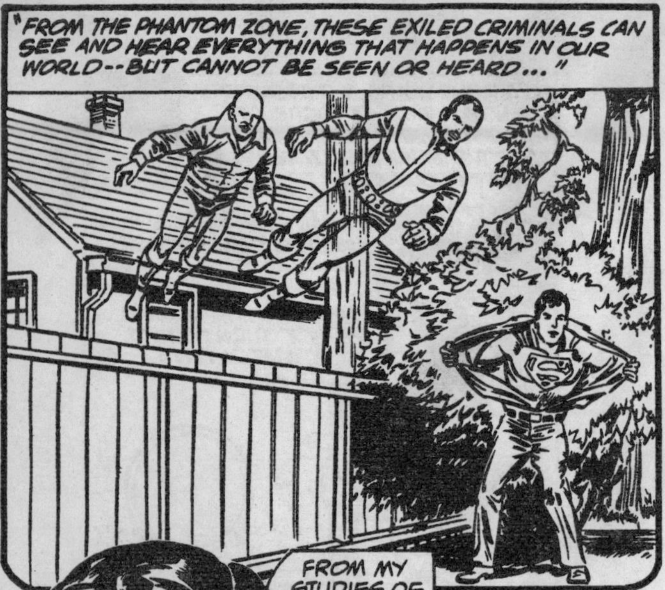
"FROM THE PHANTOM ZONE, THESE EXILED CRIMINALS CAN SEE AND HEAR EVERYTHING THAT HAPPENS IN OUR WORLD--BUT CANNOT BE SEEN OR HEARD..."

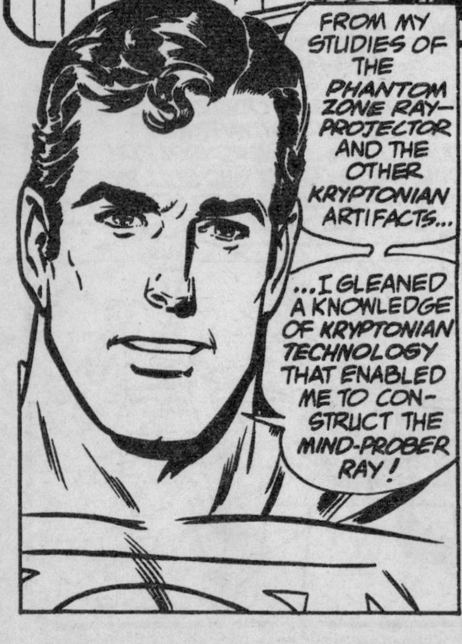
FROM MY STUDIES OF THE PHANTOM ZONE RAY-PROJECTOR AND THE OTHER KRYPTONIAN ARTIFACTS...
...I GLEANED A KNOWLEDGE OF KRYPTONIAN TECHNOLOGY THAT ENABLED ME TO CONSTRUCT THE MIND-PROBER RAY!

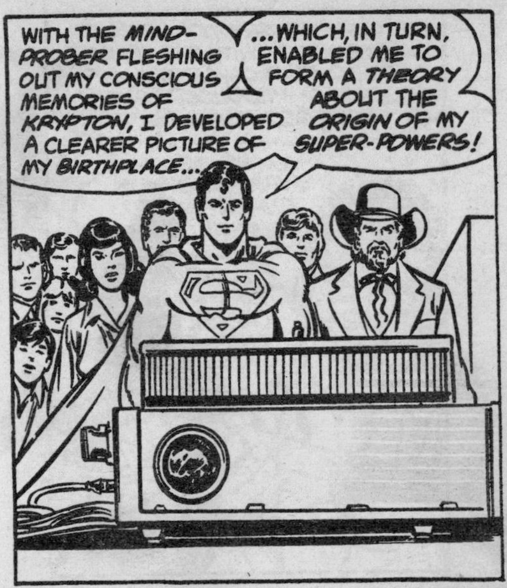
WITH THE MIND-PROBER FLESHING OUT MY CONSCIOUS MEMORIES OF KRYPTON, I DEVELOPED A CLEARER PICTURE OF MY BIRTHPLACE...
...WHICH, IN TURN, ENABLED ME TO FORM A THEORY ABOUT THE ORIGIN OF MY SUPER-POWERS!

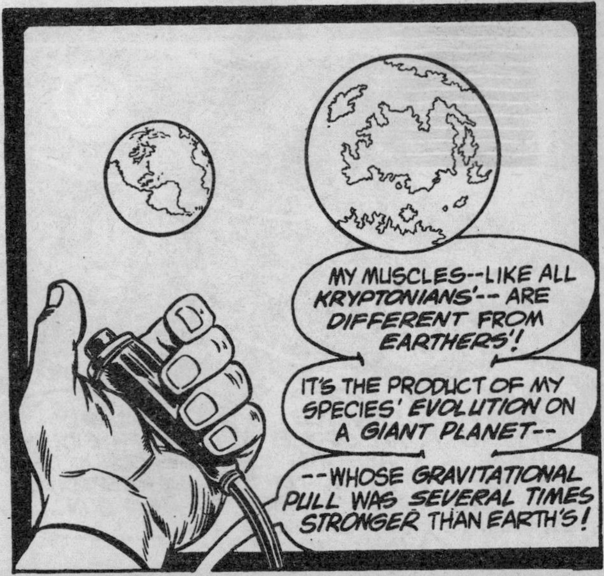
MY MUSCLES--LIKE ALL KRYPTONIANS'-- ARE DIFFERENT FROM EARTHERS'!
IT'S THE PRODUCT OF MY SPECIES' EVOLUTION ON A GIANT PLANET--
--WHOSE GRAVITATIONAL PULL WAS SEVERAL TIMES STRONGER THAN EARTH'S!

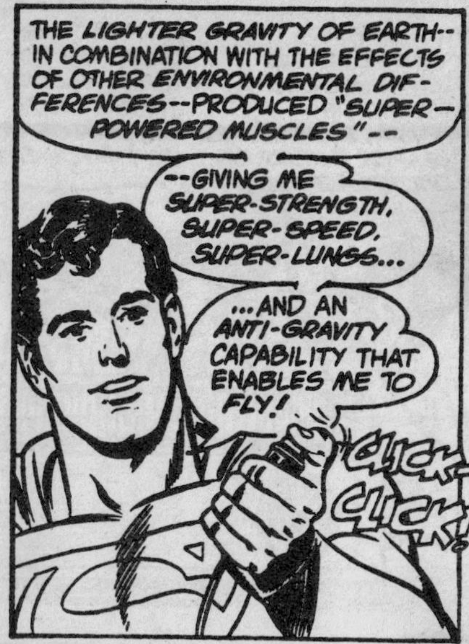
THE LIGHTER GRAVITY OF EARTH-- IN COMBINATION WITH THE EFFECTS OF OTHER ENVIRONMENTAL DIFFERENCES--PRODUCED "SUPER-POWERED MUSCLES"--
--GIVING ME SUPER-STRENGTH, SUPER-SPEED, SUPER-LUNGS...
...AND AN ANTI-GRAVITY CAPABILITY THAT ENABLES ME TO FLY!
CLICK-CLICK!

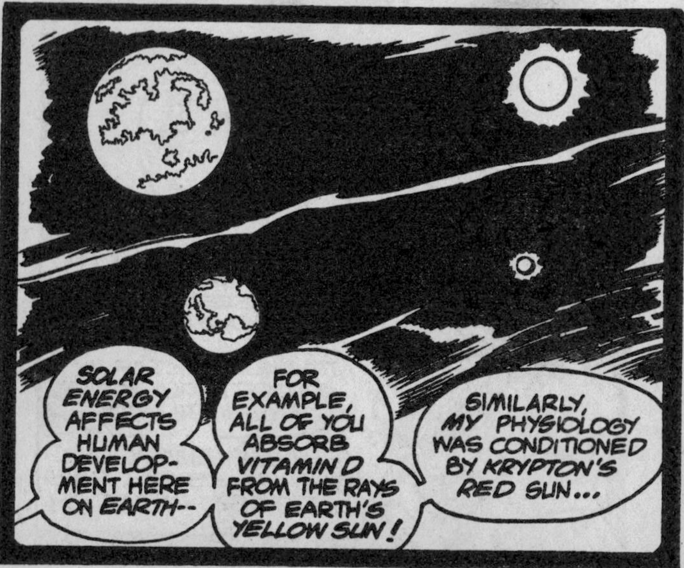
SOLAR ENERGY AFFECTS HUMAN DEVELOPMENT HERE ON EARTH--
FOR EXAMPLE, ALL OF YOU ABSORB VITAMIN D FROM THE RAYS OF EARTH'S YELLOW SUN!
SIMILARLY, MY PHYSIOLOGY WAS CONDITIONED BY KRYPTON'S RED SUN...

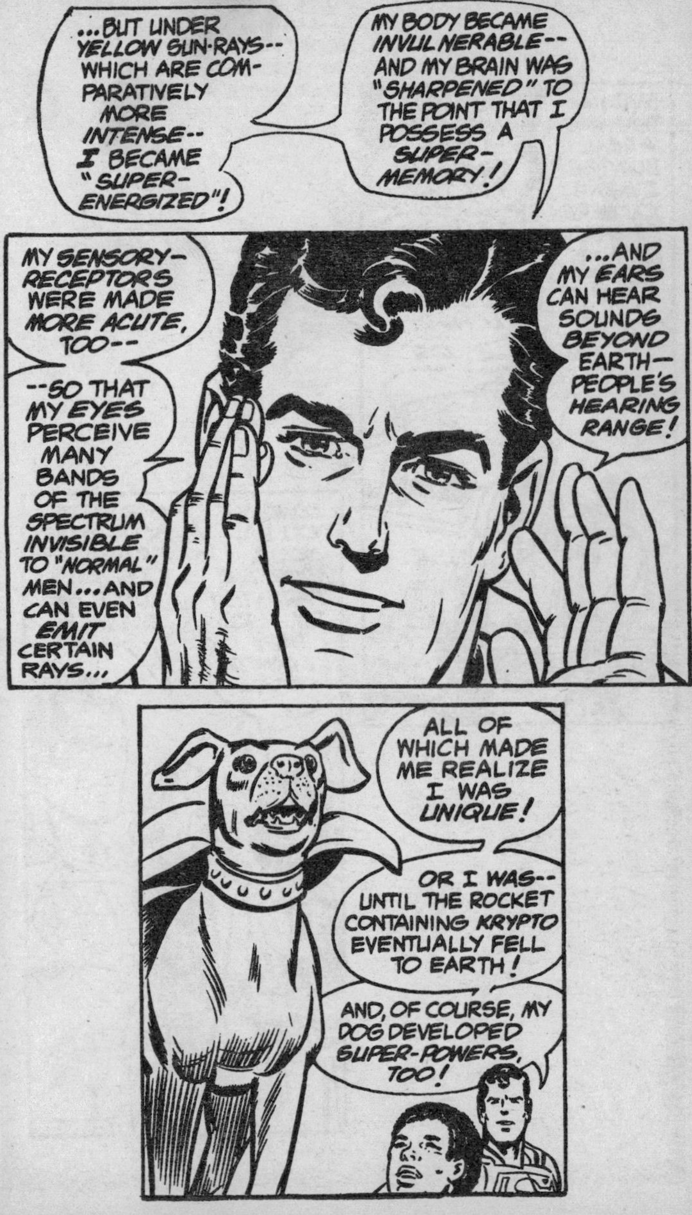
...BUT UNDER YELLOW SUN-RAYS-- WHICH ARE COMPARATIVELY MORE INTENSE-- I BECAME "SUPER-ENERGIZED"!
MY BODY BECAME INVULNERABLE-- AND MY BRAIN WAS "SHARPENED" TO THE POINT THAT I POSSESS A SUPER-MEMORY!
MY SENSORY-RECEPTORS WERE MADE MORE ACUTE, TOO--
--SO THAT MY EYES PERCEIVE MANY BANDS OF THE SPECTRUM INVISIBLE TO "NORMAL" MEN...AND CAN EVEN EMIT CERTAIN RAYS...
...AND MY EARS CAN HEAR SOUNDS BEYOND EARTH-PEOPLE'S HEARING RANGE!
ALL OF WHICH MADE ME REALIZE I WAS UNIQUE!
OR I WAS-- UNTIL THE ROCKET CONTAINING KRYPTO EVENTUALLY FELL TO EARTH!
AND, OF COURSE, MY DOG DEVELOPED SUPER-POWERS, TOO!

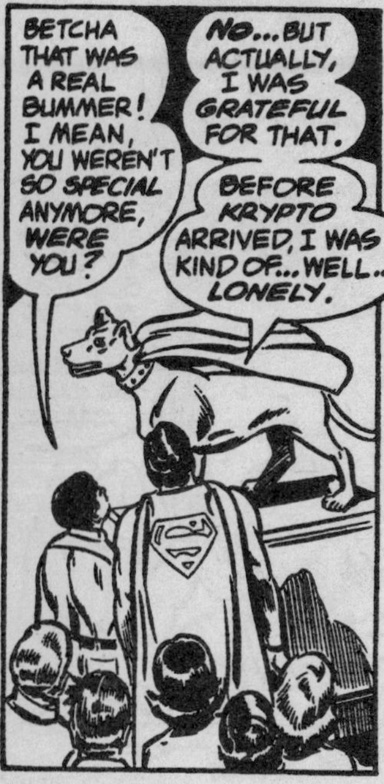
BETCHA THAT WAS A REAL BUMMER! I MEAN, YOU WEREN'T SO SPECIAL ANYMORE, WERE YOU?
NO...BUT ACTUALLY, I WAS GRATEFUL FOR THAT.
BEFORE KRYPTO ARRIVED, I WAS KIND OF...WELL... LONELY.

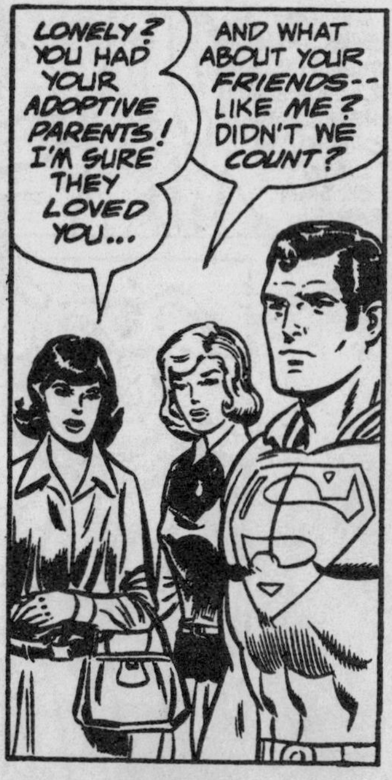
LONELY? YOU HAD YOUR ADOPTIVE PARENTS! I'M SURE THEY LOVED YOU...
AND WHAT ABOUT YOUR FRIENDS-- LIKE ME? DIDN'T WE COUNT?

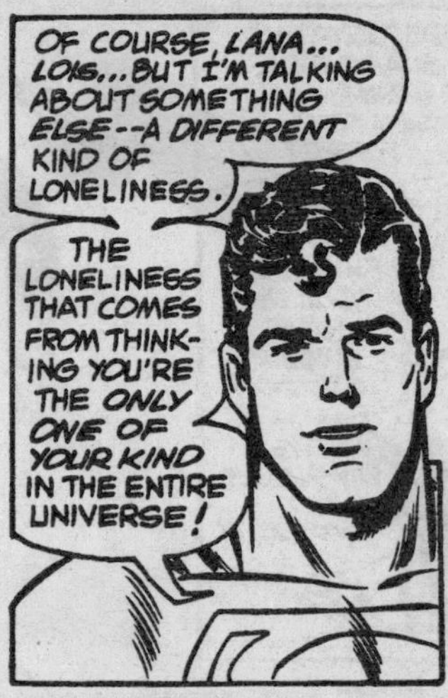
OF COURSE, LANA... LOIS...BUT I'M TALKING ABOUT SOMETHING ELSE--A DIFFERENT KIND OF LONELINESS.
THE LONELINESS THAT COMES FROM THINKING YOU'RE THE ONLY ONE OF YOUR KIND IN THE ENTIRE UNIVERSE!

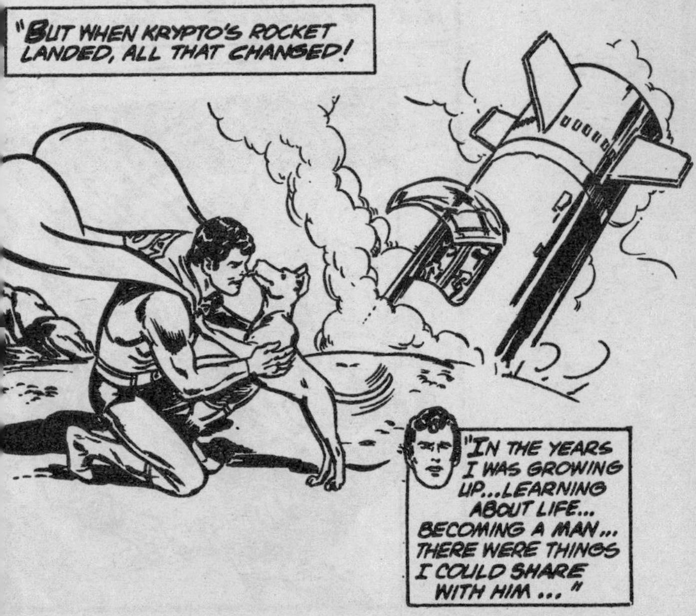
"BUT WHEN KRYPTO'S ROCKET LANDED, ALL THAT CHANGED!
"IN THE YEARS I WAS GROWING UP...LEARNING ABOUT LIFE... BECOMING A MAN... THERE WERE THINGS I COULD SHARE WITH HIM ..."

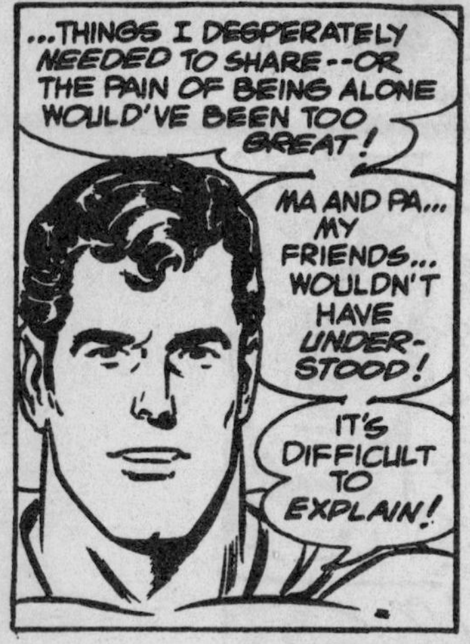
...THINGS I DESPERATELY NEEDED TO SHARE--OR THE PAIN OF BEING ALONE WOULD'VE BEEN TOO GREAT!
MA AND PA... MY FRIENDS... WOULDN'T HAVE UNDERSTOOD!
IT'S DIFFICULT TO EXPLAIN!

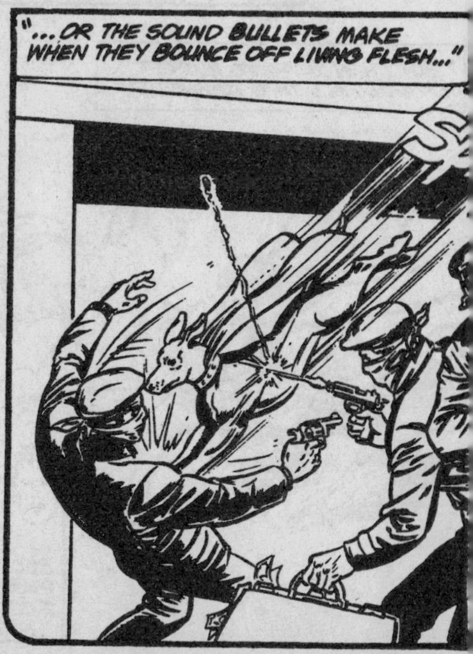
"...OR THE SOUND BULLETS MAKE WHEN THEY BOUNCE OFF LIVING FLESH..."

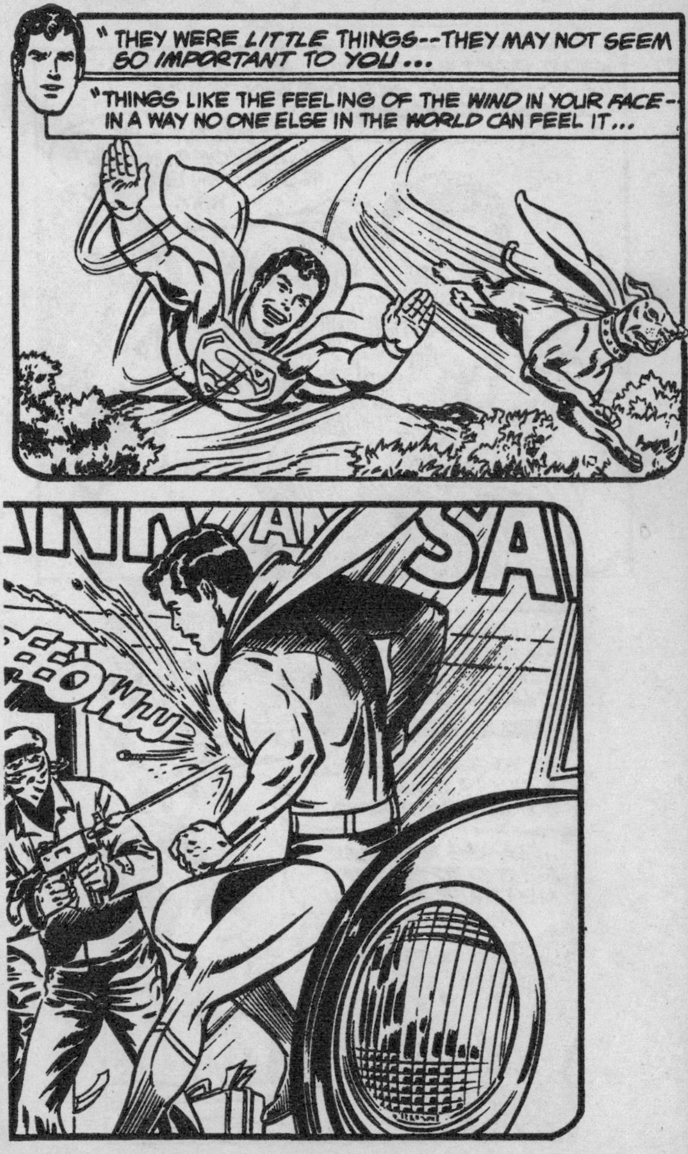
"THEY WERE LITTLE THINGS--THEY MAY NOT SEEM SO IMPORTANT TO YOU...
"THINGS LIKE THE FEELING OF THE WIND IN YOUR FACE--IN A WAY NO ONE ELSE IN THE WORLD CAN FEEL IT...

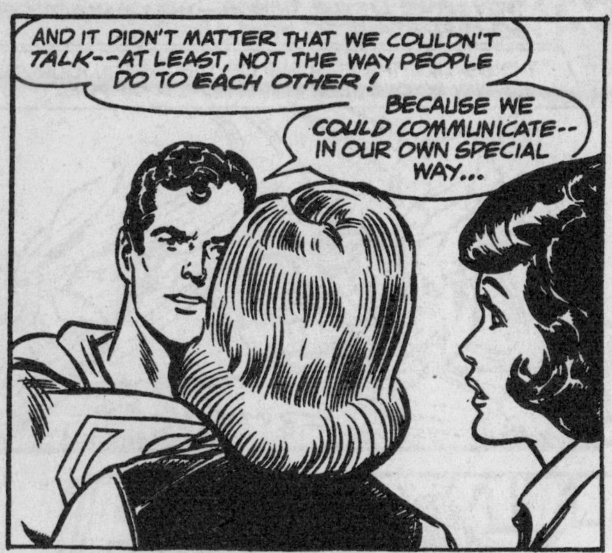
AND IT DIDN'T MATTER THAT WE COULDN'T TALK--AT LEAST, NOT THE WAY PEOPLE DO TO EACH OTHER!
BECAUSE WE COULD COMMUNICATE--IN OUR OWN SPECIAL WAY...

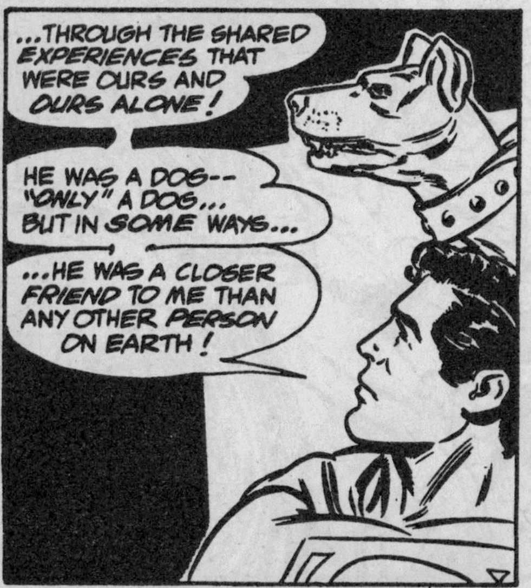
...THROUGH THE SHARED EXPERIENCES THAT WERE OURS AND OURS ALONE!
HE WAS A DOG--"ONLY" A DOG... BUT IN SOME WAYS...
...HE WAS A CLOSER FRIEND TO ME THAN ANY OTHER PERSON ON EARTH!

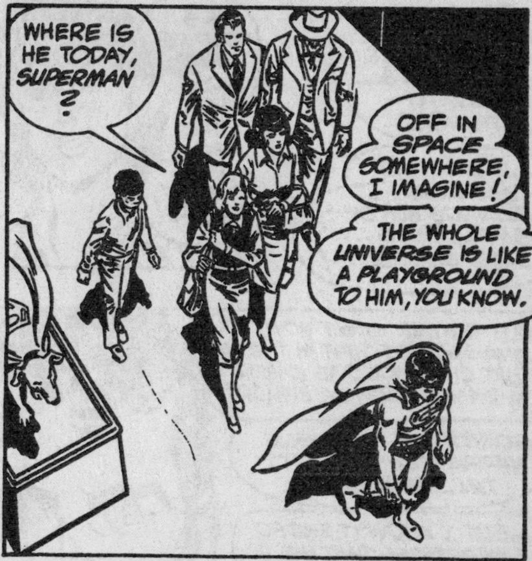
WHERE IS HE TODAY, SUPERMAN ?
OFF IN SPACE SOMEWHERE, I IMAGINE!
THE WHOLE UNIVERSE IS LIKE A PLAYGROUND TO HIM, YOU KNOW.

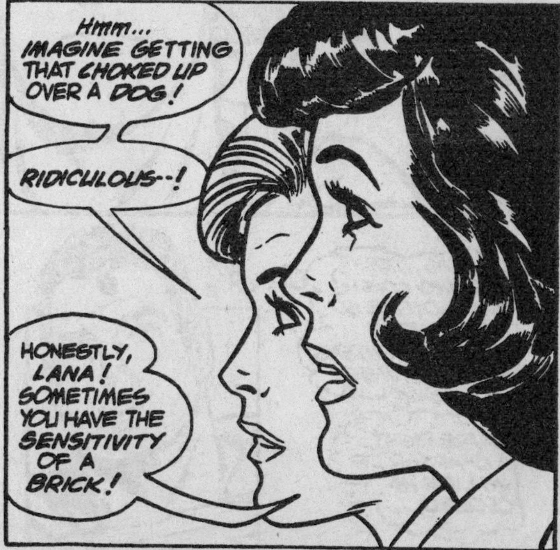
Hmm... IMAGINE GETTING THAT CHOKED UP OVER A DOG!
RIDICULOUS--!
HONESTLY, LANA! SOMETIMES YOU HAVE THE SENSITIVITY OF A BRICK!

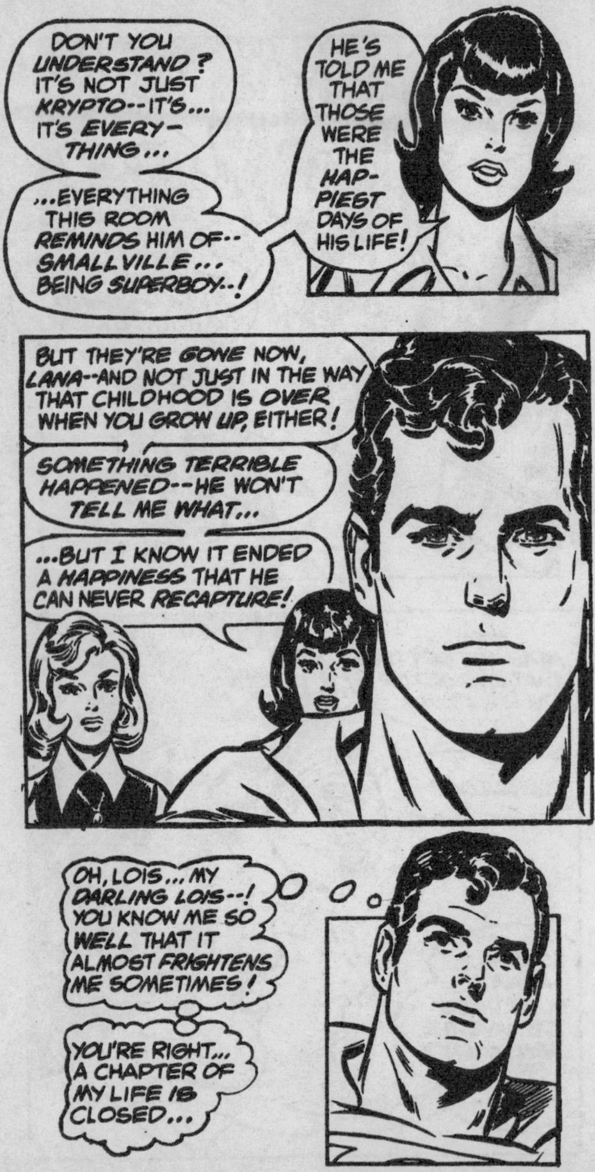
DON'T YOU UNDERSTAND? IT'S NOT JUST KRYPTO--IT'S... IT'S EVERY-THING...
...EVERYTHING THIS ROOM REMINDS HIM OF--SMALLVILLE... BEING SUPERBOY--!
HE'S TOLD ME THAT THOSE WERE THE HAP-PIEST DAYS OF HIS LIFE!
BUT THEY'RE GONE NOW, LANA--AND NOT JUST IN THE WAY THAT CHILDHOOD IS OVER WHEN YOU GROW UP, EITHER!
SOMETHING TERRIBLE HAPPENED--HE WON'T TELL ME WHAT...
...BUT I KNOW IT ENDED A HAPPINESS THAT HE CAN NEVER RECAPTURE!
OH, LOIS... MY DARLING LOIS--! YOU KNOW ME SO WELL THAT IT ALMOST FRIGHTENS ME SOMETIMES!
YOU'RE RIGHT... A CHAPTER OF MY LIFE IS CLOSED...

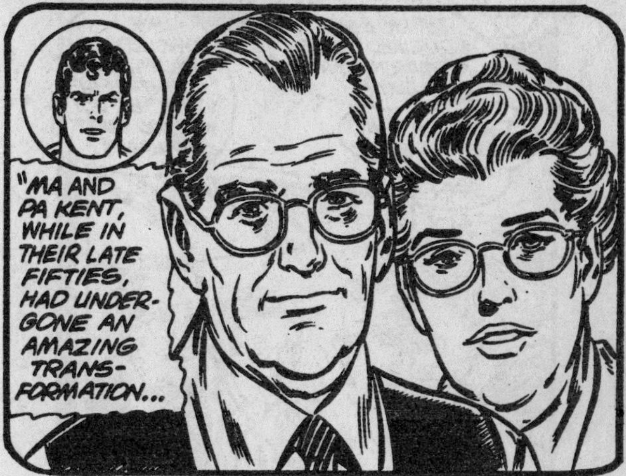
"MA AND PA KENT, WHILE IN THEIR LATE FIFTIES, HAD UNDERGONE AN AMAZING TRANSFORMATION...

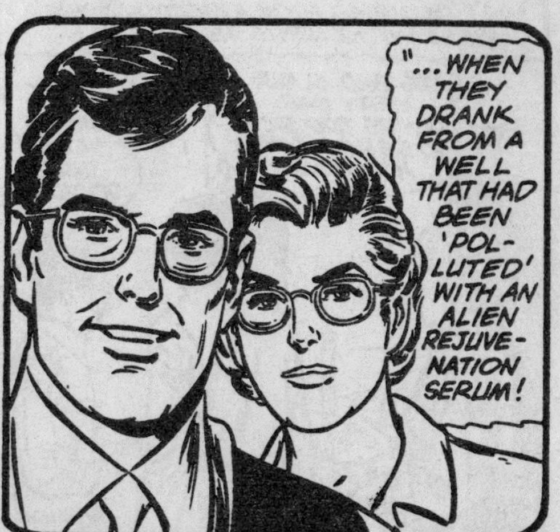
"...WHEN THEY DRANK FROM A WELL THAT HAD BEEN 'POLLUTED' WITH AN ALIEN REJUVENATION SERUM!

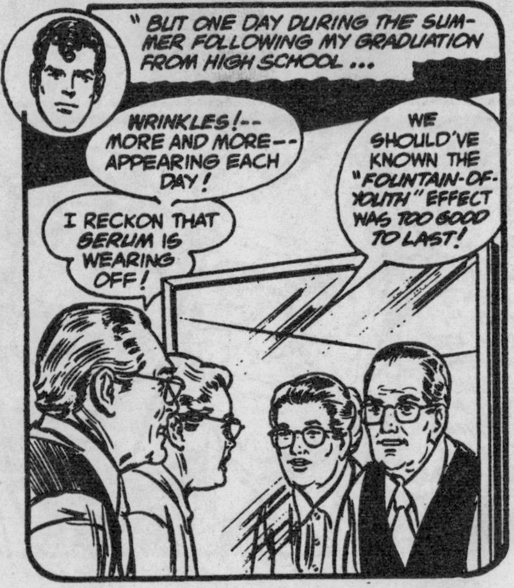
"BUT ONE DAY DURING THE SUMMER FOLLOWING MY GRADUATION FROM HIGH SCHOOL ...
WRINKLES!-- MORE AND MORE-- APPEARING EACH DAY!
I RECKON THAT SERUM IS WEARING OFF!
WE SHOULD'VE KNOWN THE "FOUNTAIN-OF-YOUTH" EFFECT WAS TOO GOOD TO LAST!

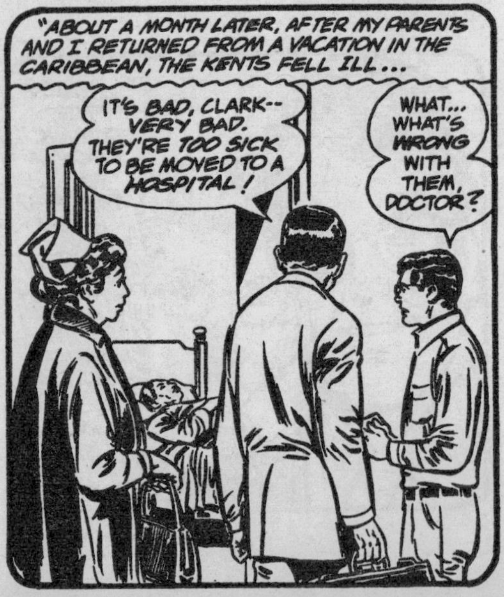
"ABOUT A MONTH LATER, AFTER MY PARENTS AND I RETURNED FROM A VACATION IN THE CARIBBEAN, THE KENTS FELL ILL ...
IT'S BAD, CLARK-- VERY BAD. THEY'RE TOO SICK TO BE MOVED TO A HOSPITAL!
WHAT... WHAT'S WRONG WITH THEM, DOCTOR?

I DON'T KNOW WHAT IT IS--IT RESEMBLES SCARLET FEVER, BUT IT'S SOMETHING ELSE.

SULFA DRUGS... STEROIDS-- I'VE TRIED EVERYTHING I KNOW...

...BUT THEY'RE NOT RESPONDING!

"I TRIED TO FIND THE CAUSE OF THE MYSTERIOUS DISEASE THEY'D CONTRACTED--AND FAILED...

"I DID EVERYTHING I COULD TO SAVE THEM--BUT A CRUEL FATE THWARTED ME AT EVERY TURN...

MA...DAD! I'VE BEEN ALL OVER THE UNIVERSE TO FIND A CURE FOR YOU--

--BUT NOTHING I'VE FOUND SEEMS TO BE WORKING--!

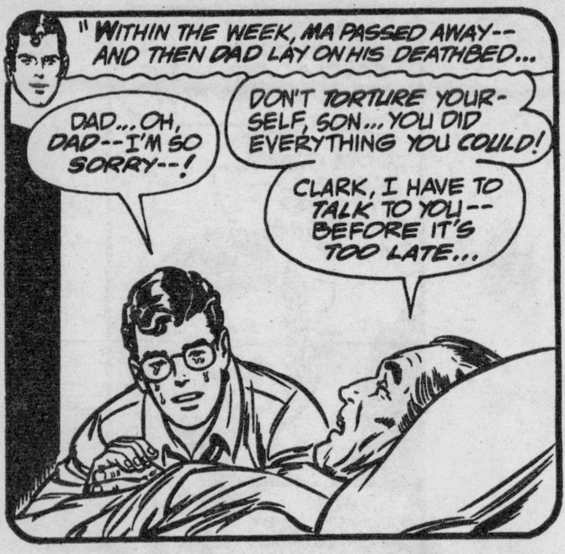
"WITHIN THE WEEK, MA PASSED AWAY--
AND THEN DAD LAY ON HIS DEATHBED...
DAD... OH, DAD--I'M SO SORRY--!
DON'T TORTURE YOURSELF, SON... YOU DID EVERYTHING YOU COULD!
CLARK, I HAVE TO TALK TO YOU--BEFORE IT'S TOO LATE...

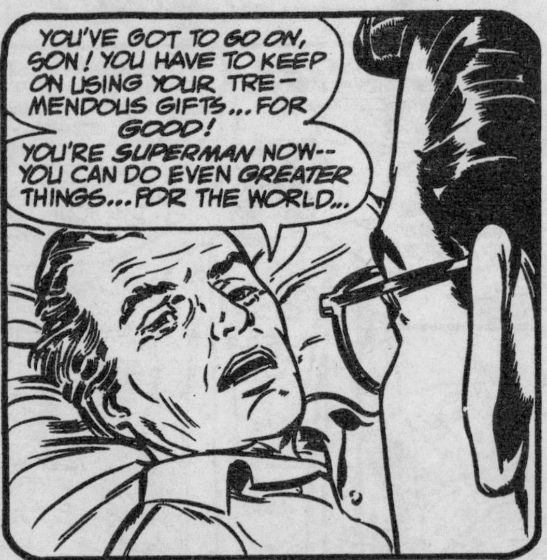
YOU'VE GOT TO GO ON, SON! YOU HAVE TO KEEP ON USING YOUR TREMENDOUS GIFTS... FOR GOOD!
YOU'RE SUPERMAN NOW--YOU CAN DO EVEN GREATER THINGS... FOR THE WORLD...

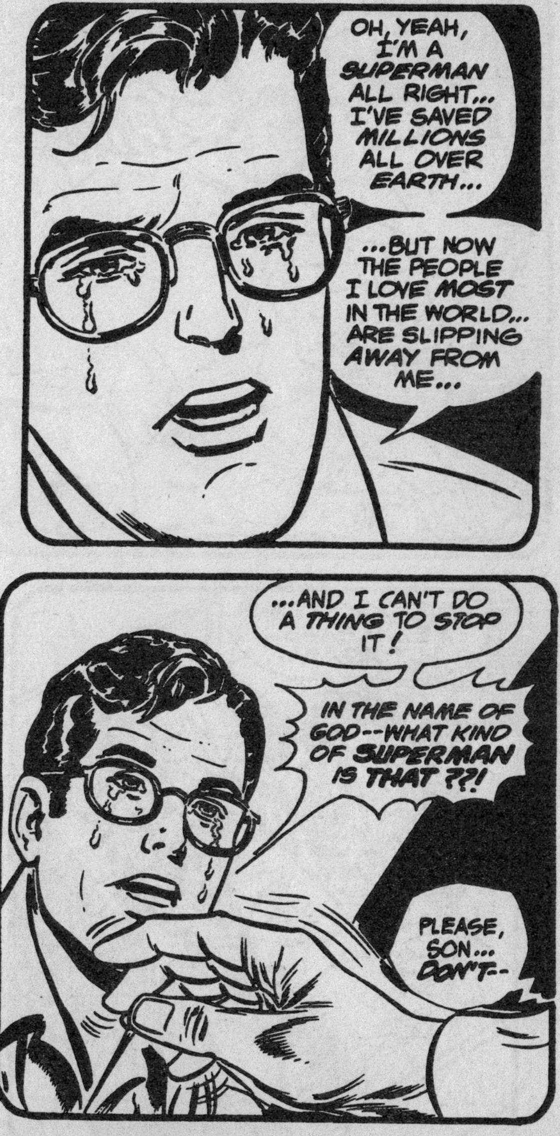
OH, YEAH, I'M A SUPERMAN ALL RIGHT... I'VE SAVED MILLIONS ALL OVER EARTH...
...BUT NOW THE PEOPLE I LOVE MOST IN THE WORLD... ARE SLIPPING AWAY FROM ME...
...AND I CAN'T DO A THING TO STOP IT!
IN THE NAME OF GOD--WHAT KIND OF SUPERMAN IS THAT ??!
PLEASE, SON... DON'T--

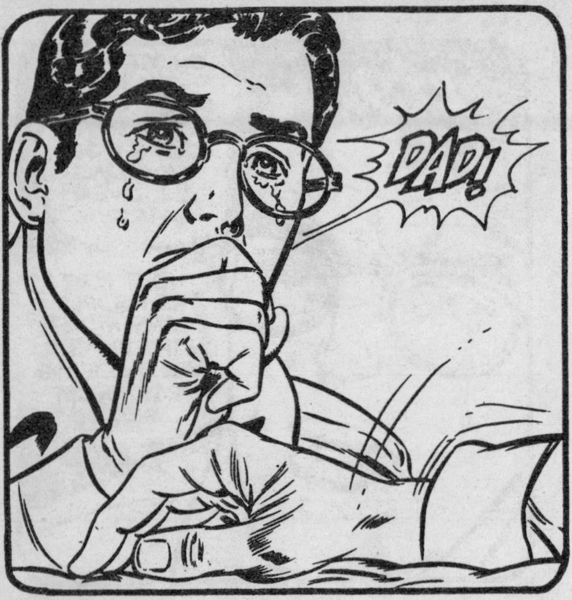
DAD!

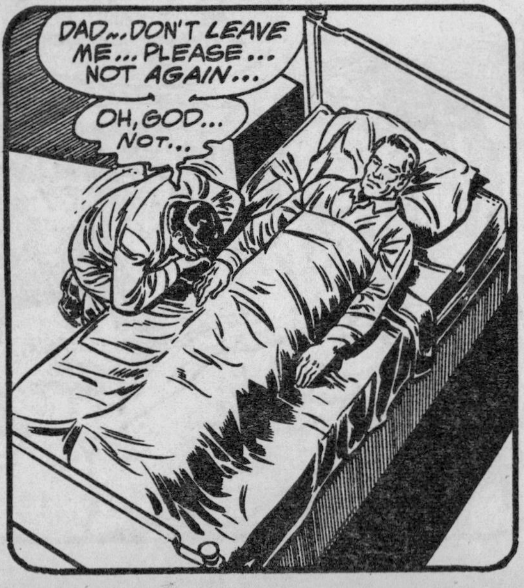
DAD...DON'T LEAVE ME... PLEASE... NOT AGAIN...
OH, GOD... NOT...

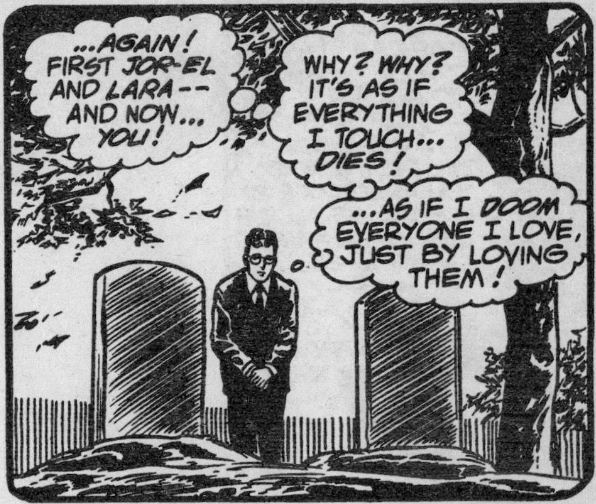
...AGAIN! FIRST JOR-EL AND LARA-- AND NOW... YOU!
WHY? WHY? IT'S AS IF EVERYTHING I TOUCH... DIES!
...AS IF I DOOM EVERYONE I LOVE, JUST BY LOVING THEM!

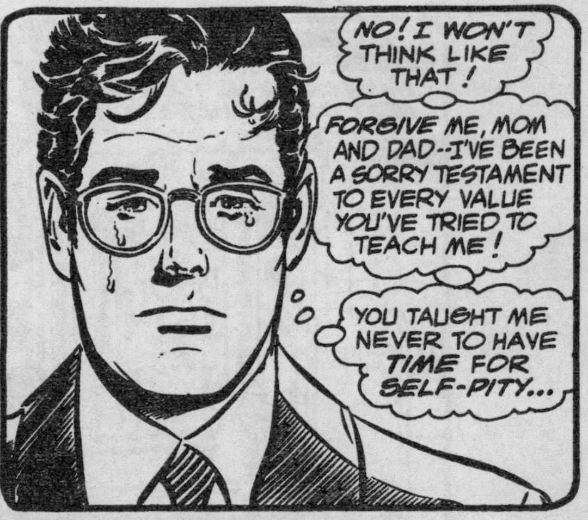
NO! I WON'T THINK LIKE THAT!
FORGIVE ME, MOM AND DAD--I'VE BEEN A SORRY TESTAMENT TO EVERY VALUE YOU'VE TRIED TO TEACH ME!
YOU TAUGHT ME NEVER TO HAVE TIME FOR SELF-PITY...

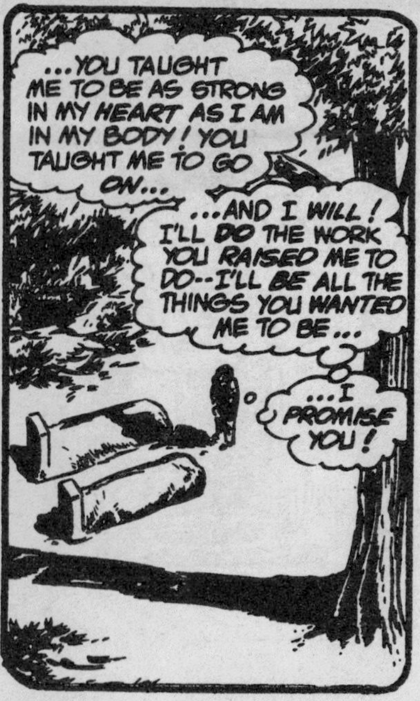
...YOU TAUGHT ME TO BE AS STRONG IN MY HEART AS I AM IN MY BODY! YOU TAUGHT ME TO GO ON...
...AND I WILL! I'LL DO THE WORK YOU RAISED ME TO DO--I'LL BE ALL THE THINGS YOU WANTED ME TO BE...
...I PROMISE YOU!

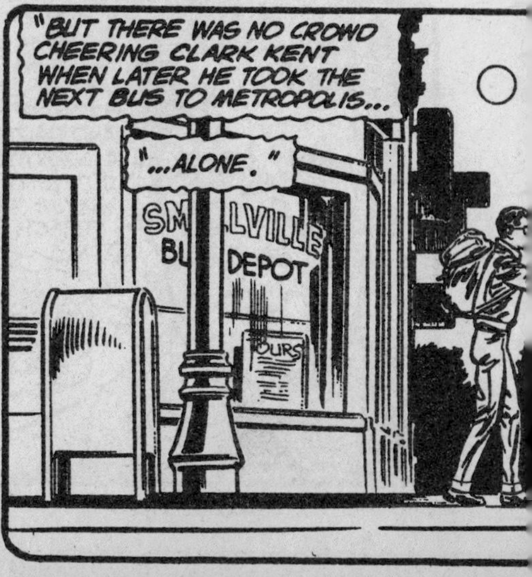
"BUT THERE WAS NO CROWD CHEERING CLARK KENT WHEN LATER HE TOOK THE NEXT BUS TO METROPOLIS...
"...ALONE."
SM LVILLE
BU DEPOT
OURS

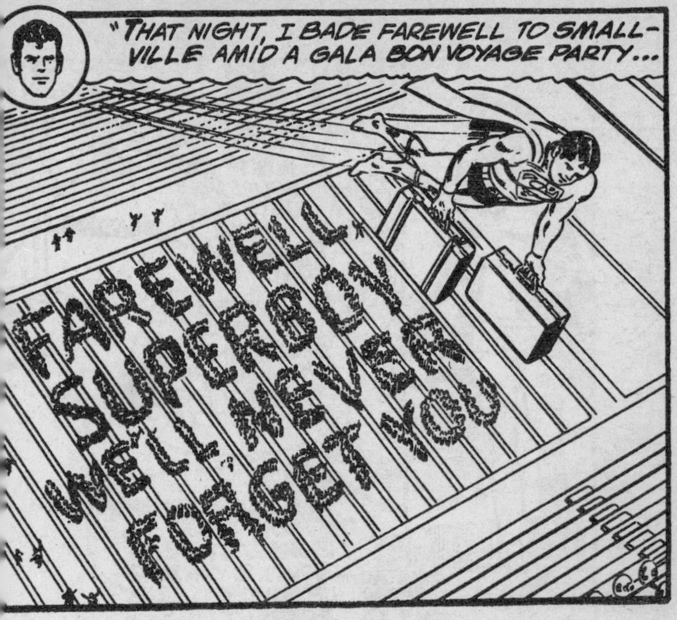
"THAT NIGHT, I BADE FAREWELL TO SMALL-VILLE AMID A GALA BON VOYAGE PARTY...
FAREWELL SUPERBOY WE'LL NEVER FORGET YOU

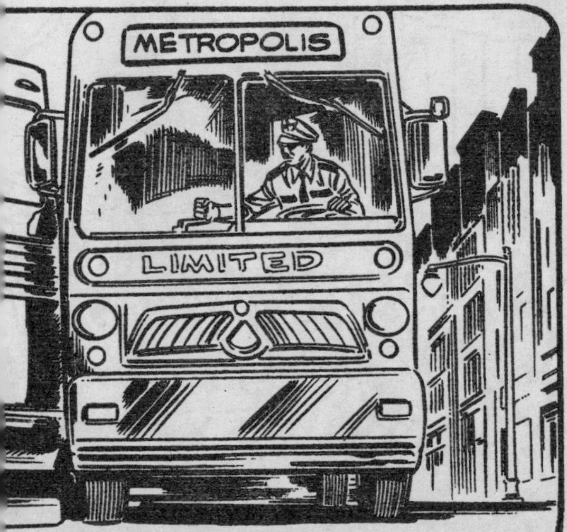
METROPOLIS
LIMITED

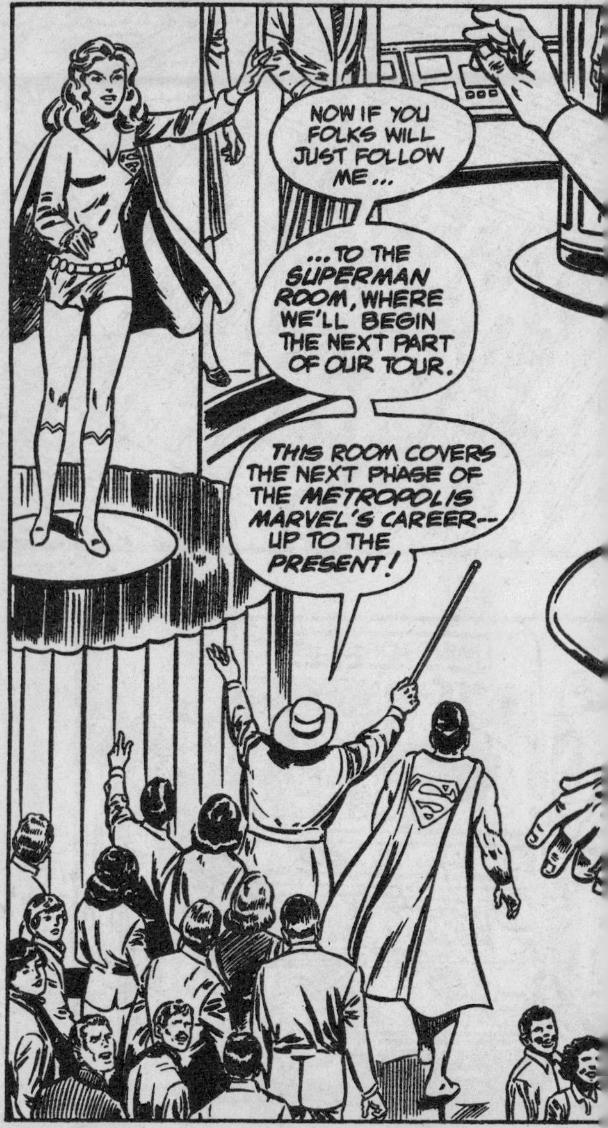
NOW IF YOU FOLKS WILL JUST FOLLOW ME...
...TO THE SUPERMAN ROOM, WHERE WE'LL BEGIN THE NEXT PART OF OUR TOUR.
THIS ROOM COVERS THE NEXT PHASE OF THE METROPOLIS MARVEL'S CAREER--UP TO THE PRESENT!

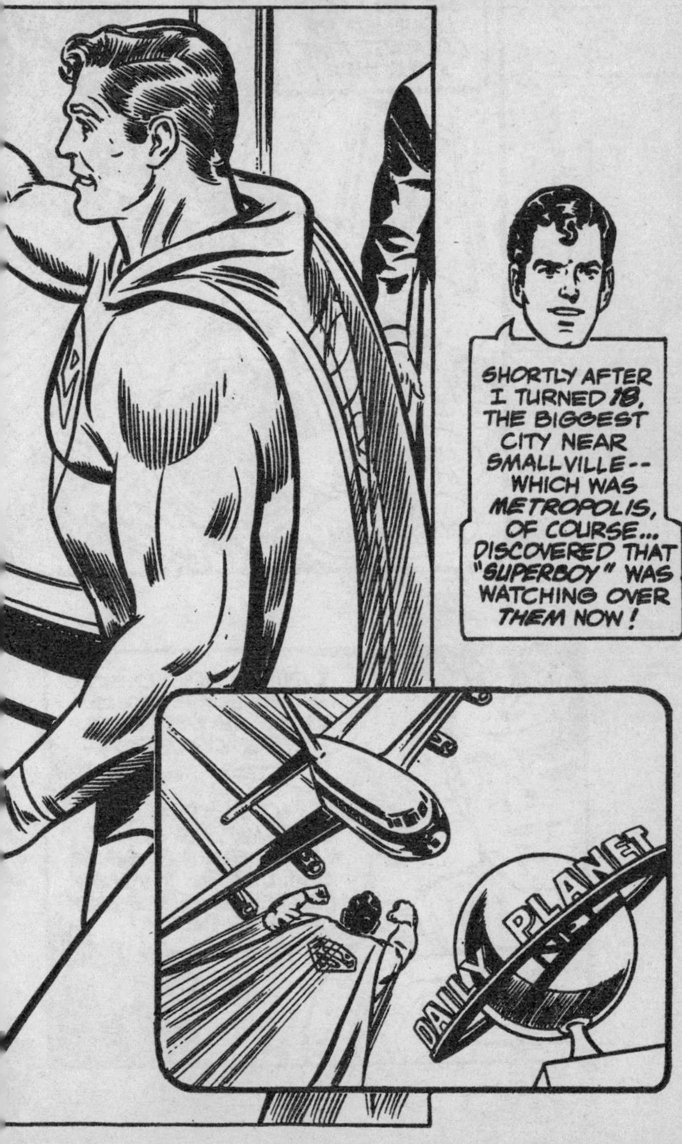
SHORTLY AFTER I TURNED 18, THE BIGGEST CITY NEAR SMALLVILLE-- WHICH WAS METROPOLIS, OF COURSE... DISCOVERED THAT "SUPERBOY" WAS WATCHING OVER THEM NOW!
DAILY PLANET

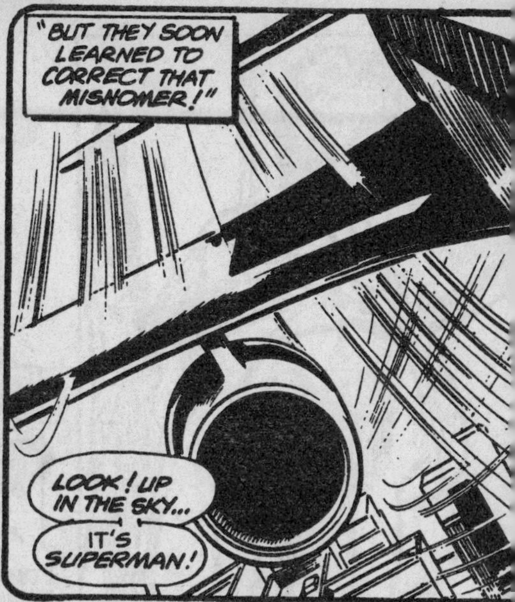
"BUT THEY SOON LEARNED TO CORRECT THAT MISNOMER!"
LOOK! UP IN THE SKY...
IT'S SUPERMAN!

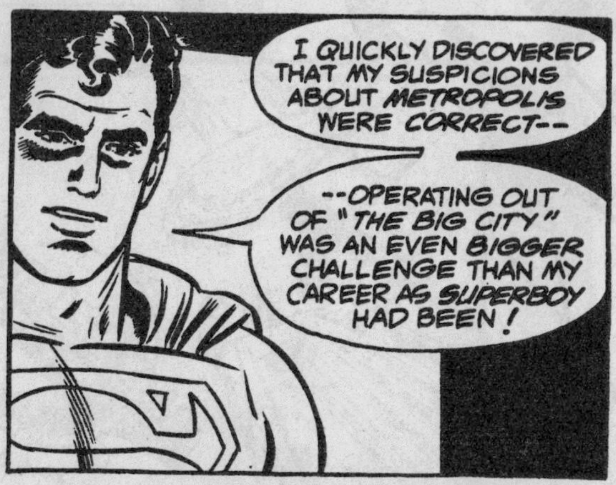
I QUICKLY DISCOVERED THAT MY SUSPICIONS ABOUT METROPOLIS WERE CORRECT--
--OPERATING OUT OF "THE BIG CITY" WAS AN EVEN BIGGER CHALLENGE THAN MY CAREER AS SUPERBOY HAD BEEN!

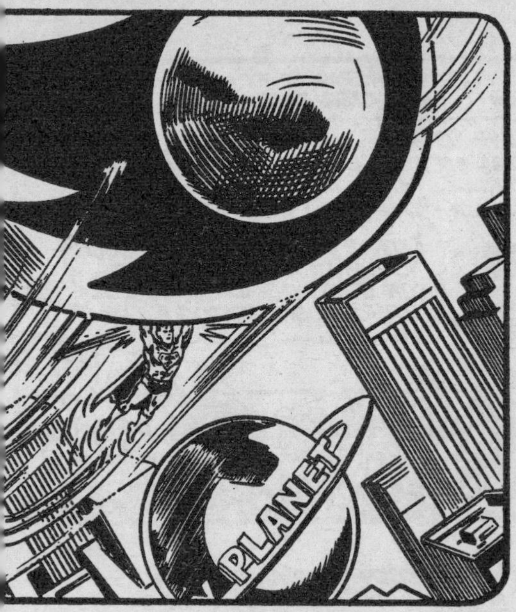
PLANET

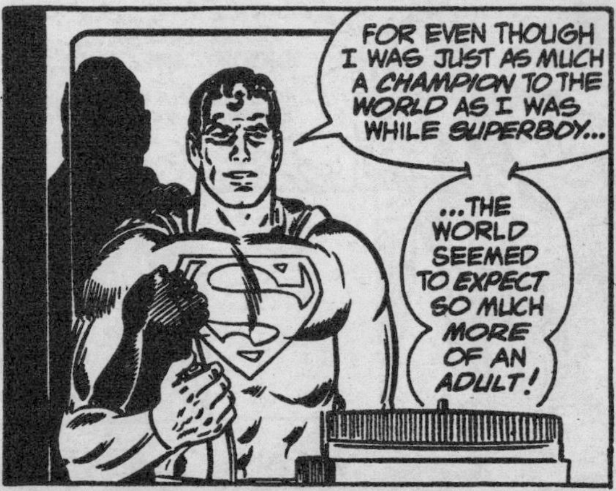
FOR EVEN THOUGH I WAS JUST AS MUCH A *CHAMPION* TO THE *WORLD* AS I WAS WHILE *SUPERBOY...*
...THE WORLD SEEMED TO *EXPECT* SO MUCH *MORE* OF AN *ADULT*!

"BUT MY FOUR YEARS AT METROPOLIS UNIVERSITY PREPARED ME WELL FOR THE CHALLENGE OF SUPER-MANHOOD!

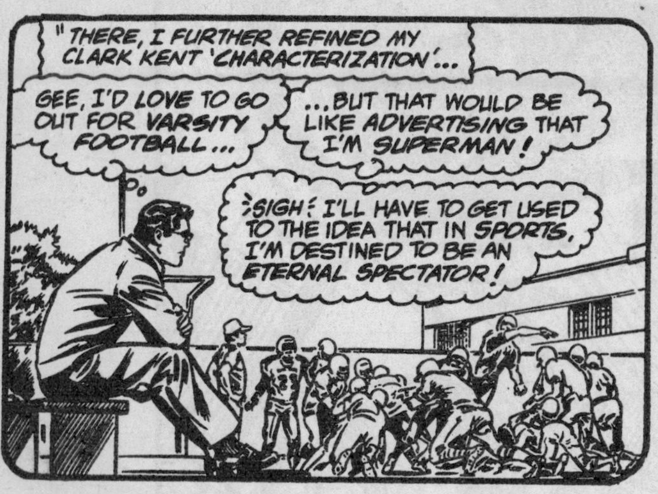
"THERE, I FURTHER REFINED MY CLARK KENT 'CHARACTERIZATION'...
GEE, I'D LOVE TO GO OUT FOR VARSITY FOOTBALL...
...BUT THAT WOULD BE LIKE ADVERTISING THAT I'M SUPERMAN!
SIGH! I'LL HAVE TO GET USED TO THE IDEA THAT IN SPORTS, I'M DESTINED TO BE AN ETERNAL SPECTATOR!

"I ALSO DISCOVERED AN 'EXTRA TOUCH' I COULD ADD TO CLARK'S PERSONALITY...

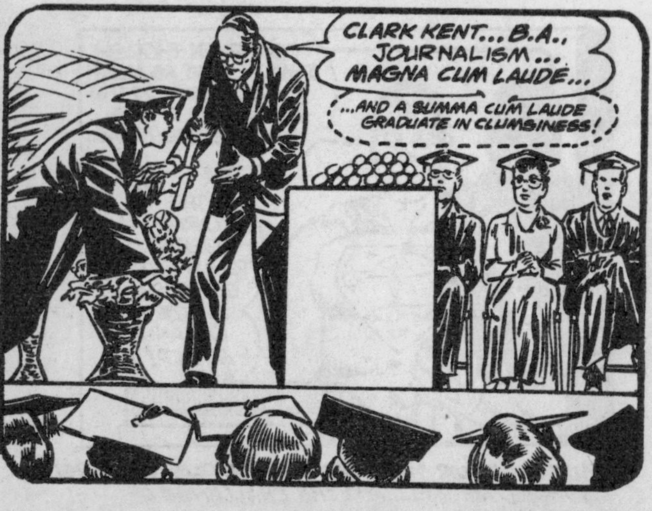
CLARK KENT... B.A., JOURNALISM... MAGNA CUM LAUDE...
...AND A SUMMA CUM LAUDE GRADUATE IN CLUMSINESS!

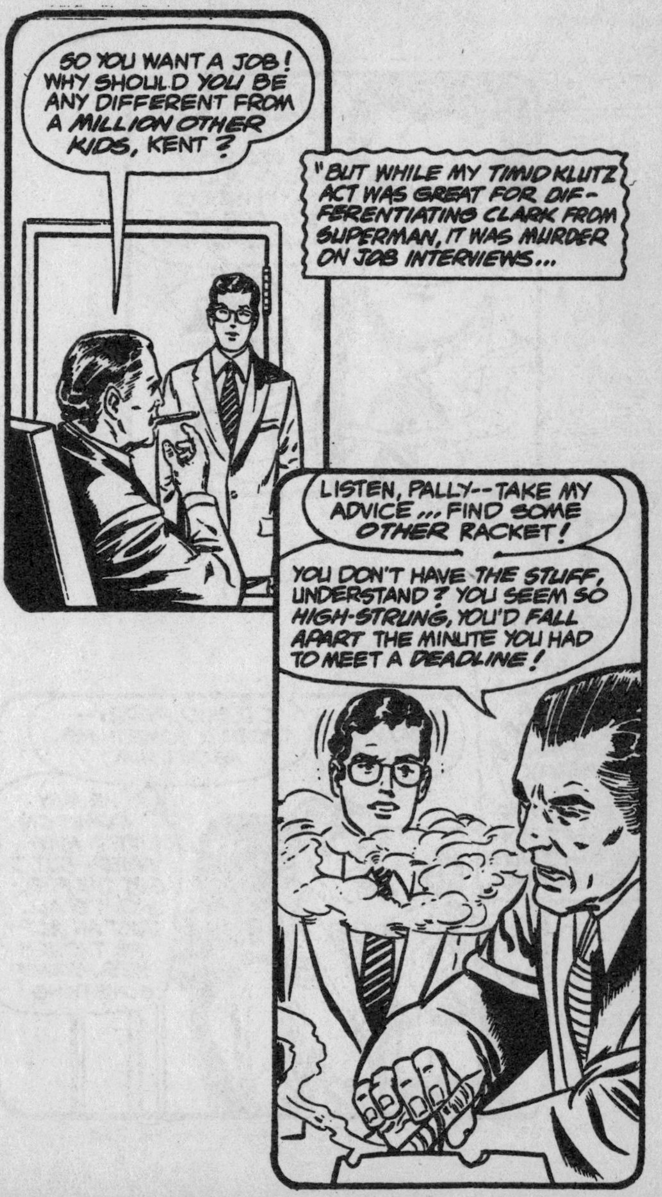
SO YOU WANT A JOB! WHY SHOULD YOU BE ANY DIFFERENT FROM A MILLION OTHER KIDS, KENT?
"BUT WHILE MY TIMID KLUTZ ACT WAS GREAT FOR DIF-FERENTIATING CLARK FROM SUPERMAN, IT WAS MURDER ON JOB INTERVIEWS...
LISTEN, PALLY--TAKE MY ADVICE... FIND SOME OTHER RACKET!
YOU DON'T HAVE THE STUFF, UNDERSTAND? YOU SEEM SO HIGH-STRUNG, YOU'D FALL APART THE MINUTE YOU HAD TO MEET A DEADLINE!

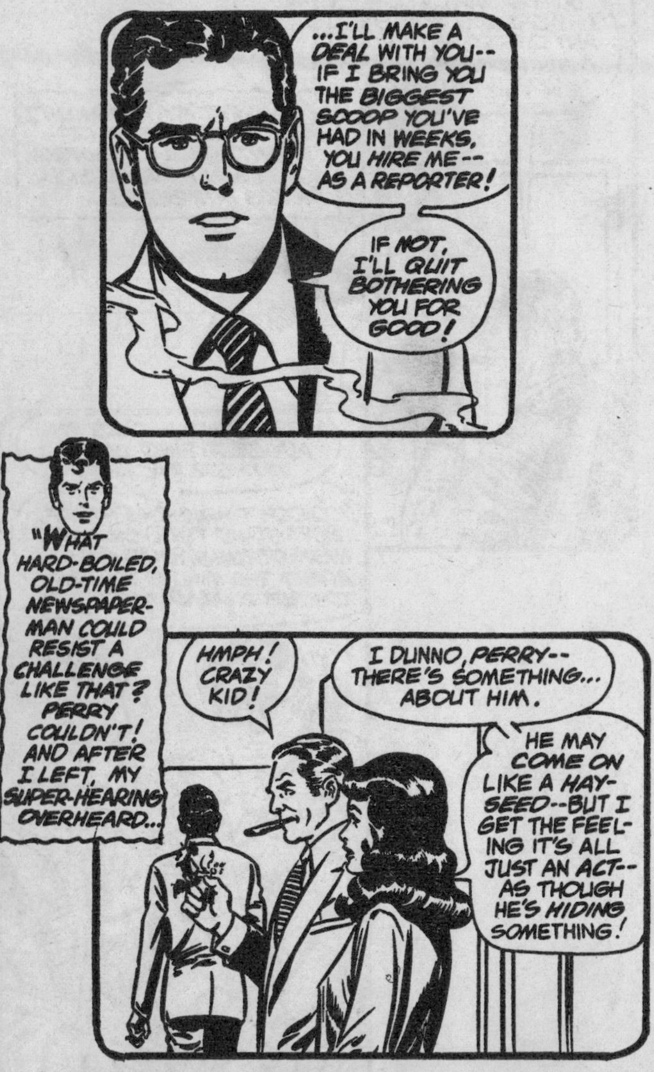
...I'LL MAKE A DEAL WITH YOU-- IF I BRING YOU THE BIGGEST SCOOP YOU'VE HAD IN WEEKS, YOU HIRE ME-- AS A REPORTER!
IF NOT, I'LL QUIT BOTHERING YOU FOR GOOD!
"WHAT HARD-BOILED, OLD-TIME NEWSPAPER-MAN COULD RESIST A CHALLENGE LIKE THAT? PERRY COULDN'T! AND AFTER I LEFT, MY SUPER-HEARING OVERHEARD...
HMPH! CRAZY KID!
I DUNNO, PERRY-- THERE'S SOMETHING... ABOUT HIM.
HE MAY COME ON LIKE A HAY-SEED--BUT I GET THE FEEL-ING IT'S ALL JUST AN ACT-- AS THOUGH HE'S HIDING SOMETHING!

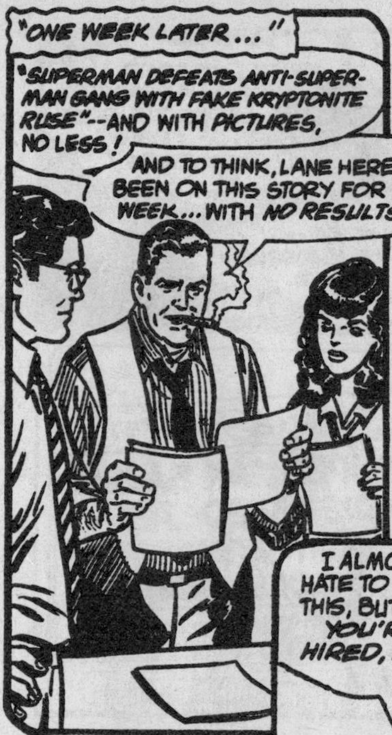
"ONE WEEK LATER ..."
"SUPERMAN DEFEATS ANTI-SUPERMAN GANGS WITH FAKE KRYPTONITE RUSE"--AND WITH PICTURES, NO LESS!
AND TO THINK, LANE HERE HAS BEEN ON THIS STORY FOR A WEEK... WITH NO RESULTS--!

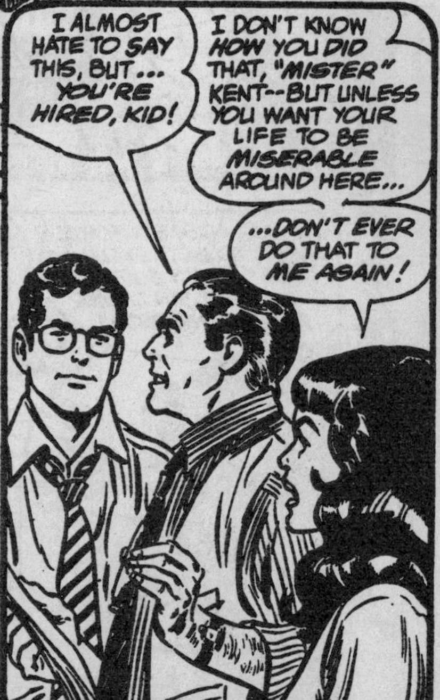
I ALMOST HATE TO SAY THIS, BUT... YOU'RE HIRED, KID!
I DON'T KNOW HOW YOU DID THAT, "MISTER" KENT--BUT UNLESS YOU WANT YOUR LIFE TO BE MISERABLE AROUND HERE...
...DON'T EVER DO THAT TO ME AGAIN!

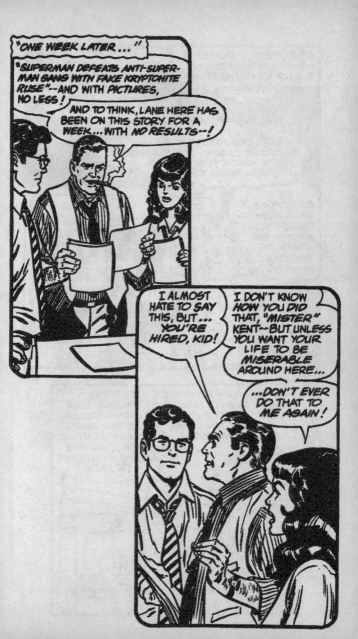

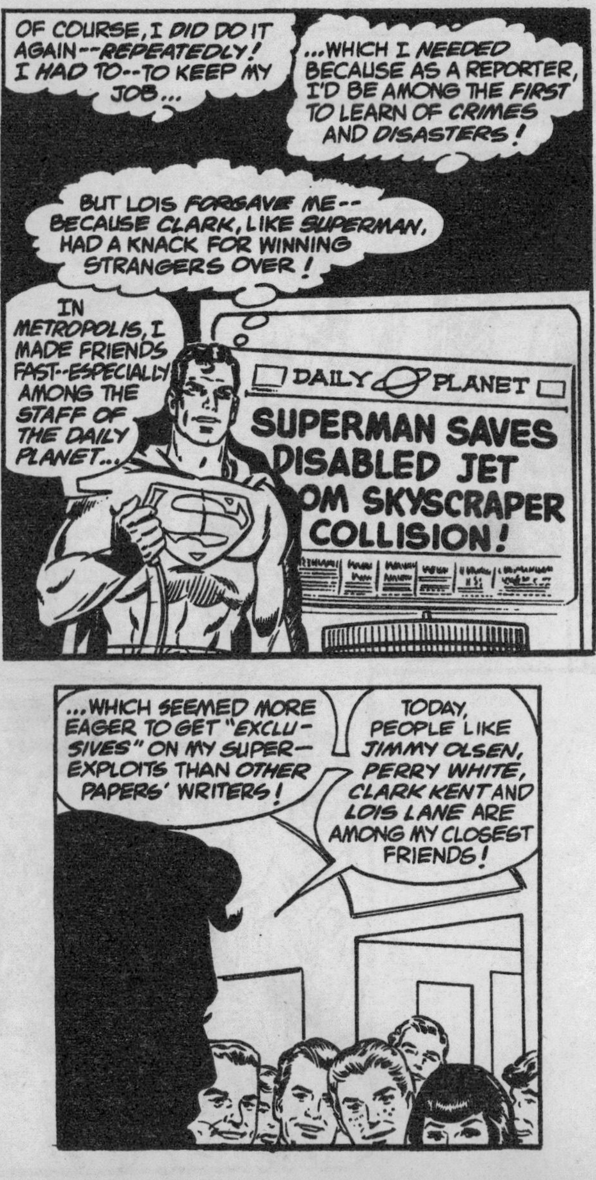
OF COURSE, I DID DO IT AGAIN--REPEATEDLY! I HAD TO--TO KEEP MY JOB...
...WHICH I NEEDED BECAUSE AS A REPORTER, I'D BE AMONG THE FIRST TO LEARN OF CRIMES AND DISASTERS!
BUT LOIS FORGAVE ME--BECAUSE CLARK, LIKE SUPERMAN, HAD A KNACK FOR WINNING STRANGERS OVER!
IN METROPOLIS, I MADE FRIENDS FAST--ESPECIALLY AMONG THE STAFF OF THE DAILY PLANET...
DAILY PLANET
SUPERMAN SAVES DISABLED JET
OM SKYSCRAPER COLLISION!
...WHICH SEEMED MORE EAGER TO GET "EXCLUSIVES" ON MY SUPER-EXPLOITS THAN OTHER PAPERS' WRITERS!
TODAY, PEOPLE LIKE JIMMY OLSEN, PERRY WHITE, CLARK KENT AND LOIS LANE ARE AMONG MY CLOSEST FRIENDS!

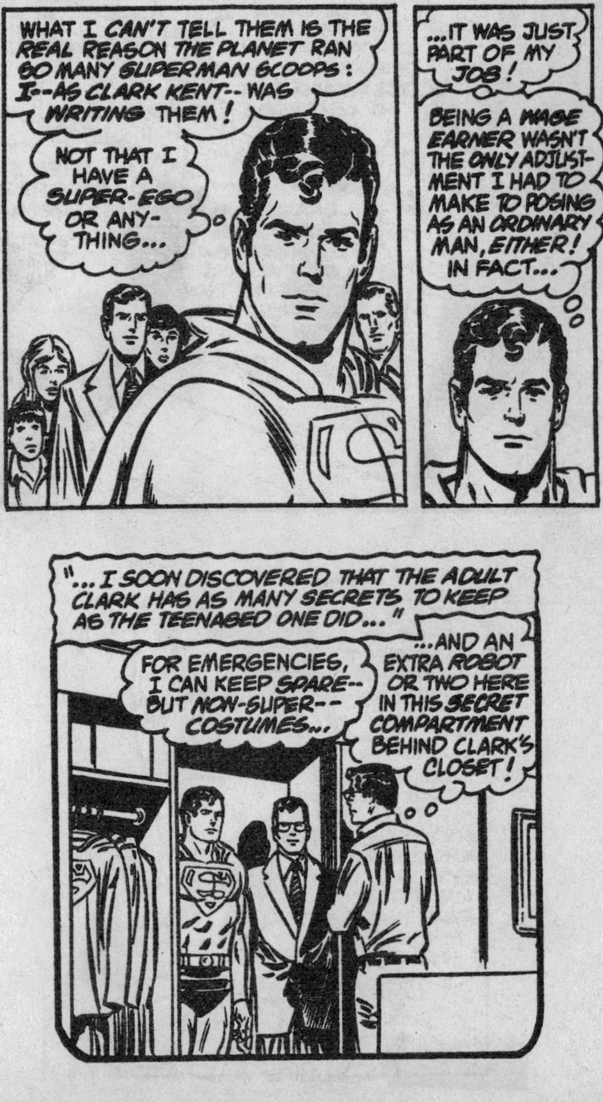
WHAT I CAN'T TELL THEM IS THE REAL REASON THE PLANET RAN SO MANY SUPERMAN SCOOPS: I--AS CLARK KENT--WAS WRITING THEM!
NOT THAT I HAVE A SUPER-EGO OR ANY-THING...
...IT WAS JUST PART OF MY JOB!
BEING A WAGE EARNER WASN'T THE ONLY ADJUST-MENT I HAD TO MAKE TO POSING AS AN ORDINARY MAN, EITHER! IN FACT...
"... I SOON DISCOVERED THAT THE ADULT CLARK HAS AS MANY SECRETS TO KEEP AS THE TEENAGED ONE DID..."
FOR EMERGENCIES, I CAN KEEP SPARE--BUT NON-SUPER--COSTUMES...
...AND AN EXTRA ROBOT OR TWO HERE IN THIS SECRET COMPARTMENT BEHIND CLARK'S CLOSET!

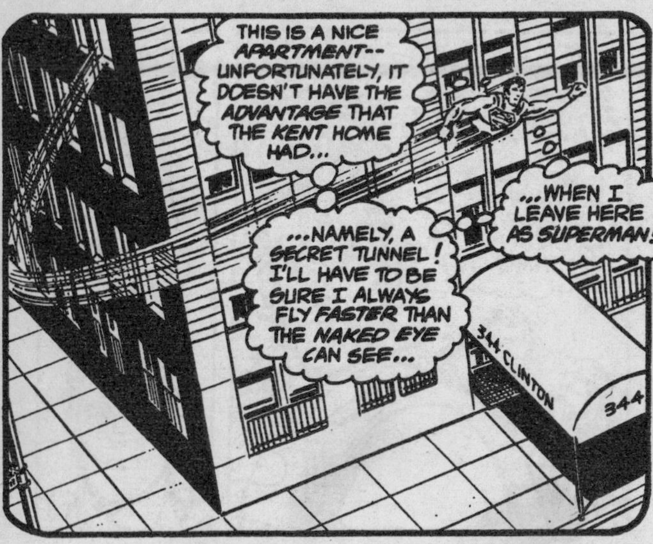
THIS IS A NICE APARTMENT--UNFORTUNATELY, IT DOESN'T HAVE THE ADVANTAGE THAT THE KENT HOME HAD...
...NAMELY, A SECRET TUNNEL! I'LL HAVE TO BE SURE I ALWAYS FLY FASTER THAN THE NAKED EYE CAN SEE...
...WHEN I LEAVE HERE AS SUPERMAN!
344 CLINTON
344

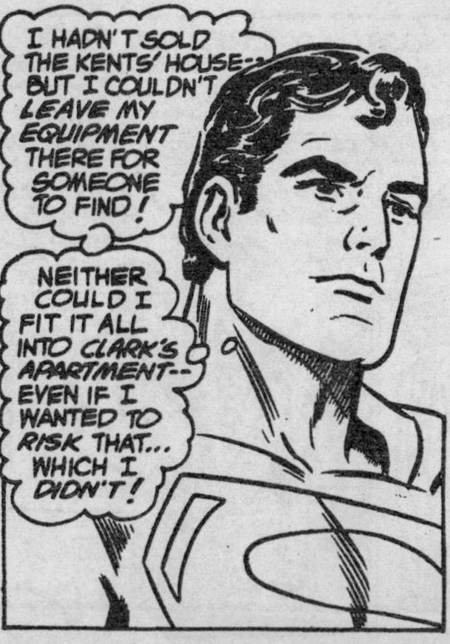
I HADN'T SOLD THE KENTS' HOUSE--BUT I COULDN'T LEAVE MY EQUIPMENT THERE FOR SOMEONE TO FIND!
NEITHER COULD I FIT IT ALL INTO CLARK'S APARTMENT--EVEN IF I WANTED TO RISK THAT... WHICH I DIDN'T!

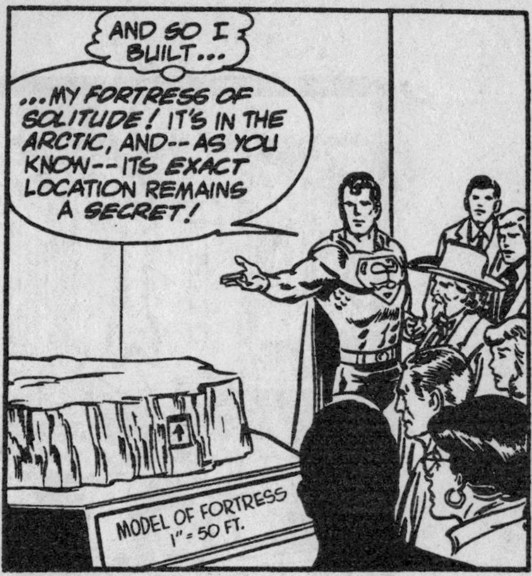
AND SO I BUILT...
...MY FORTRESS OF SOLITUDE! IT'S IN THE ARCTIC, AND--AS YOU KNOW--ITS EXACT LOCATION REMAINS A SECRET!
MODEL OF FORTRESS 1" = 50 FT.

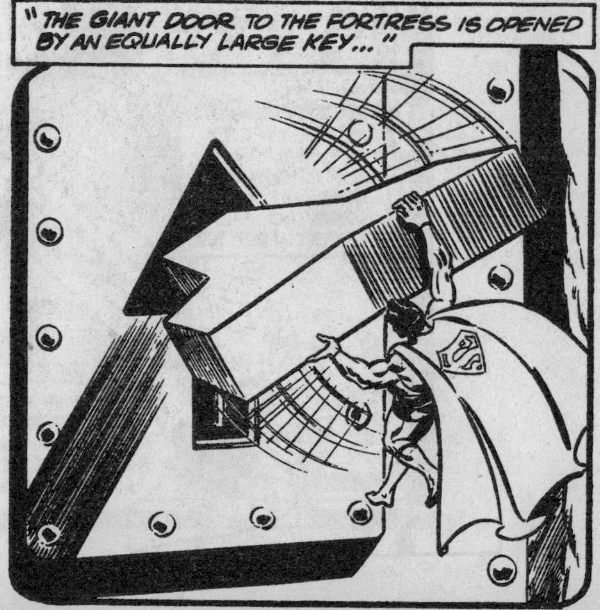
"THE GIANT DOOR TO THE FORTRESS IS OPENED BY AN EQUALLY LARGE KEY..."

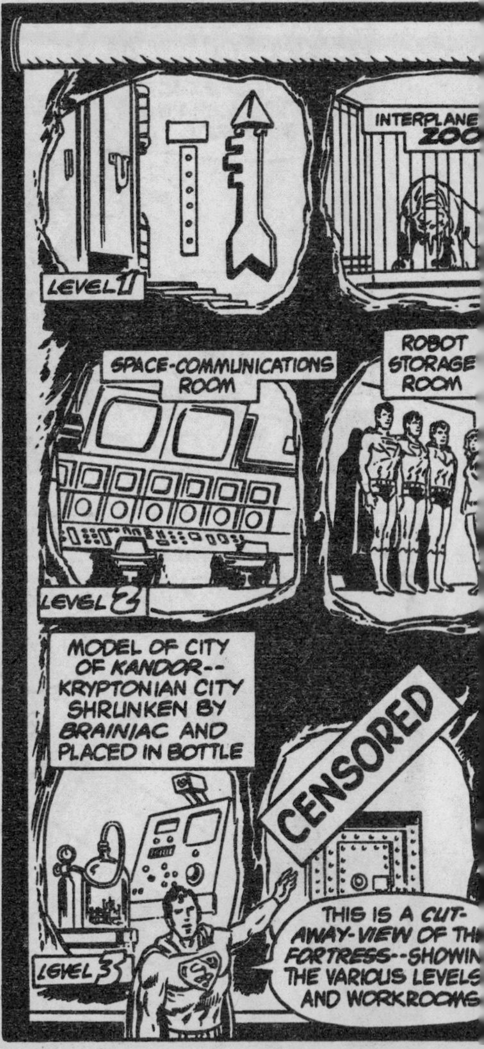

LEVEL 1
INTERPLANE
ZOO
SPACE-COMMUNICATIONS ROOM
ROBOT STORAGE ROOM
LEVEL 2
MODEL OF CITY OF KANDOR-- KRYPTONIAN CITY SHRUNKEN BY BRAINIAC AND PLACED IN BOTTLE
CENSORED
LEVEL 3
THIS IS A CUT-AWAY-VIEW OF TH FORTRESS--SHOWIN THE VARIOUS LEVELS AND WORKROOMS

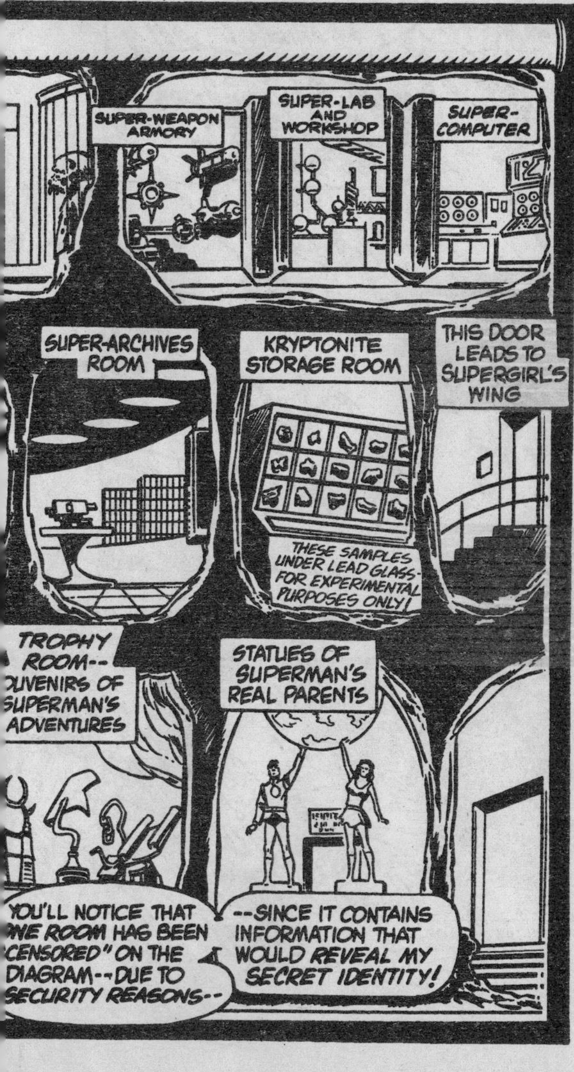
SUPER-WEAPON ARMORY
SUPER-LAB AND WORKSHOP
SUPER-COMPUTER
SUPER-ARCHIVES ROOM
KRYPTONITE STORAGE ROOM
THESE SAMPLES UNDER LEAD GLASS-FOR EXPERIMENTAL PURPOSES ONLY!
THIS DOOR LEADS TO SUPERGIRL'S WING
TROPHY ROOM--
UVENIRS OF SUPERMAN'S ADVENTURES
STATUES OF SUPERMAN'S REAL PARENTS
YOU'LL NOTICE THAT
NE ROOM HAS BEEN
CENSORED" ON THE
DIAGRAM--DUE TO
ECURITY REASONS--
--SINCE IT CONTAINS INFORMATION THAT WOULD REVEAL MY SECRET IDENTITY!

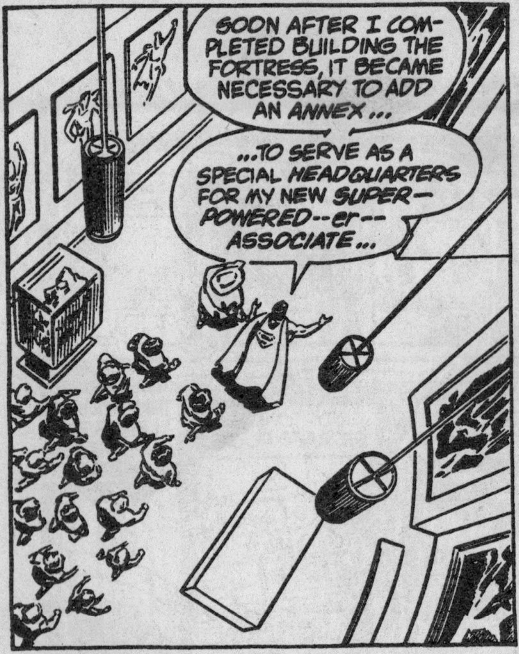
SOON AFTER I COMPLETED BUILDING THE FORTRESS, IT BECAME NECESSARY TO ADD AN ANNEX...
...TO SERVE AS A SPECIAL HEADQUARTERS FOR MY NEW SUPER-POWERED--er--ASSOCIATE...

...FOR IT WAS THEN THAT *SUPERGIRL* CAME TO EARTH!

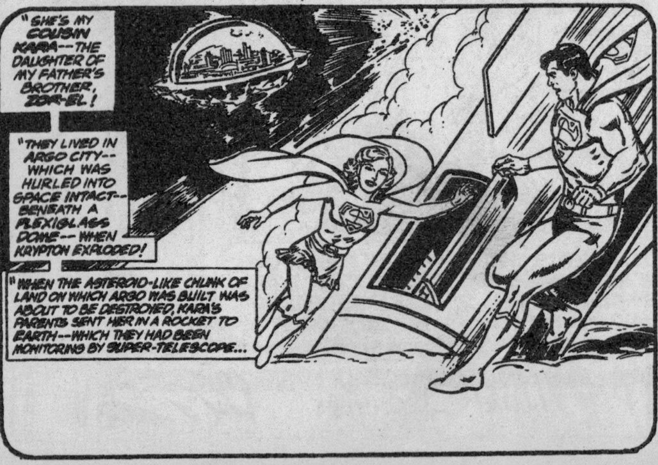
"SHE'S MY COUSIN KARA--THE DAUGHTER OF MY FATHER'S BROTHER, ZOR-EL!
"THEY LIVED IN ARGO CITY--WHICH WAS HURLED INTO SPACE INTACT--BENEATH A PLEXIGLASS DOME--WHEN KRYPTON EXPLODED!
"WHEN THE ASTEROID-LIKE CHUNK OF LAND ON WHICH ARGO WAS BUILT WAS ABOUT TO BE DESTROYED, KARA'S PARENTS SENT HER IN A ROCKET TO EARTH--WHICH THEY HAD BEEN MONITORING BY SUPER-TELESCOPE...

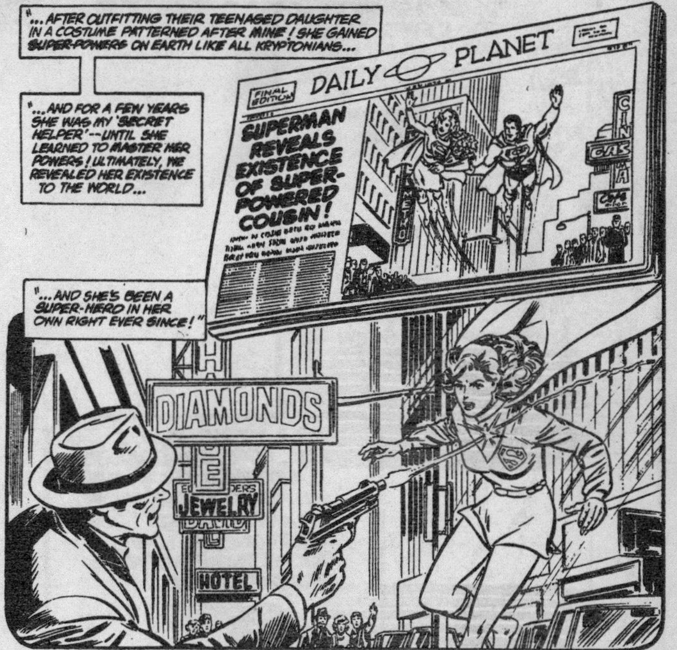
"... AFTER OUTFITTING THEIR TEENAGED DAUGHTER IN A COSTUME PATTERNED AFTER MINE! SHE GAINED SUPER-POWERS ON EARTH LIKE ALL KRYPTONIANS...
"... AND FOR A FEW YEARS SHE WAS MY 'SECRET HELPER'--UNTIL SHE LEARNED TO MASTER HER POWERS! ULTIMATELY, WE REVEALED HER EXISTENCE TO THE WORLD...
DAILY PLANET
FINAL EDITION
SUPERMAN REVEALS EXISTENCE OF SUPER-POWERED COUSIN!
"... AND SHE'S BEEN A SUPER-HERO IN HER OWN RIGHT EVER SINCE!"
DIAMONDS
JEWELRY
HOTEL

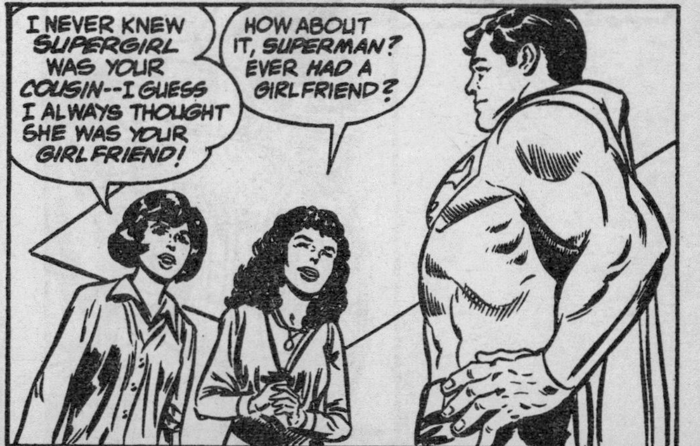
I NEVER KNEW SUPERGIRL WAS YOUR COUSIN--I GUESS I ALWAYS THOUGHT SHE WAS YOUR GIRLFRIEND!
HOW ABOUT IT, SUPERMAN? EVER HAD A GIRLFRIEND?

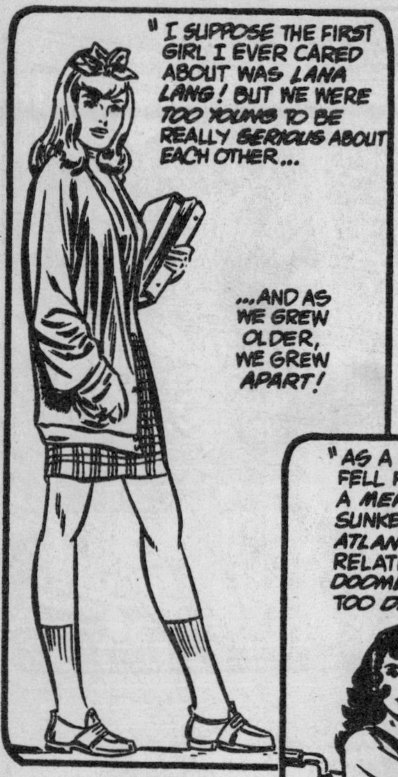
"I SUPPOSE THE FIRST GIRL I EVER CARED ABOUT WAS LANA LANG! BUT WE WERE TOO YOUNG TO BE REALLY SERIOUS ABOUT EACH OTHER...
...AND AS WE GREW OLDER, WE GREW APART!

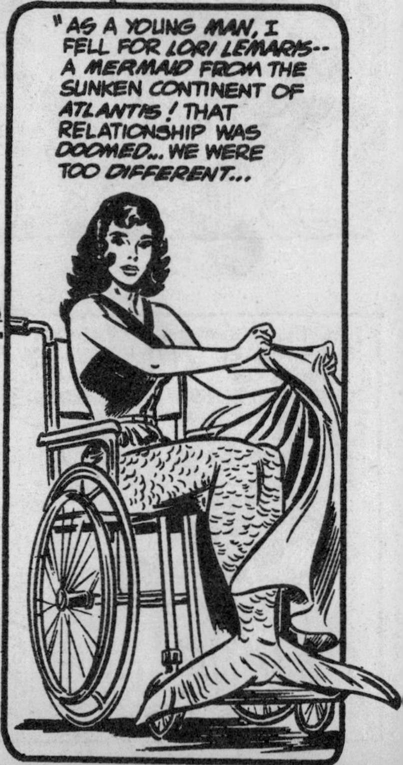
"AS A YOUNG MAN, I FELL FOR LORI LEMARIS-- A MERMAID FROM THE SUNKEN CONTINENT OF ATLANTIS! THAT RELATIONSHIP WAS DOOMED... WE WERE TOO DIFFERENT...

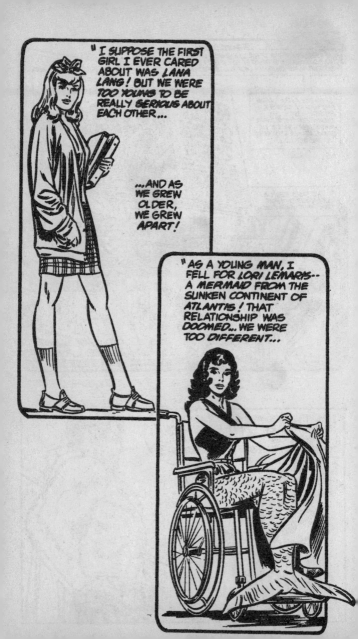

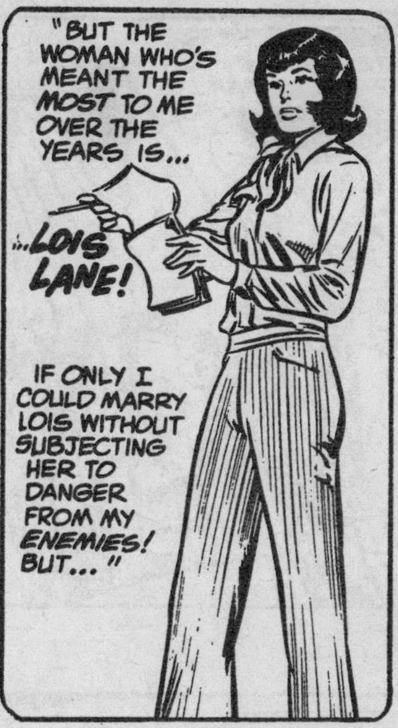
"BUT THE WOMAN WHO'S MEANT THE MOST TO ME OVER THE YEARS IS...
...LOIS LANE!
IF ONLY I COULD MARRY LOIS WITHOUT SUBJECTING HER TO DANGER FROM MY ENEMIES! BUT..."

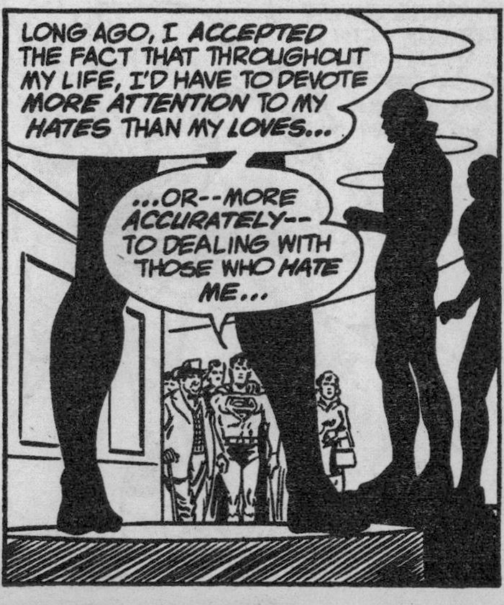
LONG AGO, I ACCEPTED THE FACT THAT THROUGHOUT MY LIFE, I'D HAVE TO DEVOTE MORE ATTENTION TO MY HATES THAN MY LOVES...
...OR--MORE ACCURATELY--TO DEALING WITH THOSE WHO HATE ME...

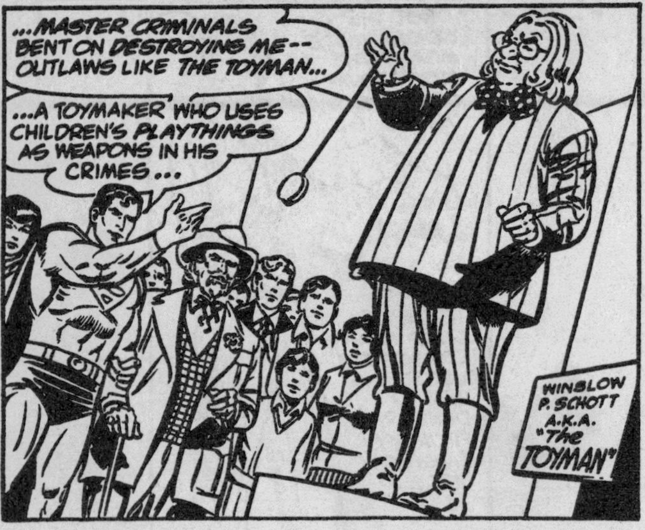
...MASTER CRIMINALS BENT ON DESTROYING ME-- OUTLAWS LIKE THE TOYMAN...
...A TOYMAKER WHO USES CHILDREN'S PLAYTHINGS AS WEAPONS IN HIS CRIMES...
WINSLOW P. SCHOTT A.K.A. "The TOYMAN"

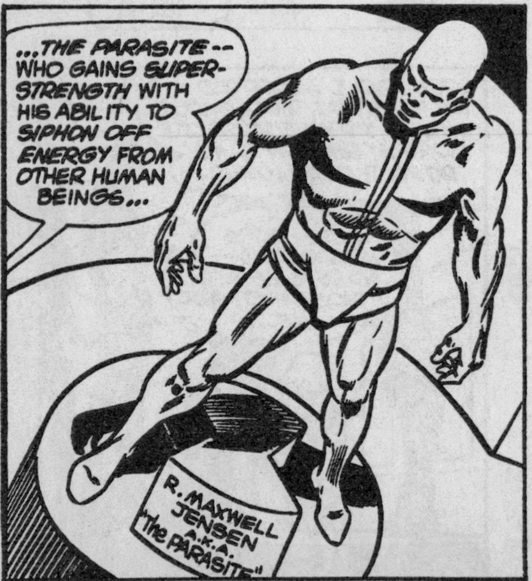
...THE PARASITE-- WHO GAINS SUPER-STRENGTH WITH HIS ABILITY TO SIPHON OFF ENERGY FROM OTHER HUMAN BEINGS...
R. MAXWELL JENSEN A.K.A. "The PARASITE"

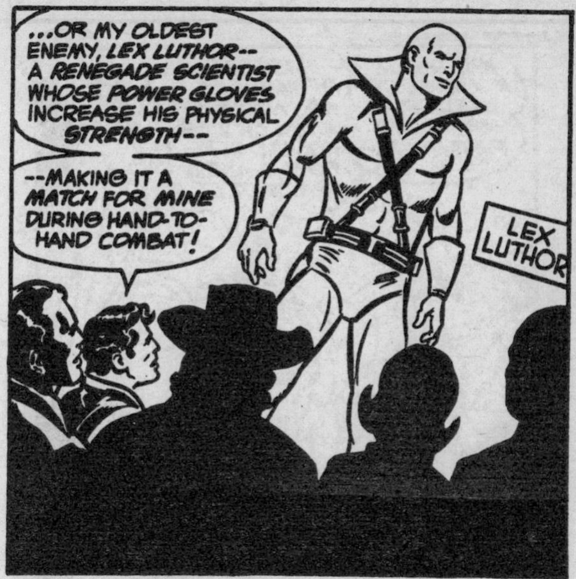
...OR MY OLDEST ENEMY, LEX LUTHOR-- A RENEGADE SCIENTIST WHOSE POWER GLOVES INCREASE HIS PHYSICAL STRENGTH--
--MAKING IT A MATCH FOR MINE DURING HAND-TO-HAND COMBAT!
LEX LUTHOR

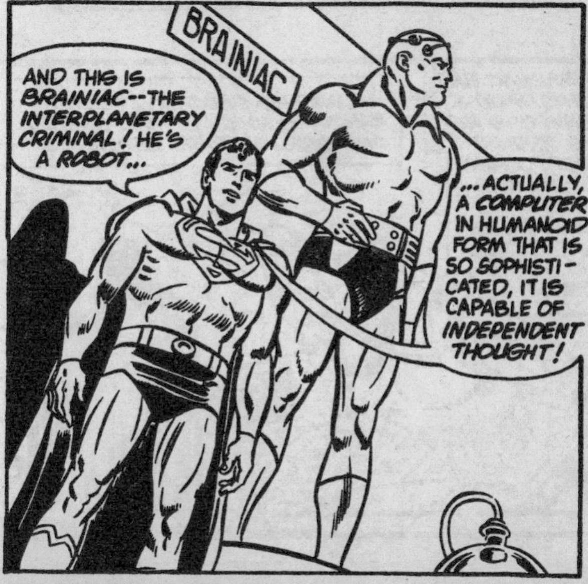
BRAINIAC
AND THIS IS BRAINIAC--THE INTERPLANETARY CRIMINAL! HE'S A ROBOT...
...ACTUALLY, A COMPUTER IN HUMANOID FORM THAT IS SO SOPHISTI-CATED, IT IS CAPABLE OF INDEPENDENT THOUGHT!

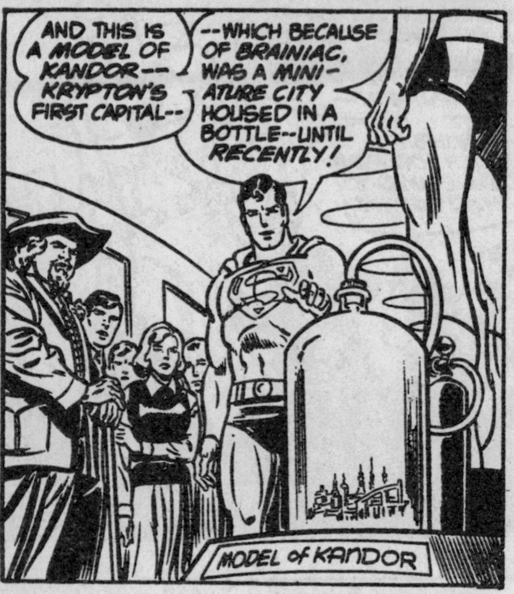
AND THIS IS A MODEL OF KANDOR-- KRYPTON'S FIRST CAPITAL--
--WHICH BECAUSE OF BRAINIAC, WAS A MINI-ATURE CITY HOUSED IN A BOTTLE--UNTIL RECENTLY!
MODEL of KANDOR

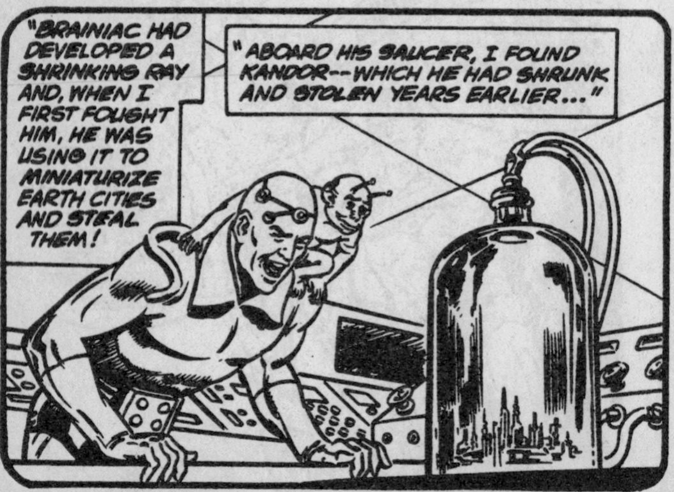
"BRAINIAC HAD DEVELOPED A SHRINKING RAY AND, WHEN I FIRST FOUGHT HIM, HE WAS USING IT TO MINIATURIZE EARTH CITIES AND STEAL THEM!
"ABOARD HIS SAUCER, I FOUND KANDOR--WHICH HE HAD SHRUNK AND STOLEN YEARS EARLIER..."

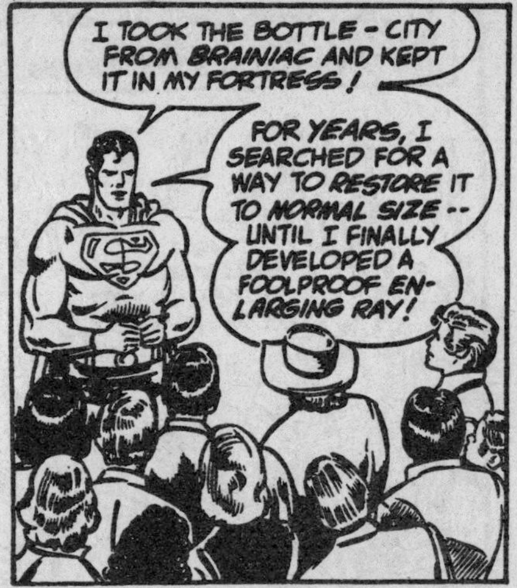
I TOOK THE BOTTLE-CITY FROM BRAINIAC AND KEPT IT IN MY FORTRESS!
FOR YEARS, I SEARCHED FOR A WAY TO RESTORE IT TO NORMAL SIZE -- UNTIL I FINALLY DEVELOPED A FOOLPROOF EN-LARGING RAY!

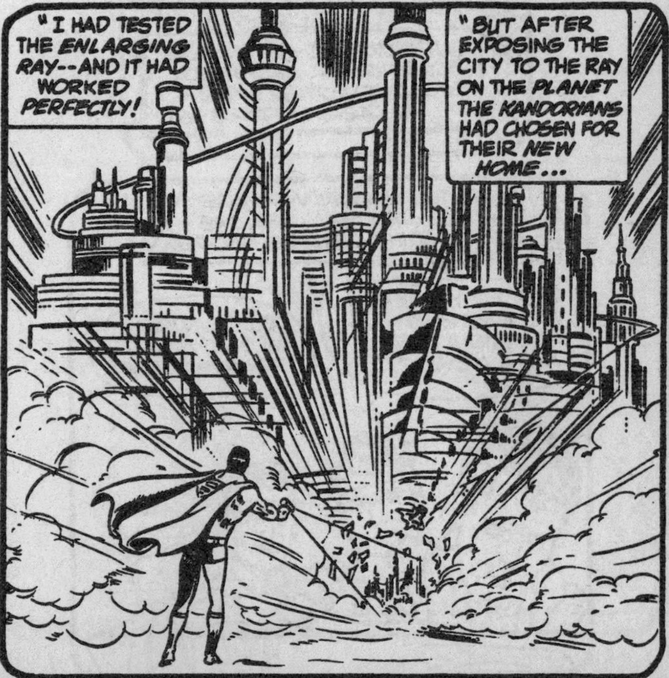
"I HAD TESTED THE ENLARGING RAY--AND IT HAD WORKED PERFECTLY!
"BUT AFTER EXPOSING THE CITY TO THE RAY ON THE PLANET THE KANDORIANS HAD CHOSEN FOR THEIR NEW HOME...

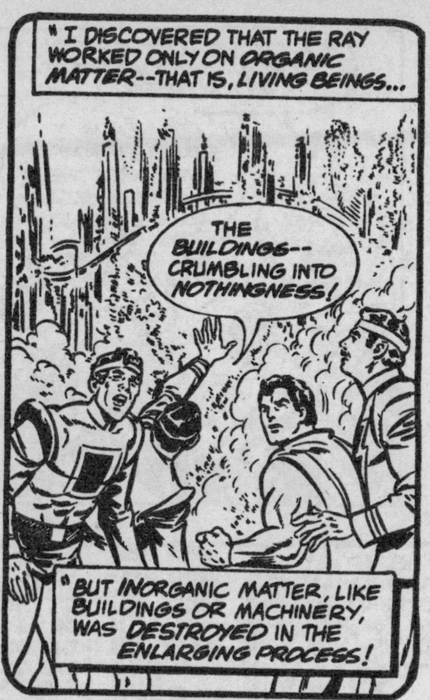
"I DISCOVERED THAT THE RAY WORKED ONLY ON ORGANIC MATTER--THAT IS, LIVING BEINGS...
THE BUILDINGS--CRUMBLING INTO NOTHINGNESS!
"BUT INORGANIC MATTER, LIKE BUILDINGS OR MACHINERY, WAS DESTROYED IN THE ENLARGING PROCESS!

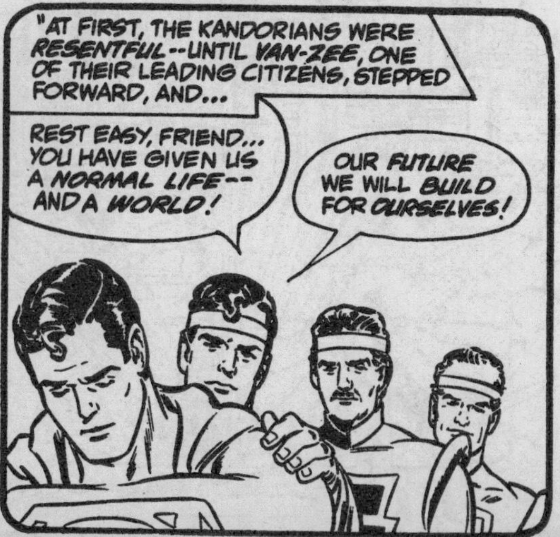
"AT FIRST, THE KANDORIANS WERE RESENTFUL--UNTIL VAN-ZEE, ONE OF THEIR LEADING CITIZENS, STEPPED FORWARD, AND...
REST EASY, FRIEND... YOU HAVE GIVEN US A NORMAL LIFE--AND A WORLD!
OUR FUTURE WE WILL BUILD FOR OURSELVES!

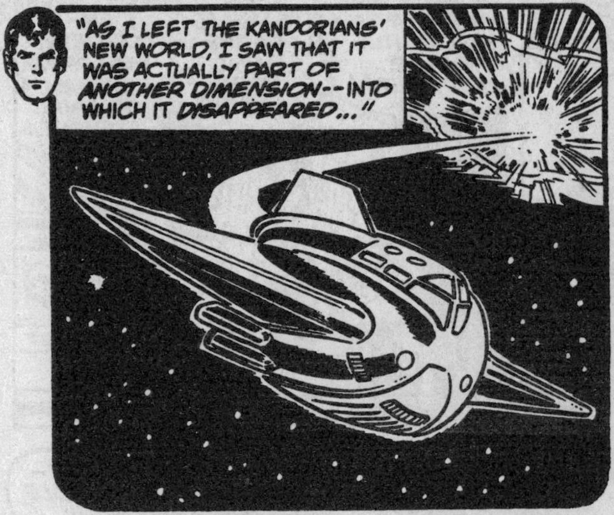
"AS I LEFT THE KANDORIANS' NEW WORLD, I SAW THAT IT WAS ACTUALLY PART OF ANOTHER DIMENSION--INTO WHICH IT DISAPPEARED..."

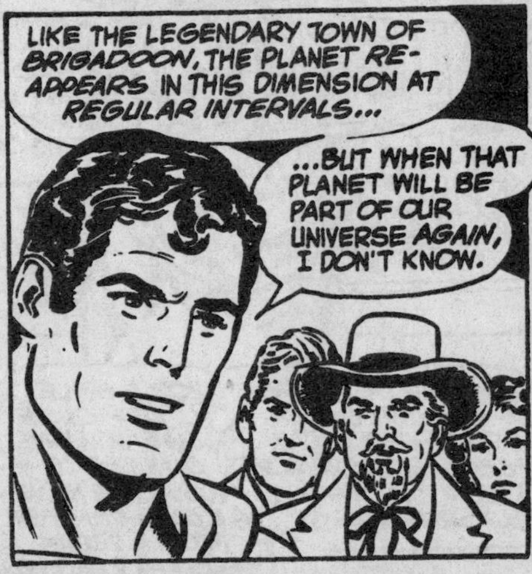
LIKE THE LEGENDARY TOWN OF BRIGADOON, THE PLANET RE-APPEARS IN THIS DIMENSION AT REGULAR INTERVALS...
...BUT WHEN THAT PLANET WILL BE PART OF OUR UNIVERSE AGAIN, I DON'T KNOW.

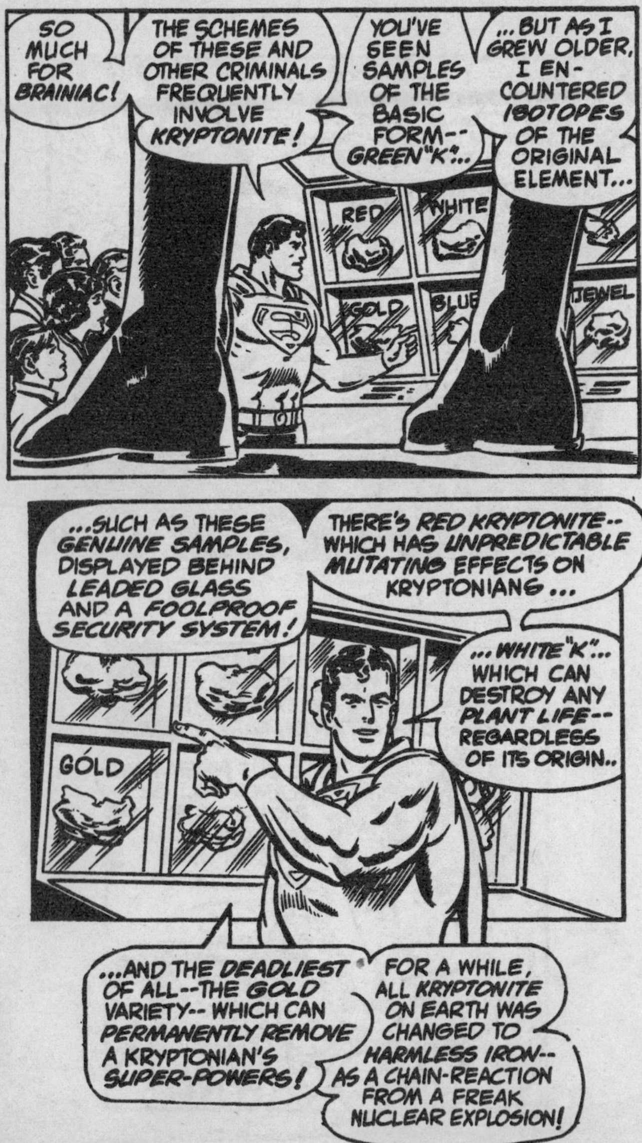
SO MUCH FOR BRAINIAC!
THE SCHEMES OF THESE AND OTHER CRIMINALS FREQUENTLY INVOLVE KRYPTONITE!
YOU'VE SEEN SAMPLES OF THE BASIC FORM-- GREEN "K"...
...BUT AS I GREW OLDER, I EN-COUNTERED ISOTOPES OF THE ORIGINAL ELEMENT...
RED
WHITE
GOLD
BLUE
JEWEL
...SUCH AS THESE GENUINE SAMPLES, DISPLAYED BEHIND LEADED GLASS AND A FOOLPROOF SECURITY SYSTEM!
THERE'S RED KRYPTONITE-- WHICH HAS UNPREDICTABLE MUTATING EFFECTS ON KRYPTONIANS...
...WHITE "K"... WHICH CAN DESTROY ANY PLANT LIFE-- REGARDLESS OF ITS ORIGIN..
GOLD
...AND THE DEADLIEST OF ALL--THE GOLD VARIETY-- WHICH CAN PERMANENTLY REMOVE A KRYPTONIAN'S SUPER-POWERS!
FOR A WHILE, ALL KRYPTONITE ON EARTH WAS CHANGED TO HARMLESS IRON-- AS A CHAIN-REACTION FROM A FREAK NUCLEAR EXPLOSION!

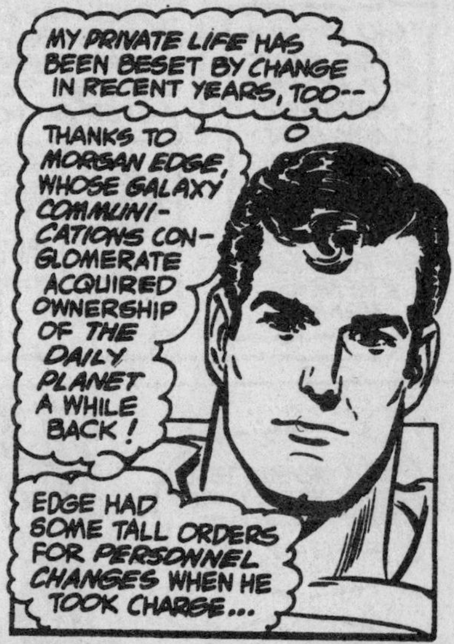
MY PRIVATE LIFE HAS BEEN BESET BY CHANGE IN RECENT YEARS, TOO--
THANKS TO MORGAN EDGE, WHOSE GALAXY COMMUNI-CATIONS CON-GLOMERATE ACQUIRED OWNERSHIP OF THE DAILY PLANET A WHILE BACK!
EDGE HAD SOME TALL ORDERS FOR PERSONNEL CHANGES WHEN HE TOOK CHARGE...

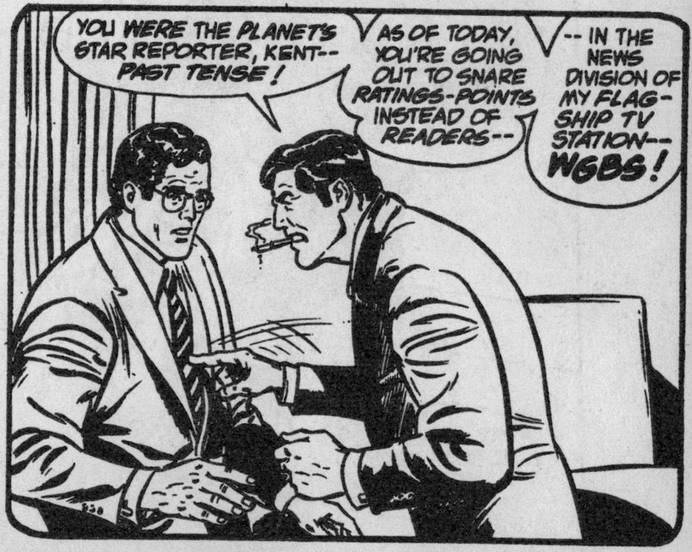
YOU WERE THE PLANET'S STAR REPORTER, KENT-- PAST TENSE!
AS OF TODAY, YOU'RE GOING OUT TO SNARE RATINGS-POINTS INSTEAD OF READERS--
-- IN THE NEWS DIVISION OF MY FLAG-SHIP TV STATION-- WGBS!

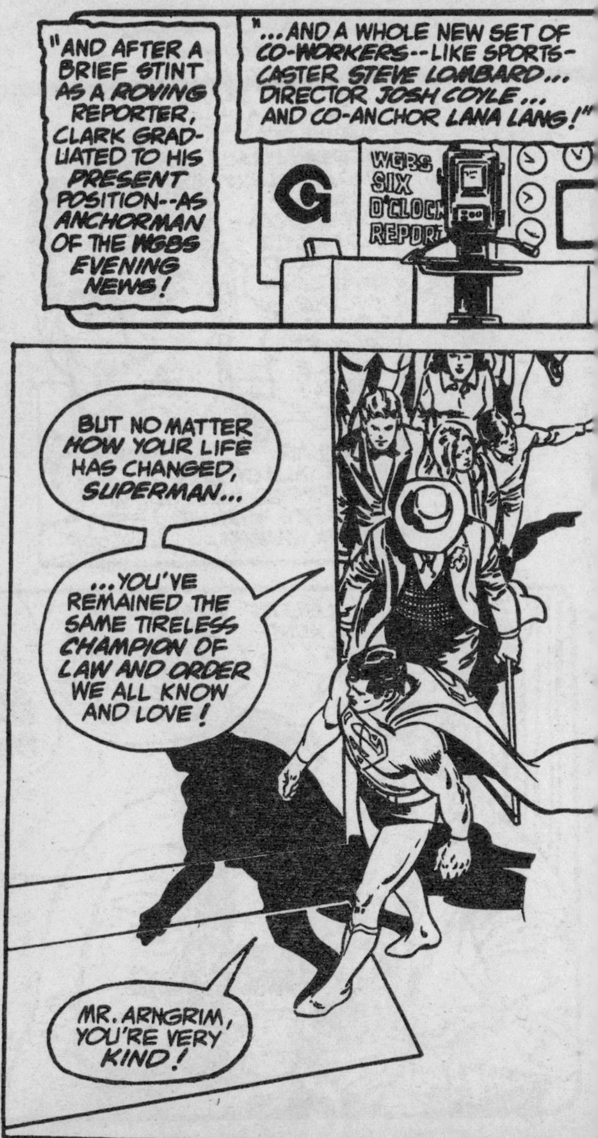
"AND AFTER A BRIEF STINT AS A ROVING REPORTER, CLARK GRADUATED TO HIS PRESENT POSITION--AS ANCHORMAN OF THE WGBS EVENING NEWS!
"...AND A WHOLE NEW SET OF CO-WORKERS--LIKE SPORTSCASTER STEVE LOMBARD... DIRECTOR JOSH COYLE... AND CO-ANCHOR LANA LANG!"
WGBS SIX O'CLOCK REPORT
BUT NO MATTER HOW YOUR LIFE HAS CHANGED, SUPERMAN...
...YOU'VE REMAINED THE SAME TIRELESS CHAMPION OF LAW AND ORDER WE ALL KNOW AND LOVE!
MR. ARNGRIM, YOU'RE VERY KIND!

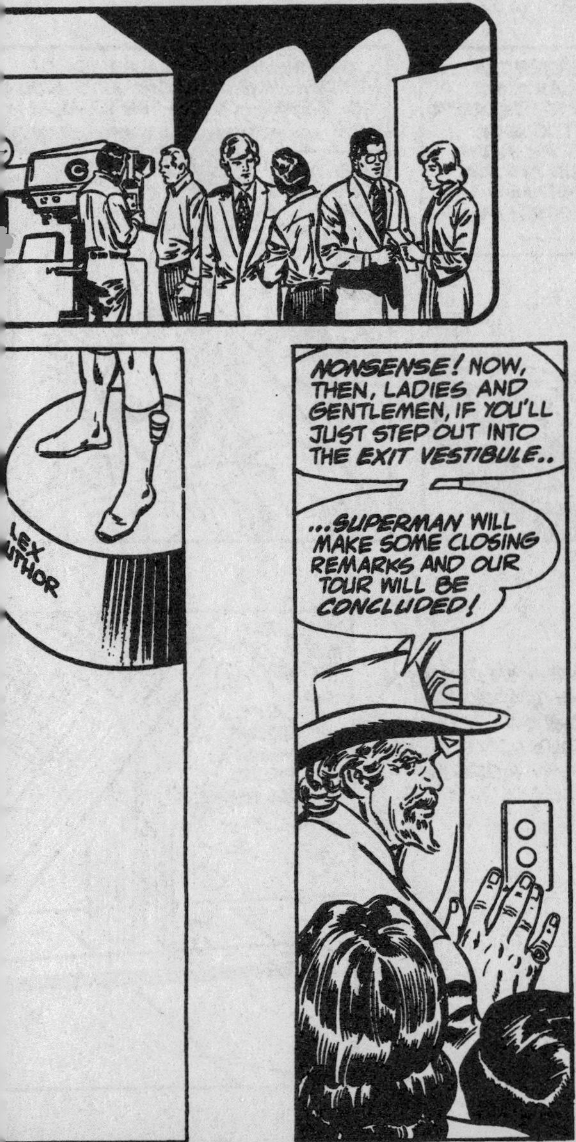

LEX
UTHOR
NONSENSE! NOW, THEN, LADIES AND GENTLEMEN, IF YOU'LL JUST STEP OUT INTO THE EXIT VESTIBULE..
...SUPERMAN WILL MAKE SOME CLOSING REMARKS AND OUR TOUR WILL BE CONCLUDED!

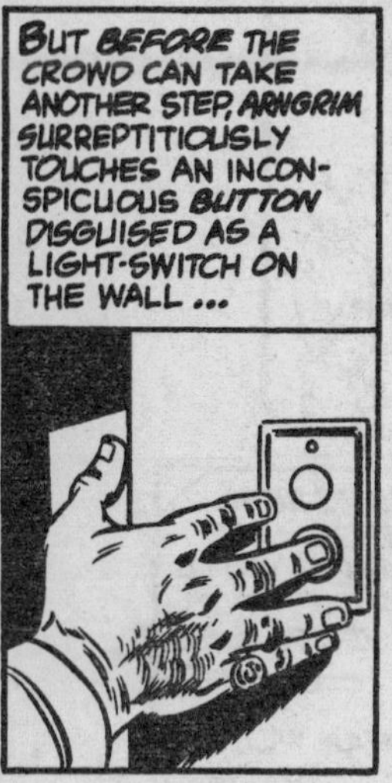
BUT BEFORE THE CROWD CAN TAKE ANOTHER STEP, ARNGRIM SURREPTITIOUSLY TOUCHES AN INCON-SPICUOUS BUTTON DISGUISED AS A LIGHT-SWITCH ON THE WALL ...

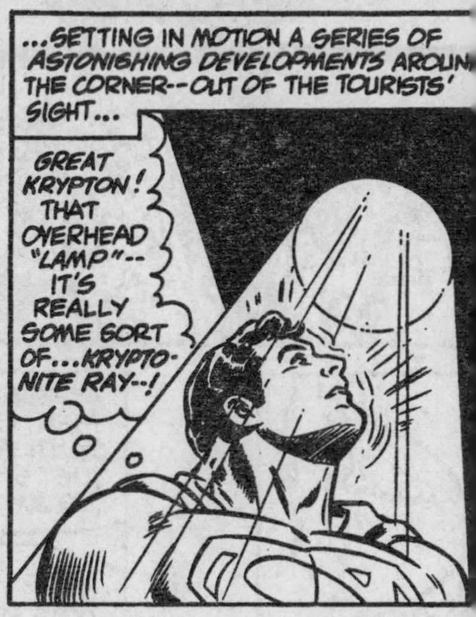
...SETTING IN MOTION A SERIES OF ASTONISHING DEVELOPMENTS AROUN THE CORNER--OUT OF THE TOURISTS' SIGHT...
GREAT KRYPTON! THAT OVERHEAD "LAMP"-- IT'S REALLY SOME SORT OF...KRYPTO-NITE RAY--!

AND AS THE MAN OF STEEL FALLS, THE TRAPDOOR FLIPS OVER--- AND AN EXACT DUPLICATE OF SUPERMAN RISES IN HIS PLACE!

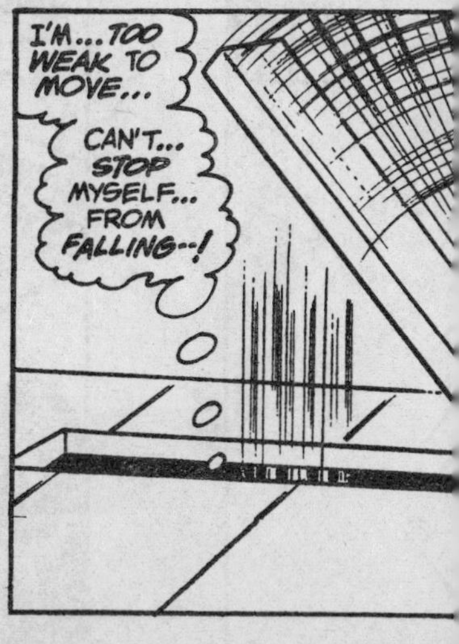
I'M...TOO WEAK TO MOVE...
CAN'T... STOP MYSELF... FROM FALLING--!

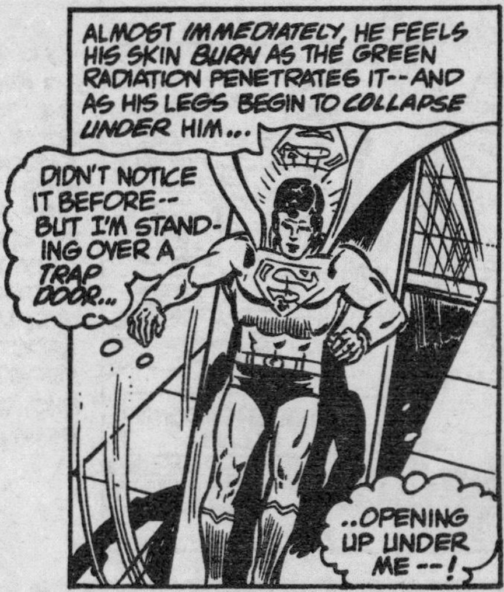
ALMOST IMMEDIATELY, HE FEELS HIS SKIN BURN AS THE GREEN RADIATION PENETRATES IT--AND AS HIS LEGS BEGIN TO COLLAPSE UNDER HIM...
DIDN'T NOTICE IT BEFORE-- BUT I'M STANDING OVER A TRAP DOOR...
..OPENING UP UNDER ME--!

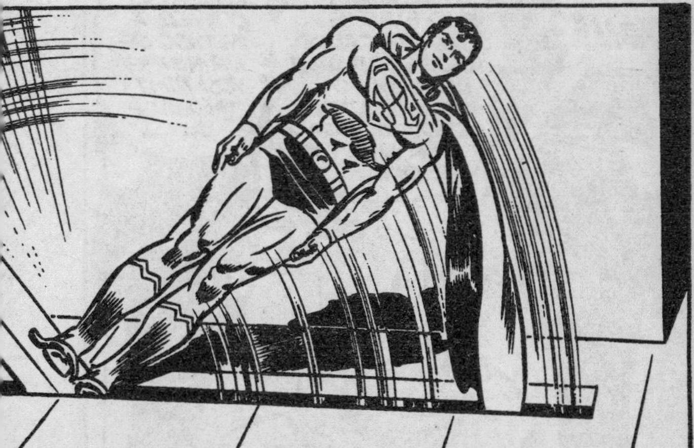

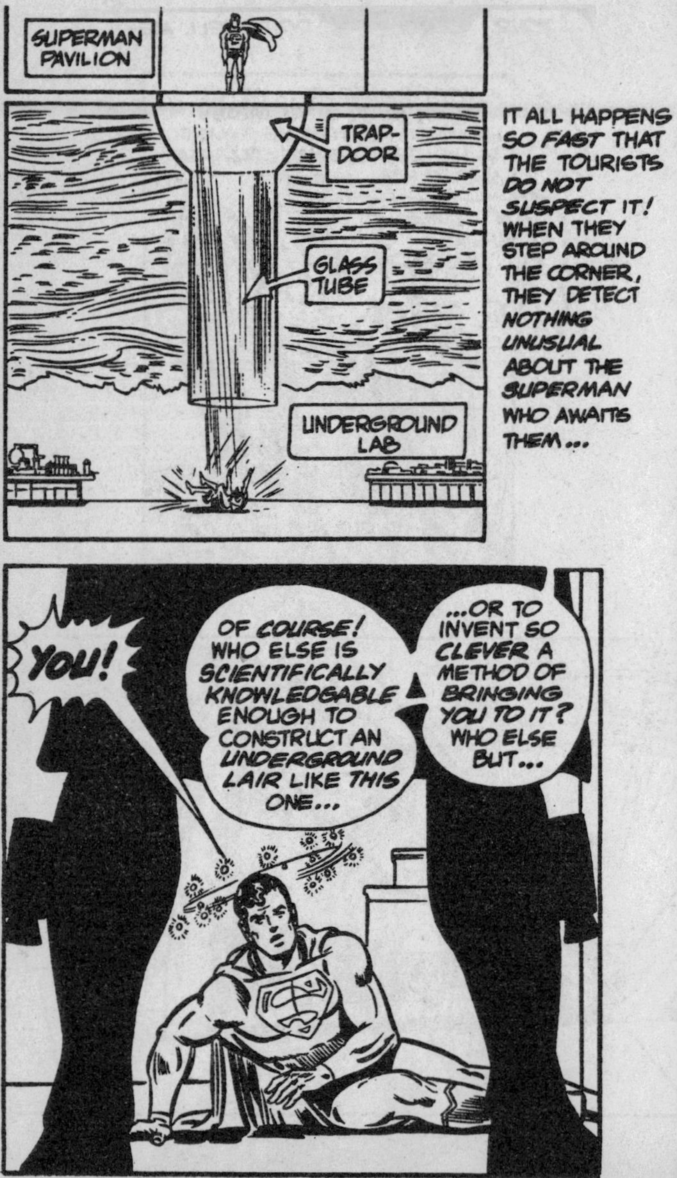
SUPERMAN PAVILION
TRAP-DOOR
GLASS TUBE
UNDERGROUND LAB
IT ALL HAPPENS SO FAST THAT THE TOURISTS DO NOT SUSPECT IT! WHEN THEY STEP AROUND THE CORNER, THEY DETECT NOTHING UNUSUAL ABOUT THE SUPERMAN WHO AWAITS THEM...
YOU!
OF COURSE! WHO ELSE IS SCIENTIFICALLY KNOWLEDGABLE ENOUGH TO CONSTRUCT AN UNDERGROUND LAIR LIKE THIS ONE...
...OR TO INVENT SO CLEVER A METHOD OF BRINGING YOU TO IT? WHO ELSE BUT...

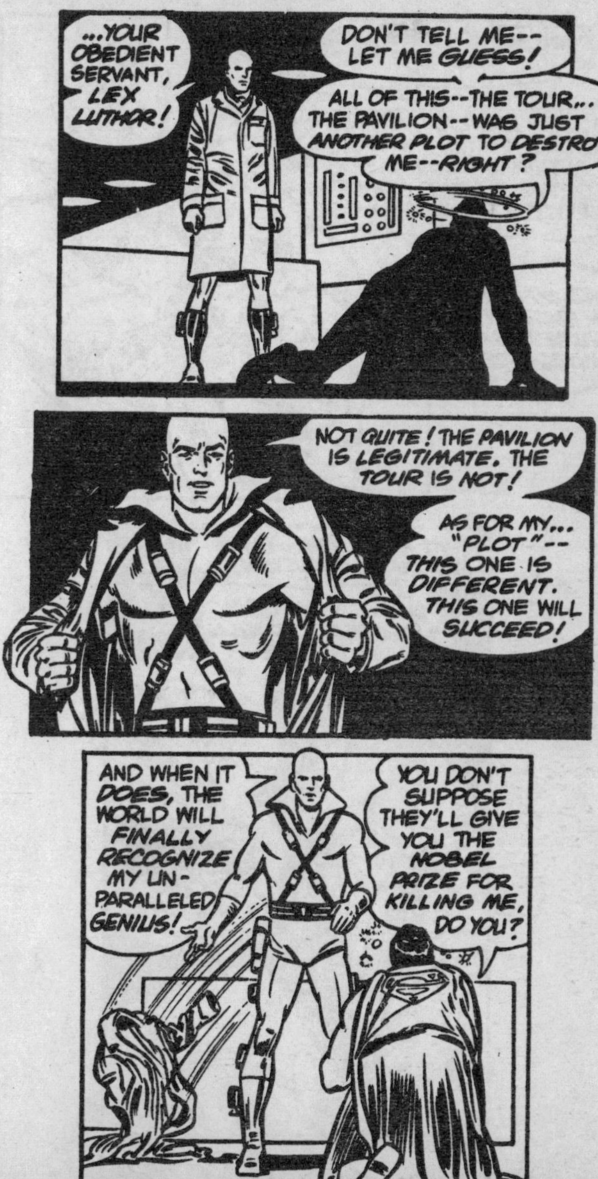
...YOUR OBEDIENT SERVANT, LEX LUTHOR!
DON'T TELL ME-- LET ME GUESS!
ALL OF THIS--THE TOUR... THE PAVILION--WAS JUST ANOTHER PLOT TO DESTROY ME--RIGHT?
NOT QUITE! THE PAVILION IS LEGITIMATE. THE TOUR IS NOT!
AS FOR MY... "PLOT"-- THIS ONE IS DIFFERENT. THIS ONE WILL SUCCEED!
AND WHEN IT DOES, THE WORLD WILL FINALLY RECOGNIZE MY UN-PARALLELED GENIUS!
YOU DON'T SUPPOSE THEY'LL GIVE YOU THE NOBEL PRIZE FOR KILLING ME, DO YOU?

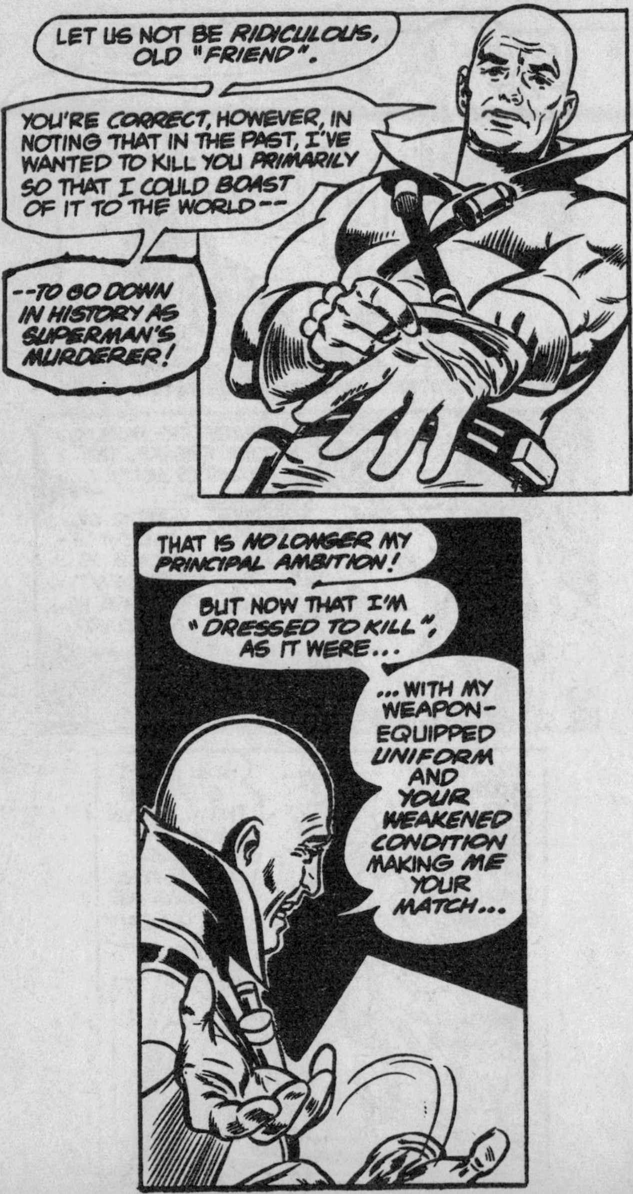
LET US NOT BE *RIDICULOUS*, OLD "*FRIEND*".
YOU'RE *CORRECT*, HOWEVER, IN NOTING THAT IN THE PAST, I'VE WANTED TO KILL YOU *PRIMARILY* SO THAT I COULD *BOAST* OF IT TO THE WORLD--
--*TO GO DOWN IN HISTORY AS SUPERMAN'S MURDERER!*
THAT IS *NO LONGER* MY *PRINCIPAL AMBITION!*
BUT NOW THAT I'M "*DRESSED TO KILL*", AS IT WERE...
...WITH MY WEAPON-EQUIPPED *UNIFORM* AND *YOUR WEAKENED CONDITION* MAKING ME *YOUR MATCH...*

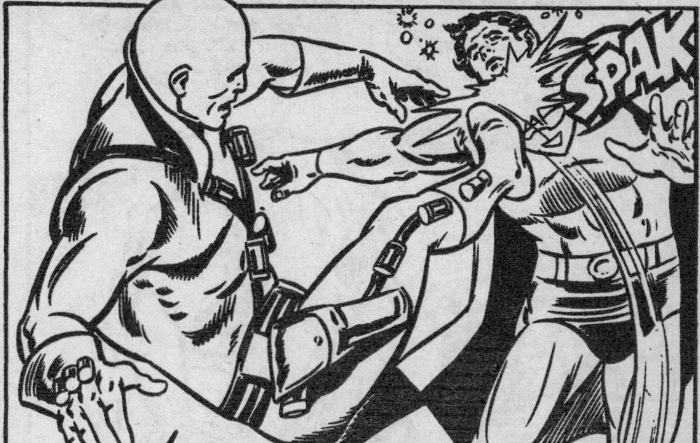
SPAK
...I CAN'T RESIST THE TEMPTATION TO ROUGH YOU UP A BIT!!

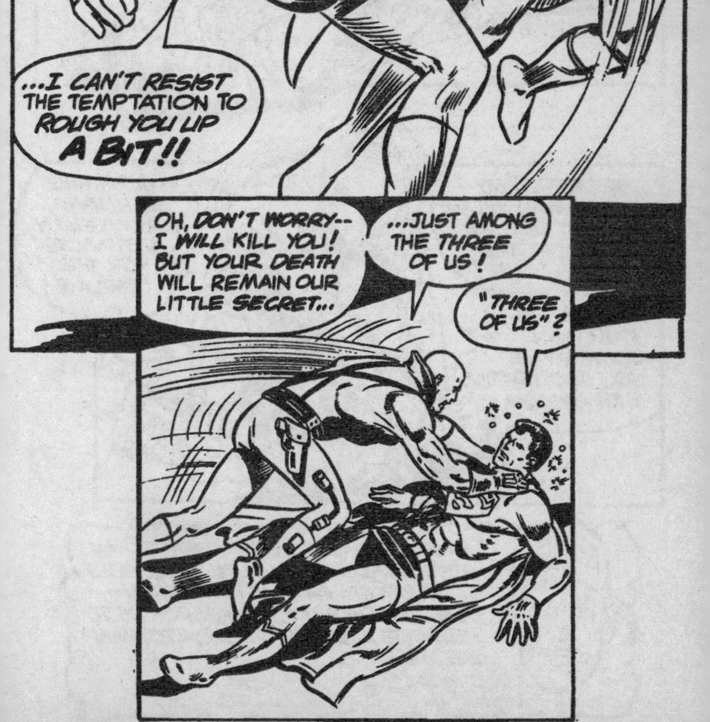
OH, DON'T WORRY-- I WILL KILL YOU! BUT YOUR DEATH WILL REMAIN OUR LITTLE SECRET...
...JUST AMONG THE THREE OF US!
"THREE OF US"?

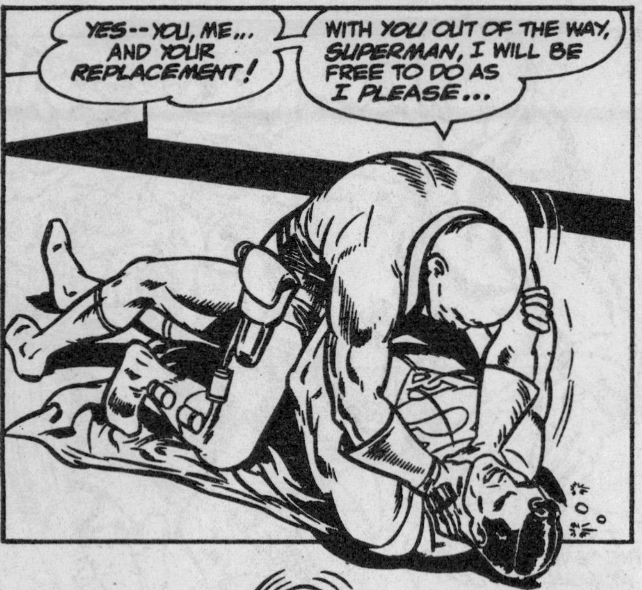
YES--YOU, ME... AND YOUR REPLACEMENT!
WITH YOU OUT OF THE WAY, SUPERMAN, I WILL BE FREE TO DO AS I PLEASE...
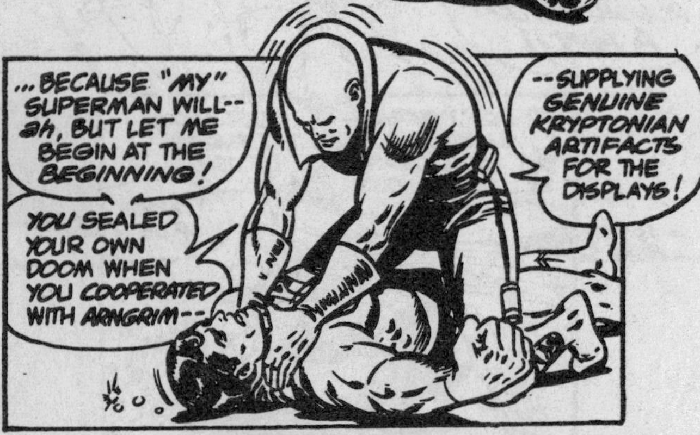
...BECAUSE "MY" SUPERMAN WILL--ah, BUT LET ME BEGIN AT THE BEGINNING!
YOU SEALED YOUR OWN DOOM WHEN YOU COOPERATED WITH ARNGRIM--
--SUPPLYING GENUINE KRYPTONIAN ARTIFACTS FOR THE DISPLAYS!
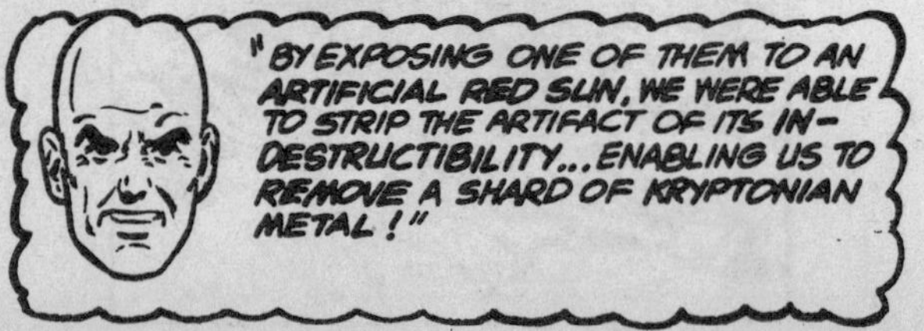
"BY EXPOSING ONE OF THEM TO AN ARTIFICIAL RED SUN, WE WERE ABLE TO STRIP THE ARTIFACT OF ITS INDESTRUCTIBILITY...ENABLING US TO REMOVE A SHARD OF KRYPTONIAN METAL!"

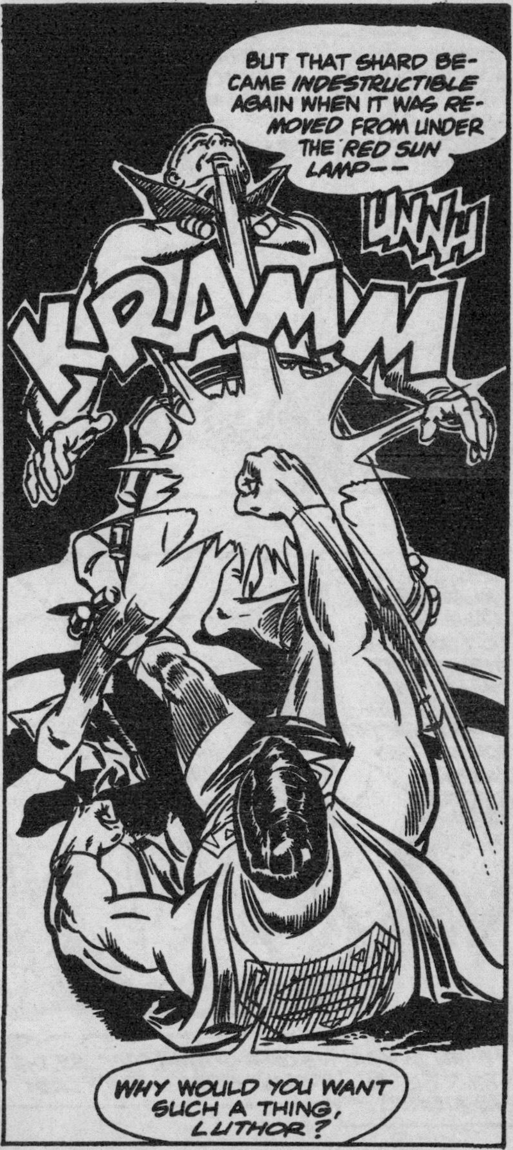
BUT THAT SHARD BE-CAME INDESTRUCTIBLE AGAIN WHEN IT WAS RE-MOVED FROM UNDER THE RED SUN LAMP--
UNNH
KRAMM
WHY WOULD YOU WANT SUCH A THING, LUTHOR?

"BECAUSE ONLY A KRYPTONIAN OBJECT WOULD BE HARD ENOUGH TO PUNCTURE YOUR NORMALLY INVULNERABLE SKIN!

"REMEMBER WHEN YOU SHOOK HANDS WITH ARNGRIM AT THE BEGINNING OF THE TOUR?

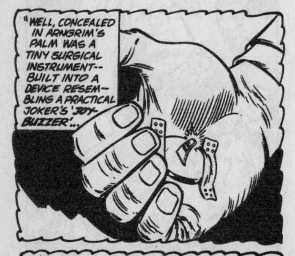

"WELL, CONCEALED IN ARNGRIM'S PALM WAS A TINY SURGICAL INSTRUMENT-- BUILT INTO A DEVICE RESEM- BLING A PRACTICAL JOKER'S 'JOY- BUZZER'...

"WHEN ARNGRIM SLIPPED AWAY BEFORE THE TOUR BEGAN, HE CAME HERE--TO MY LAB- ORATORY..."

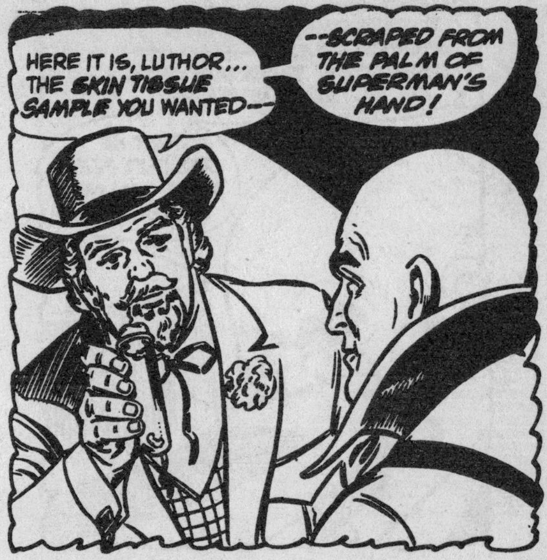
HERE IT IS, LUTHOR... THE SKIN TISSUE SAMPLE YOU WANTED--
--SCRAPED FROM THE PALM OF SUPERMAN'S HAND!

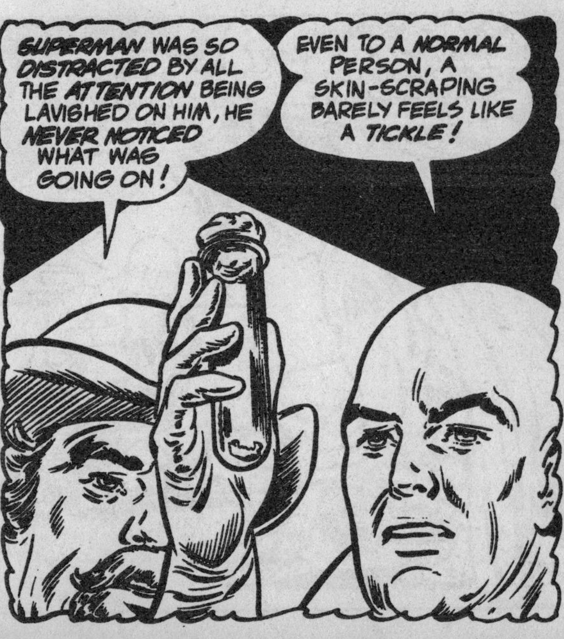
SUPERMAN WAS SO DISTRACTED BY ALL THE ATTENTION BEING LAVISHED ON HIM, HE NEVER NOTICED WHAT WAS GOING ON!
EVEN TO A NORMAL PERSON, A SKIN-SCRAPING BARELY FEELS LIKE A TICKLE!

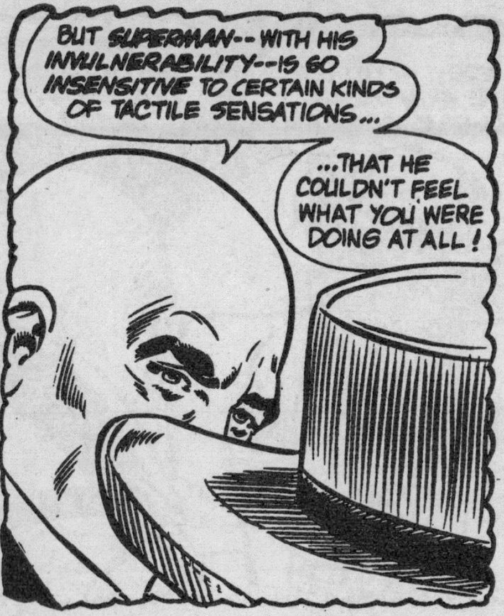
BUT SUPERMAN-- WITH HIS INVULNERABILITY--IS SO INSENSITIVE TO CERTAIN KINDS OF TACTILE SENSATIONS...
...THAT HE COULDN'T FEEL WHAT YOU WERE DOING AT ALL!

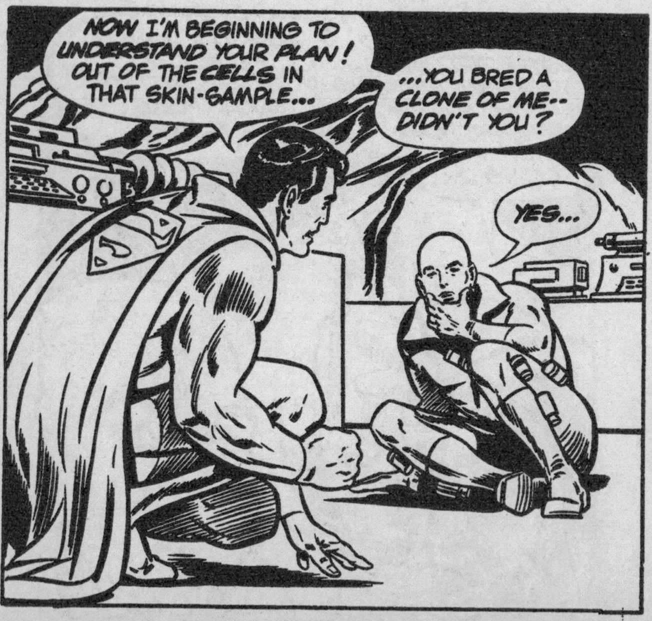
NOW I'M BEGINNING TO UNDERSTAND YOUR PLAN! OUT OF THE CELLS IN THAT SKIN-SAMPLE...
...YOU BRED A CLONE OF ME-- DIDN'T YOU?
YES...

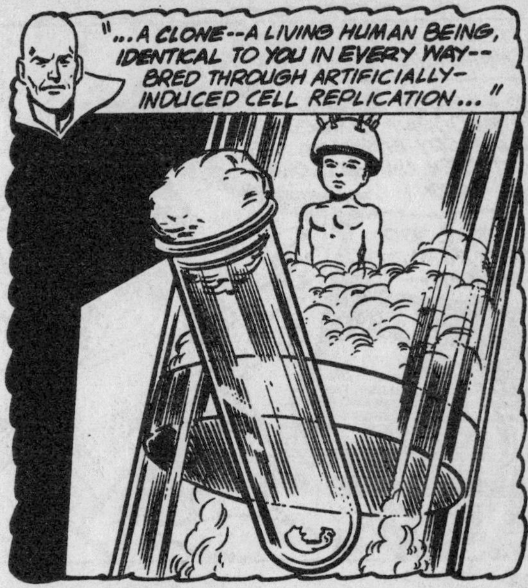
"...A CLONE--A LIVING HUMAN BEING, IDENTICAL TO YOU IN EVERY WAY--BRED THROUGH ARTIFICIALLY-INDUCED CELL REPLICATION..."

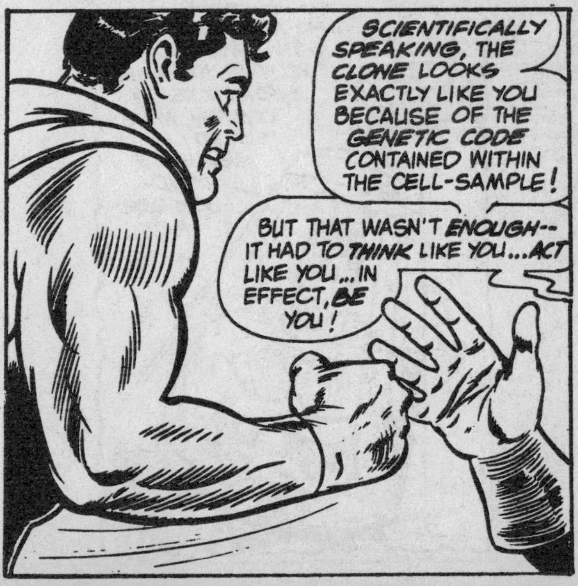
SCIENTIFICALLY SPEAKING, THE CLONE LOOKS EXACTLY LIKE YOU BECAUSE OF THE GENETIC CODE CONTAINED WITHIN THE CELL-SAMPLE!
BUT THAT WASN'T ENOUGH--IT HAD TO THINK LIKE YOU...ACT LIKE YOU...IN EFFECT, BE YOU!

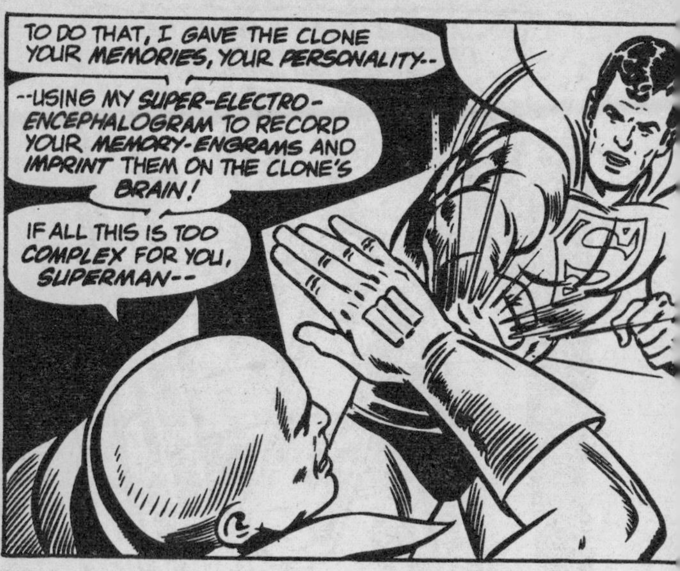
TO DO THAT, I GAVE THE CLONE YOUR MEMORIES, YOUR PERSONALITY--
--USING MY SUPER-ELECTRO-ENCEPHALOGRAM TO RECORD YOUR MEMORY-ENGRAMS AND IMPRINT THEM ON THE CLONE'S BRAIN!
IF ALL THIS IS TOO COMPLEX FOR YOU, SUPERMAN--

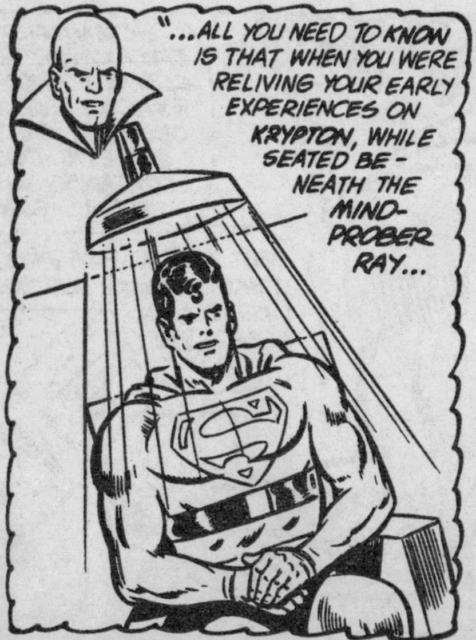
"...ALL YOU NEED TO KNOW IS THAT WHEN YOU WERE RELIVING YOUR EARLY EXPERIENCES ON KRYPTON, WHILE SEATED BE-NEATH THE MIND-PROBER RAY...

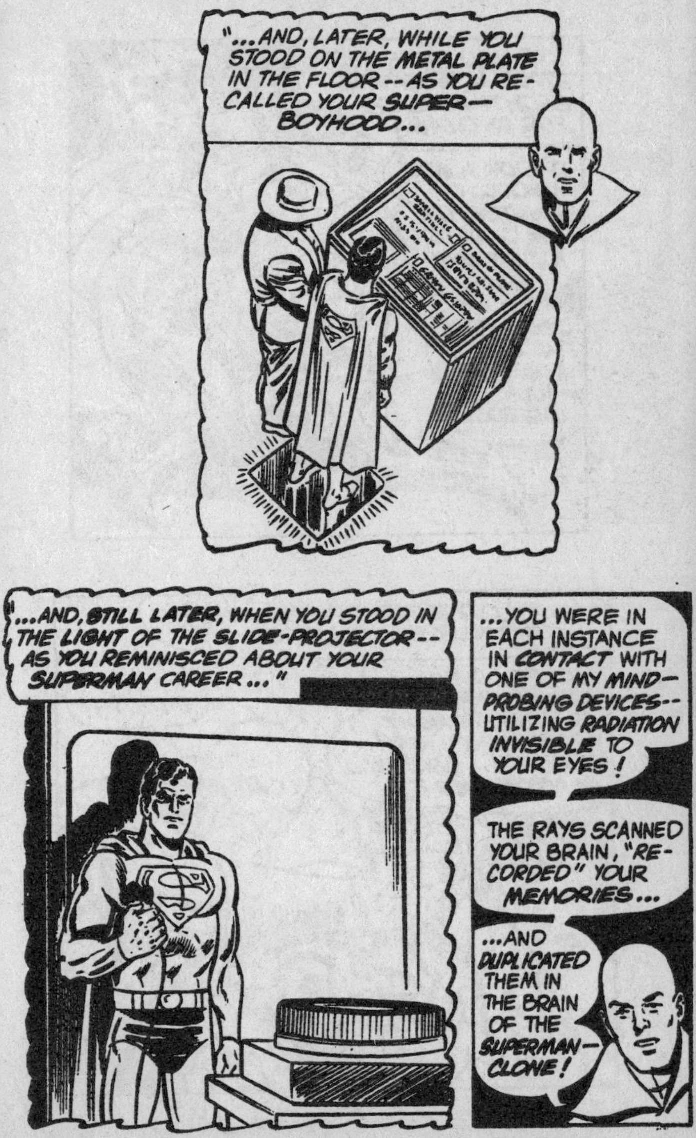
"...AND, LATER, WHILE YOU STOOD ON THE METAL PLATE IN THE FLOOR -- AS YOU RE-CALLED YOUR SUPER-BOYHOOD...
"...AND, STILL LATER, WHEN YOU STOOD IN THE LIGHT OF THE SLIDE-PROJECTOR -- AS YOU REMINISCED ABOUT YOUR SUPERMAN CAREER..."
...YOU WERE IN EACH INSTANCE IN CONTACT WITH ONE OF MY MIND-PROBING DEVICES -- UTILIZING RADIATION INVISIBLE TO YOUR EYES!
THE RAYS SCANNED YOUR BRAIN, "RE-CORDED" YOUR MEMORIES...
...AND DUPLICATED THEM IN THE BRAIN OF THE SUPERMAN-CLONE!

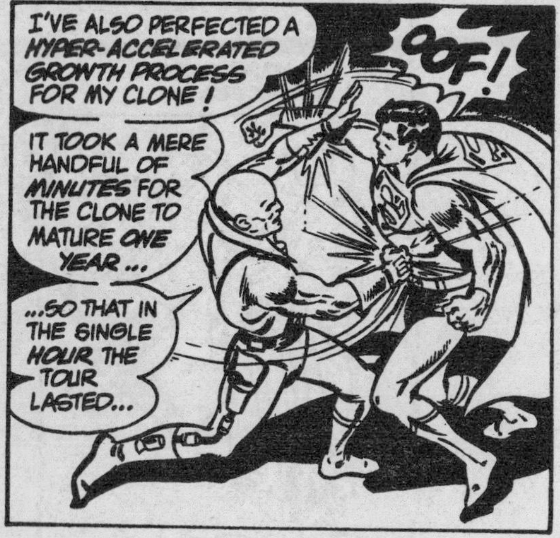
I'VE ALSO PERFECTED A HYPER-ACCELERATED GROWTH PROCESS FOR MY CLONE!
OOF!
IT TOOK A MERE HANDFUL OF MINUTES FOR THE CLONE TO MATURE ONE YEAR...
...SO THAT IN THE SINGLE HOUR THE TOUR LASTED...

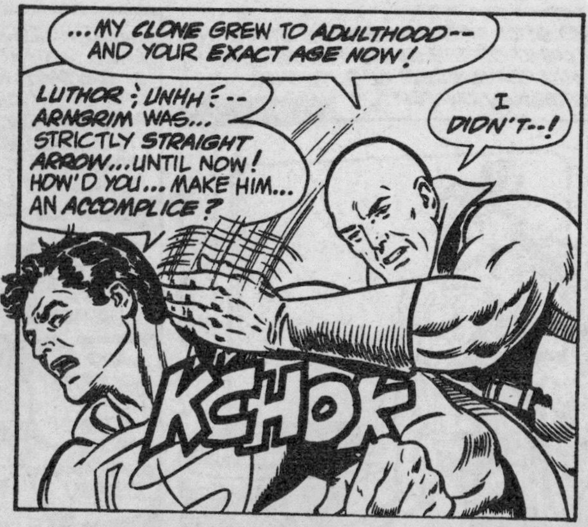
...MY CLONE GREW TO ADULTHOOD-- AND YOUR EXACT AGE NOW!
LUTHOR ; UNHH ; -- ARNGRIM WAS... STRICTLY STRAIGHT ARROW...UNTIL NOW! HOW'D YOU... MAKE HIM... AN ACCOMPLICE?
I DIDN'T--!
KCHOK

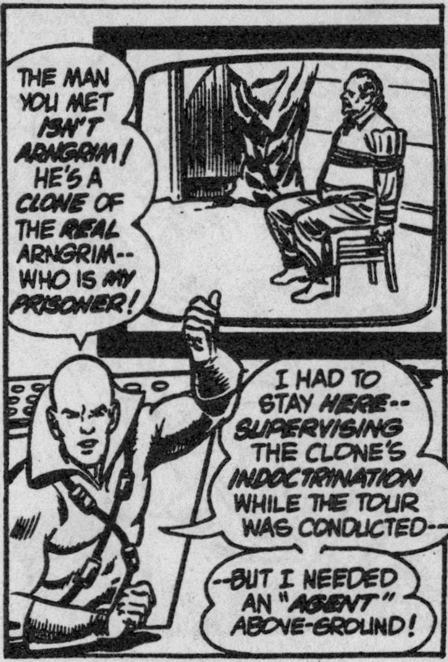
THE MAN YOU MET ISN'T ARNGRIM! HE'S A CLONE OF THE REAL ARNGRIM--WHO IS MY PRISONER!
I HAD TO STAY HERE--SUPERVISING THE CLONE'S INDOCTRINATION WHILE THE TOUR WAS CONDUCTED--
--BUT I NEEDED AN "AGENT" ABOVE-GROUND!

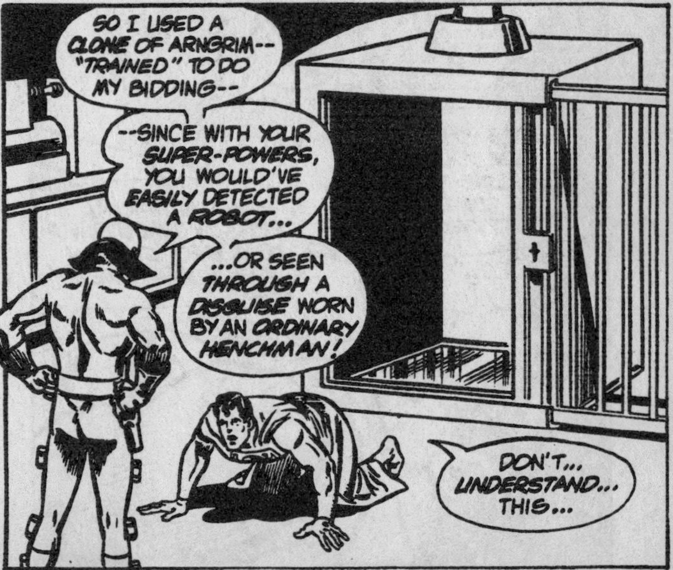
SO I USED A CLONE OF ARNGRIM--"TRAINED" TO DO MY BIDDING--
--SINCE WITH YOUR SUPER-POWERS, YOU WOULD'VE EASILY DETECTED A ROBOT...
...OR SEEN THROUGH A DISGUISE WORN BY AN ORDINARY HENCHMAN!
DON'T... UNDERSTAND... THIS...

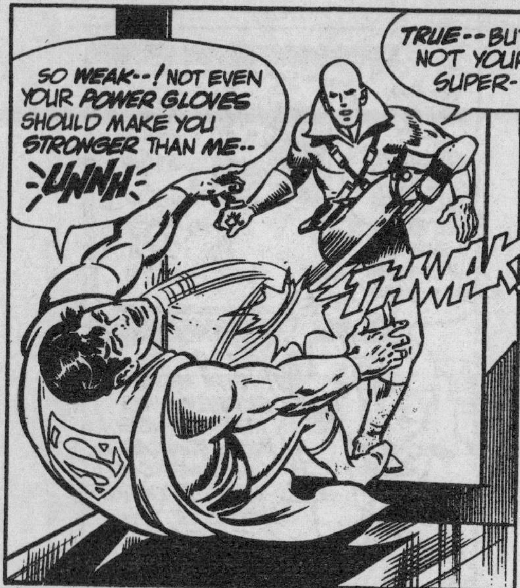
SO WEAK--! NOT EVEN YOUR POWER GLOVES SHOULD MAKE YOU STRONGER THAN ME-- UNNH
TRUE--BUT YOU'RE NOT YOUR USUAL SUPER-SELF--!
THWAK!

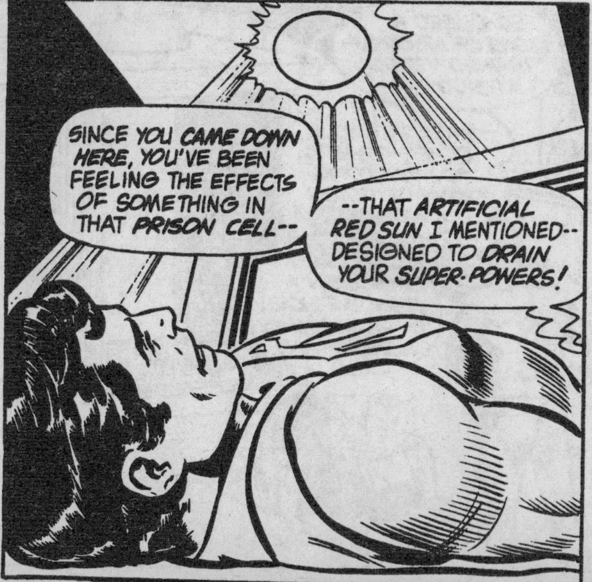
SINCE YOU CAME DOWN HERE, YOU'VE BEEN FEELING THE EFFECTS OF SOMETHING IN THAT PRISON CELL--
--THAT ARTIFICIAL RED SUN I MENTIONED--DESIGNED TO DRAIN YOUR SUPER-POWERS!

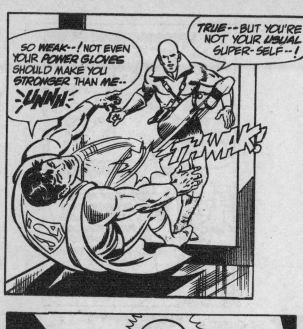

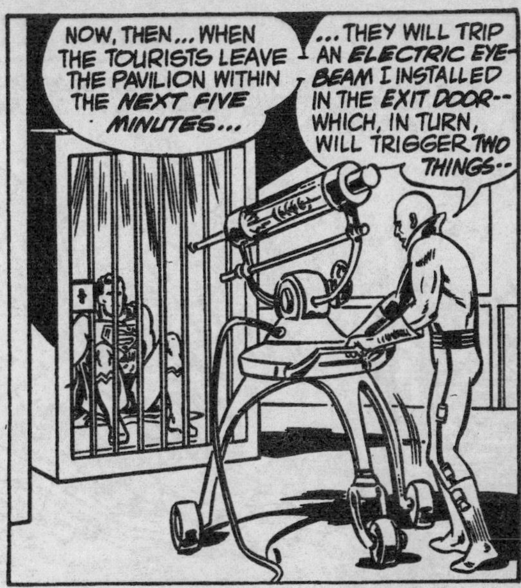
NOW, THEN... WHEN THE TOURISTS LEAVE THE PAVILION WITHIN THE *NEXT FIVE MINUTES*...
...THEY WILL TRIP AN *ELECTRIC EYE-BEAM* I INSTALLED IN THE *EXIT DOOR*--WHICH, IN TURN, WILL TRIGGER *TWO THINGS*--

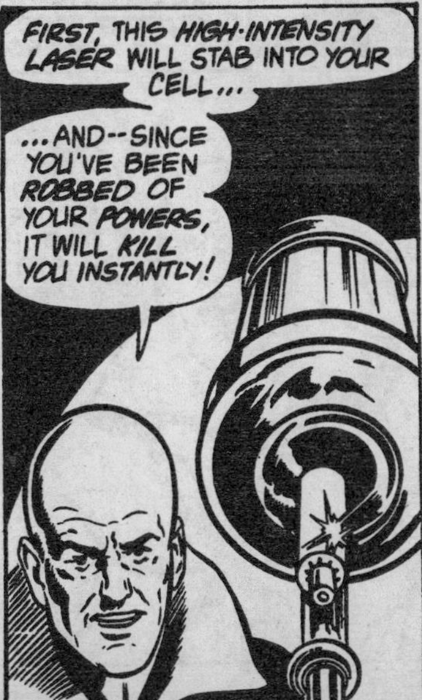
FIRST, THIS *HIGH-INTENSITY LASER* WILL STAB INTO *YOUR* CELL...
...AND--SINCE YOU'VE BEEN *ROBBED* OF YOUR *POWERS*, IT WILL *KILL* YOU INSTANTLY!

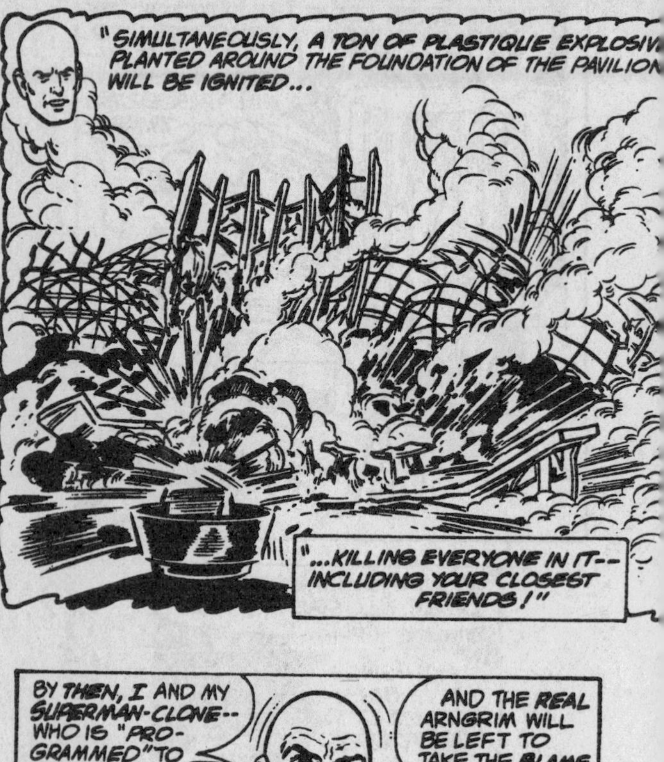
"SIMULTANEOUSLY, A TON OF PLASTIQUE EXPLOSIV
PLANTED AROUND THE FOUNDATION OF THE PAVILION
WILL BE IGNITED...
"...KILLING EVERYONE IN IT--
INCLUDING YOUR CLOSEST
FRIENDS!"

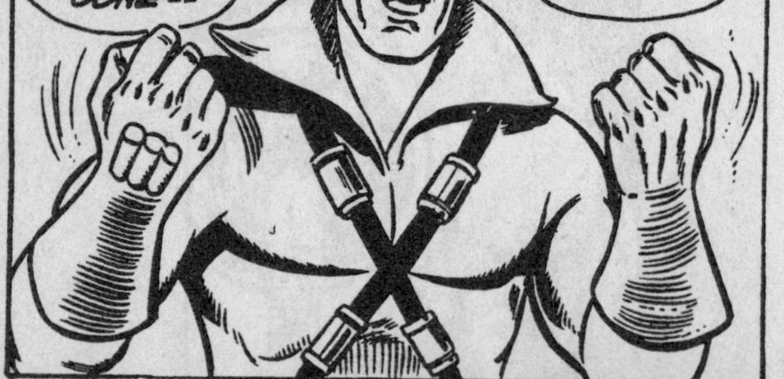
BY THEN, I AND MY SUPERMAN-CLONE--WHO IS "PROGRAMMED" TO SERVE ME--WILL BE LONG GONE--
AND THE REAL ARNGRIM WILL BE LEFT TO TAKE THE BLAME FOR THE DISASTER!

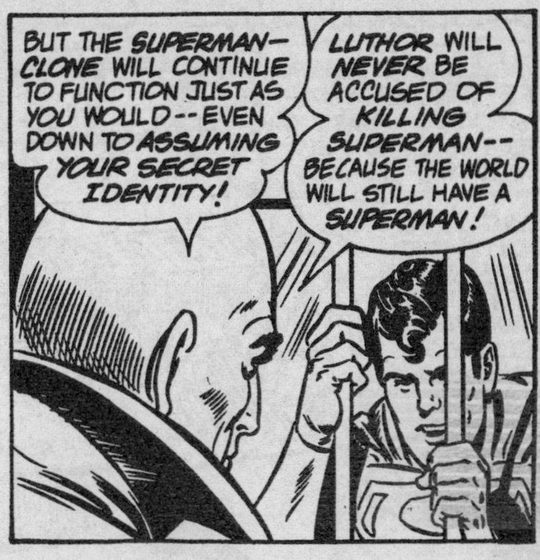
BUT THE SUPERMAN-CLONE WILL CONTINUE TO FUNCTION JUST AS YOU WOULD--EVEN DOWN TO ASSUMING YOUR SECRET IDENTITY!
LUTHOR WILL NEVER BE ACCUSED OF KILLING SUPERMAN--BECAUSE THE WORLD WILL STILL HAVE A SUPERMAN!

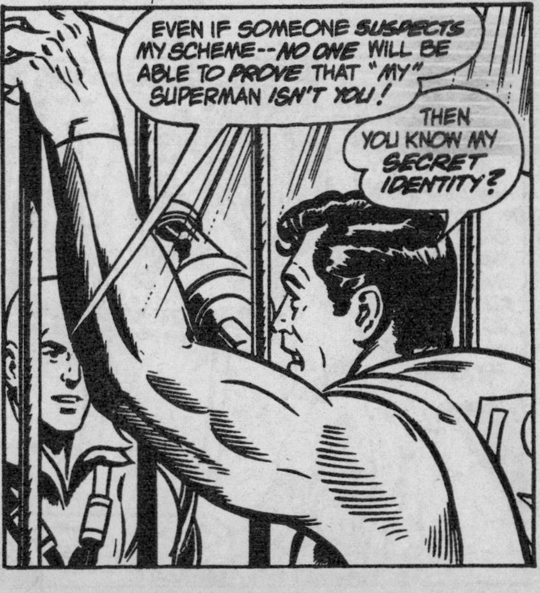
EVEN IF SOMEONE SUSPECTS MY SCHEME--NO ONE WILL BE ABLE TO PROVE THAT "MY" SUPERMAN ISN'T YOU!
THEN YOU KNOW MY SECRET IDENTITY?

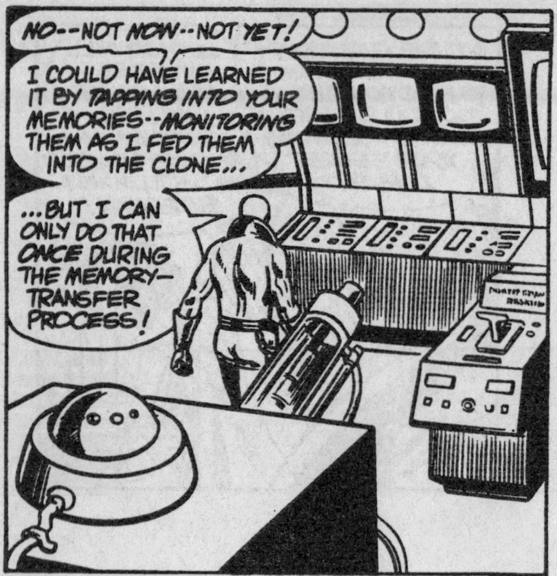
NO--NOT NOW--NOT YET!
I COULD HAVE LEARNED IT BY TAPPING INTO YOUR MEMORIES--MONITORING THEM AS I FED THEM INTO THE CLONE...
...BUT I CAN ONLY DO THAT ONCE DURING THE MEMORY-TRANSFER PROCESS!

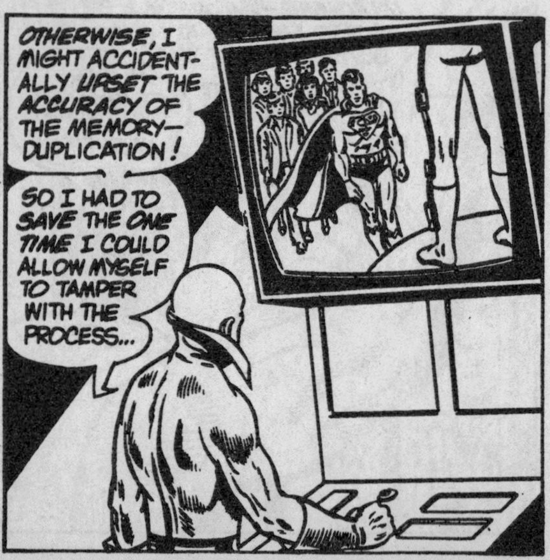
OTHERWISE, I MIGHT ACCIDENT-ALLY UPSET THE ACCURACY OF THE MEMORY-DUPLICATION!
SO I HAD TO SAVE THE ONE TIME I COULD ALLOW MYSELF TO TAMPER WITH THE PROCESS...

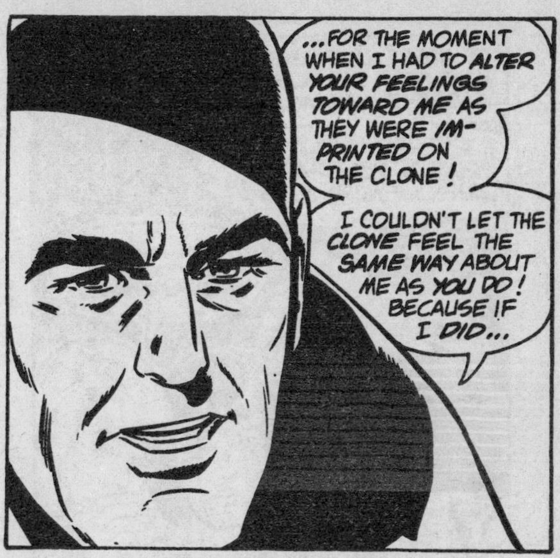
...FOR THE MOMENT WHEN I HAD TO ALTER YOUR FEELINGS TOWARD ME AS THEY WERE IM-PRINTED ON THE CLONE!
I COULDN'T LET THE CLONE FEEL THE SAME WAY ABOUT ME AS YOU DO! BECAUSE IF I DID...

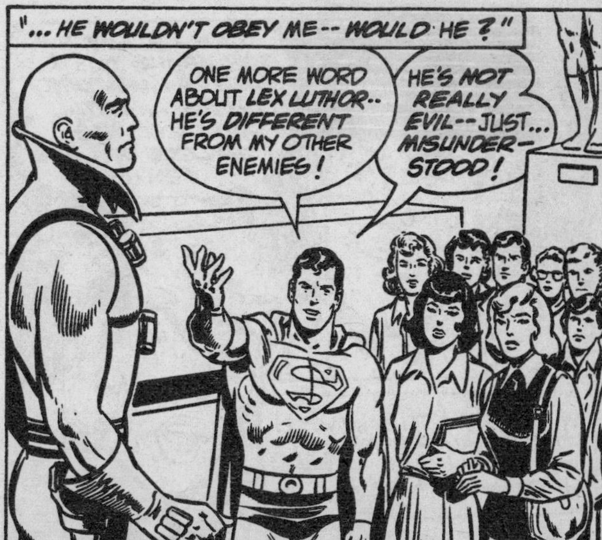
"... HE WOULDN'T OBEY ME -- WOULD HE ?"
ONE MORE WORD ABOUT LEX LUTHOR.. HE'S DIFFERENT FROM MY OTHER ENEMIES!
HE'S NOT REALLY EVIL -- JUST... MISUNDER-STOOD!

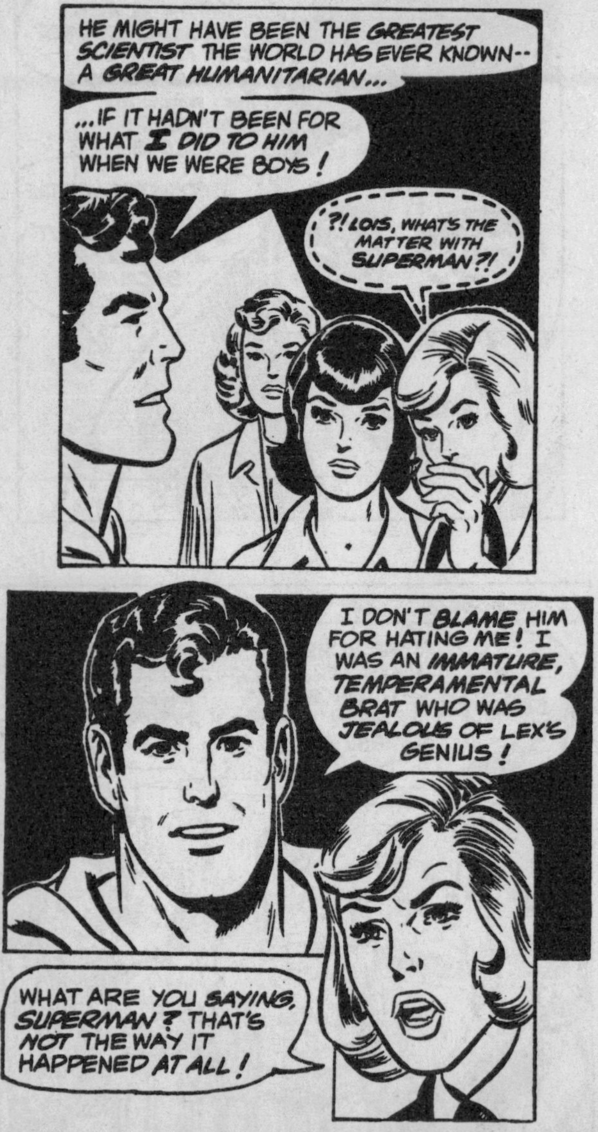
HE MIGHT HAVE BEEN THE GREATEST SCIENTIST THE WORLD HAS EVER KNOWN-- A GREAT HUMANITARIAN...
...IF IT HADN'T BEEN FOR WHAT I DID TO HIM WHEN WE WERE BOYS!
?! LOIS, WHAT'S THE MATTER WITH SUPERMAN?!
I DON'T BLAME HIM FOR HATING ME! I WAS AN IMMATURE, TEMPERAMENTAL BRAT WHO WAS JEALOUS OF LEX'S GENIUS!
WHAT ARE YOU SAYING, SUPERMAN? THAT'S NOT THE WAY IT HAPPENED AT ALL!

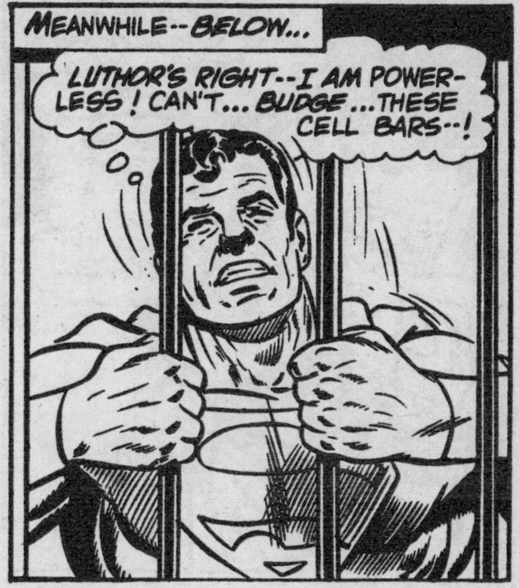
MEANWHILE--BELOW...
LUTHOR'S RIGHT--I AM POWER-LESS! CAN'T... BUDGE... THESE CELL BARS--!

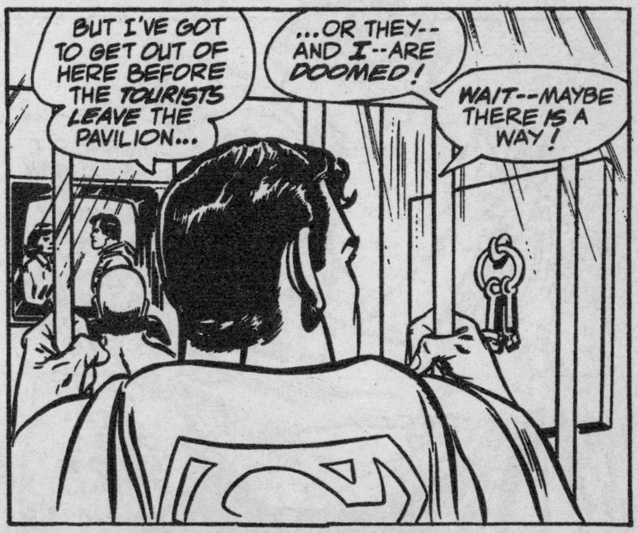
BUT I'VE GOT TO GET OUT OF HERE BEFORE THE TOURISTS LEAVE THE PAVILION...
...OR THEY--AND I--ARE DOOMED!
WAIT--MAYBE THERE IS A WAY!

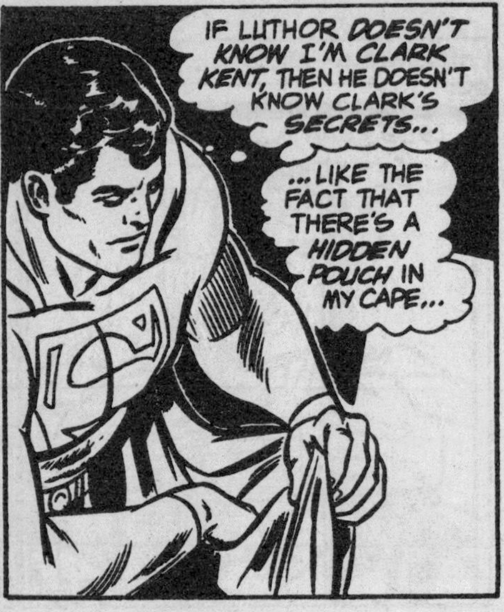
IF LUTHOR DOESN'T KNOW I'M CLARK KENT, THEN HE DOESN'T KNOW CLARK'S SECRETS...
...LIKE THE FACT THAT THERE'S A HIDDEN POUCH IN MY CAPE...

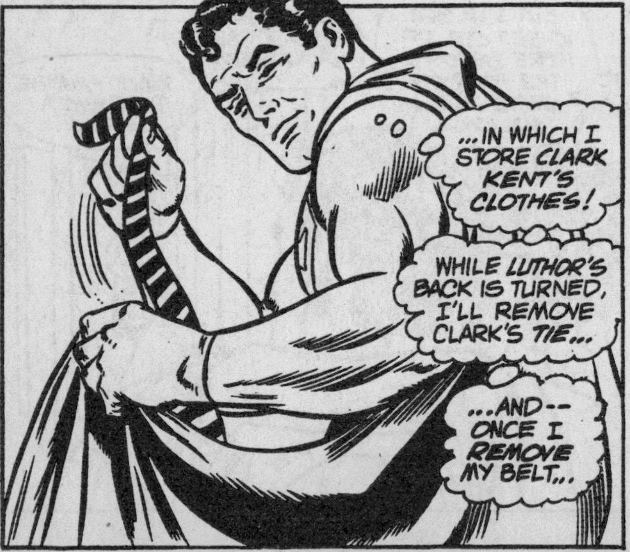
...IN WHICH I STORE CLARK KENT'S CLOTHES!
WHILE LUTHOR'S BACK IS TURNED, I'LL REMOVE CLARK'S TIE...
...AND-- ONCE I REMOVE MY BELT...

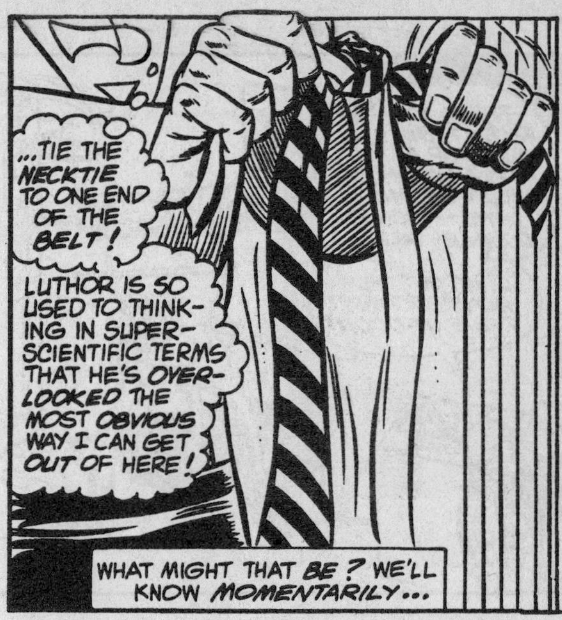
...TIE THE NECKTIE TO ONE END OF THE BELT!
LUTHOR IS SO USED TO THINKING IN SUPER-SCIENTIFIC TERMS THAT HE'S OVERLOOKED THE MOST OBVIOUS WAY I CAN GET OUT OF HERE!
WHAT MIGHT THAT BE? WE'LL KNOW MOMENTARILY...

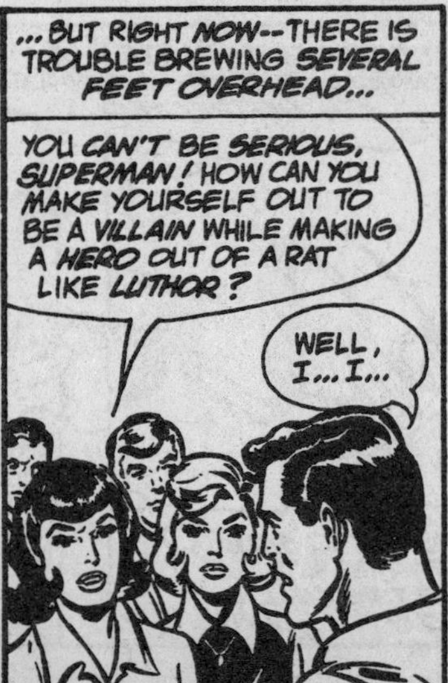
...BUT RIGHT NOW--THERE IS TROUBLE BREWING SEVERAL FEET OVERHEAD...
YOU CAN'T BE SERIOUS, SUPERMAN! HOW CAN YOU MAKE YOURSELF OUT TO BE A VILLAIN WHILE MAKING A HERO OUT OF A RAT LIKE LUTHOR?
WELL, I... I...

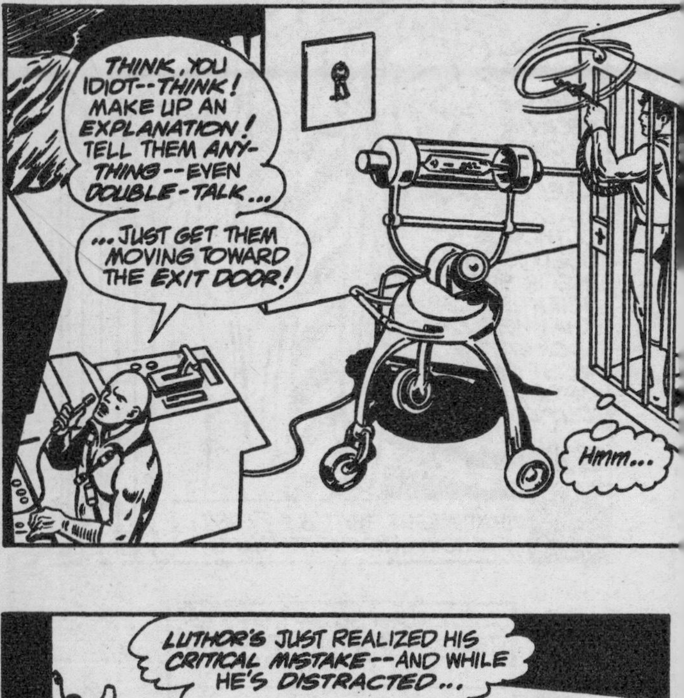
THINK, YOU IDIOT--THINK! MAKE UP AN EXPLANATION! TELL THEM ANYTHING--EVEN DOUBLE-TALK...
...JUST GET THEM MOVING TOWARD THE EXIT DOOR!
Hmm...

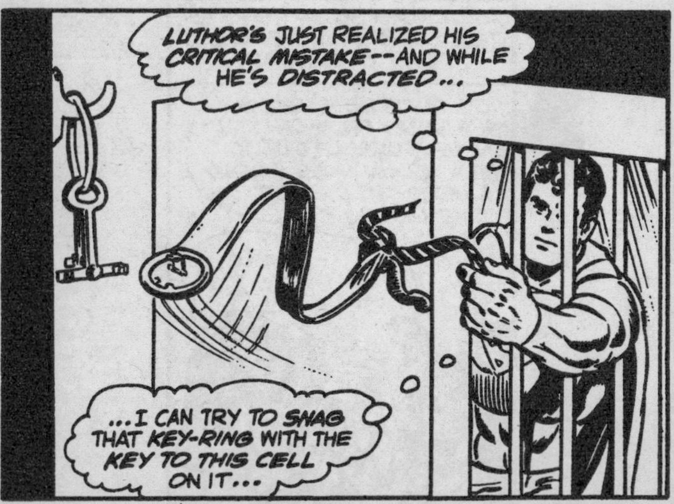
LUTHOR'S JUST REALIZED HIS CRITICAL MISTAKE--AND WHILE HE'S DISTRACTED...
...I CAN TRY TO SNAG THAT KEY-RING WITH THE KEY TO THIS CELL ON IT...

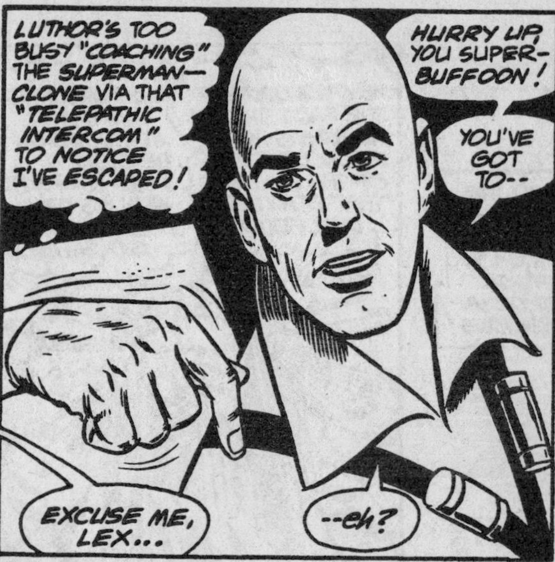
LUTHOR'S TOO BUSY "COACHING" THE SUPERMAN-CLONE VIA THAT "TELEPATHIC INTERCOM" TO NOTICE I'VE ESCAPED!
HURRY UP, YOU SUPER-BUFFOON!
YOU'VE GOT TO--
EXCUSE ME, LEX...
--eh?
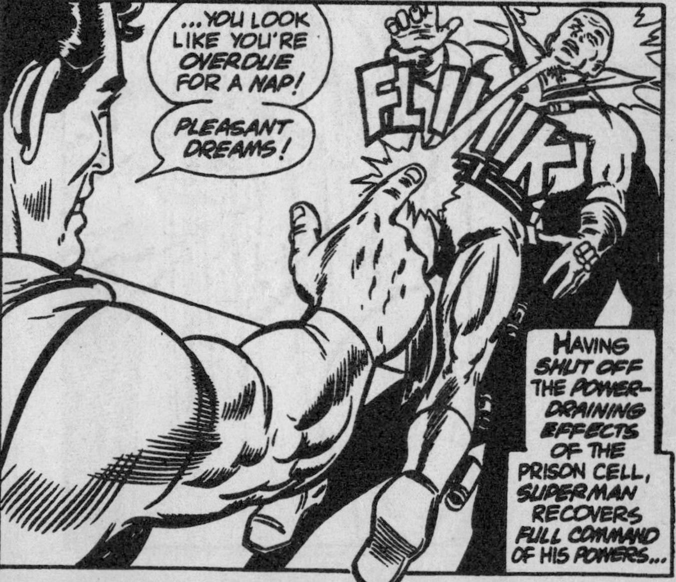
...YOU LOOK LIKE YOU'RE OVERDUE FOR A NAP!
PLEASANT DREAMS!
FLIIIK
HAVING SHUT OFF THE POWER-DRAINING EFFECTS OF THE PRISON CELL, SUPERMAN RECOVERS FULL COMMAND OF HIS POWERS...

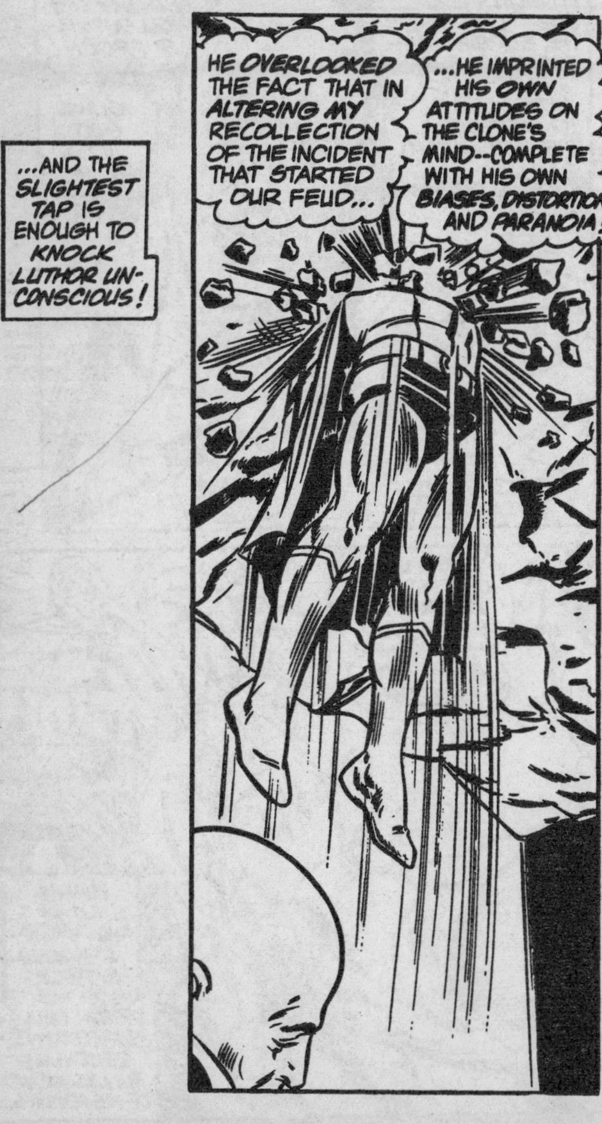
...AND THE SLIGHTEST TAP IS ENOUGH TO KNOCK LUTHOR UN-CONSCIOUS!
HE OVERLOOKED THE FACT THAT IN ALTERING MY RECOLLECTION OF THE INCIDENT THAT STARTED OUR FEUD...
...HE IMPRINTED HIS OWN ATTITUDES ON THE CLONE'S MIND--COMPLETE WITH HIS OWN BIASES, DISTORTIONS, AND PARANOIA!

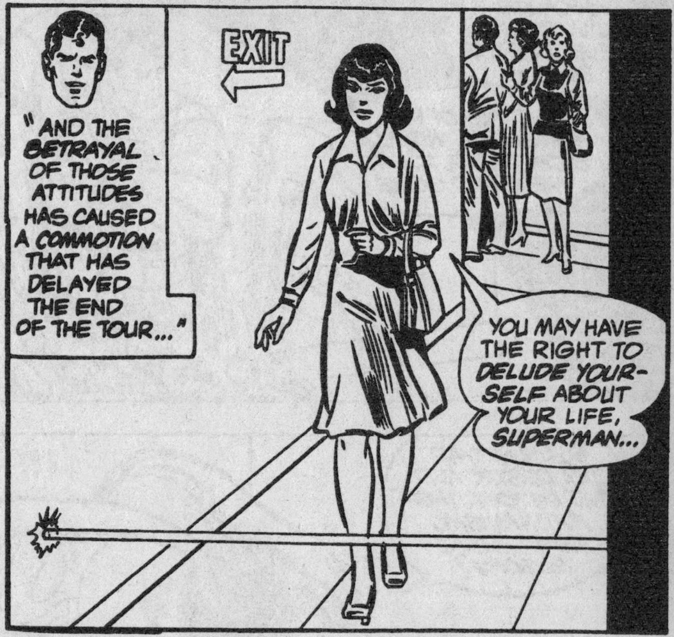
"AND THE BETRAYAL OF THOSE ATTITUDES HAS CAUSED A COMMOTION THAT HAS DELAYED THE END OF THE TOUR..."
EXIT
YOU MAY HAVE THE RIGHT TO DELUDE YOURSELF ABOUT YOUR LIFE, SUPERMAN...

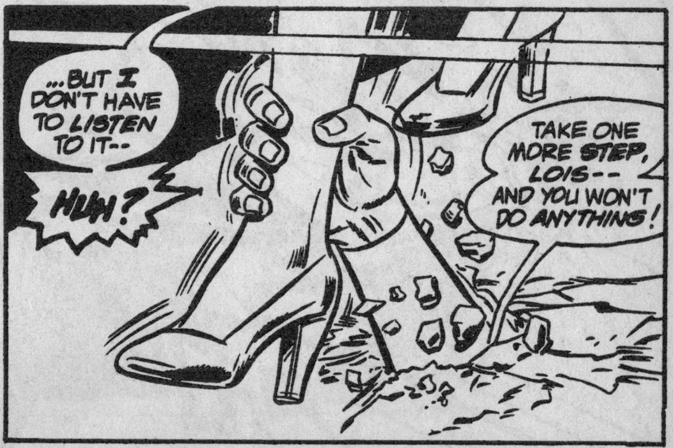
...BUT I DON'T HAVE TO LISTEN TO IT--
HUH?
TAKE ONE MORE STEP, LOIS-- AND YOU WON'T DO ANYTHING!

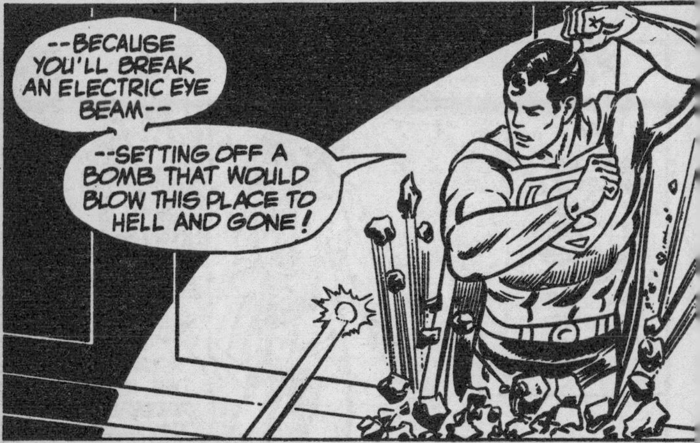
--BECAUSE YOU'LL BREAK AN ELECTRIC EYE BEAM--
--SETTING OFF A BOMB THAT WOULD BLOW THIS PLACE TO HELL AND GONE!

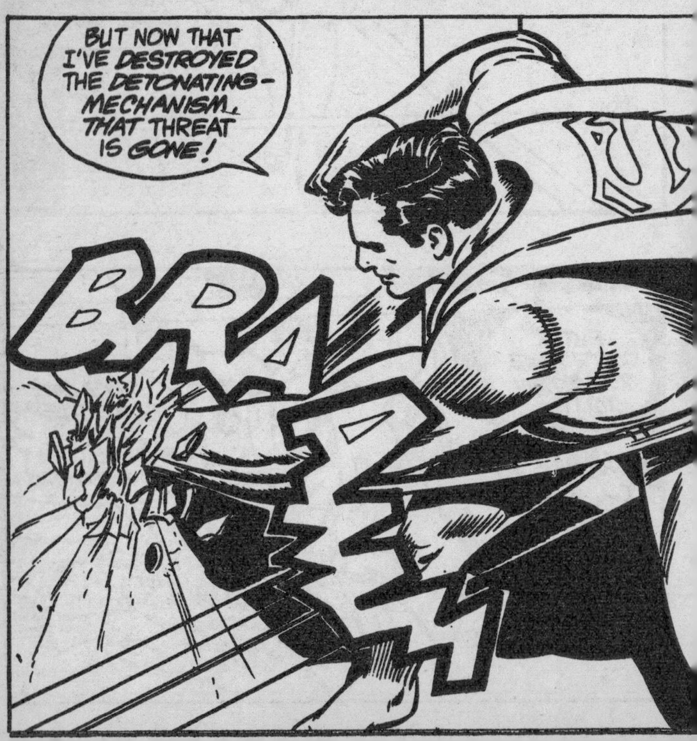
BUT NOW THAT I'VE DESTROYED THE DETONATING-MECHANISM, THAT THREAT IS GONE!

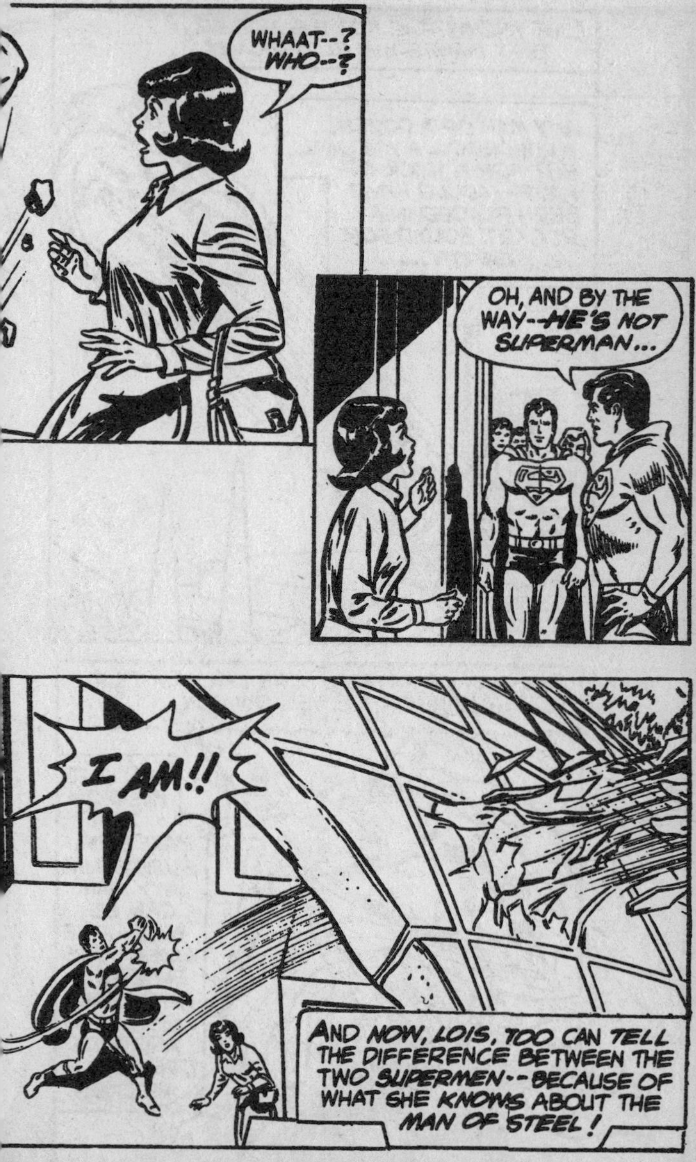
WHAAT--? WHO--?
OH, AND BY THE WAY--HE'S NOT SUPERMAN...
I AM!!
AND NOW, LOIS, TOO CAN TELL THE DIFFERENCE BETWEEN THE TWO SUPERMEN--BECAUSE OF WHAT SHE KNOWS ABOUT THE MAN OF STEEL!

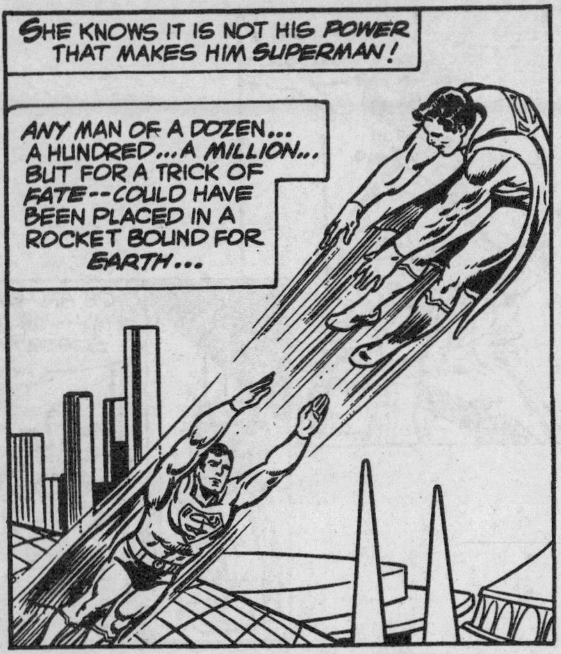
SHE KNOWS IT IS NOT HIS POWER THAT MAKES HIM SUPERMAN!
ANY MAN OF A DOZEN... A HUNDRED...A MILLION... BUT FOR A TRICK OF FATE--COULD HAVE BEEN PLACED IN A ROCKET BOUND FOR EARTH...

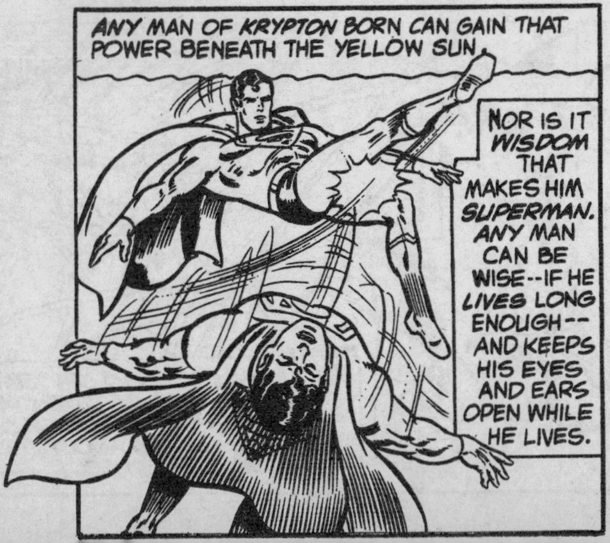
ANY MAN OF KRYPTON BORN CAN GAIN THAT POWER BENEATH THE YELLOW SUN.
NOR IS IT WISDOM THAT MAKES HIM SUPERMAN. ANY MAN CAN BE WISE--IF HE LIVES LONG ENOUGH--AND KEEPS HIS EYES AND EARS OPEN WHILE HE LIVES.

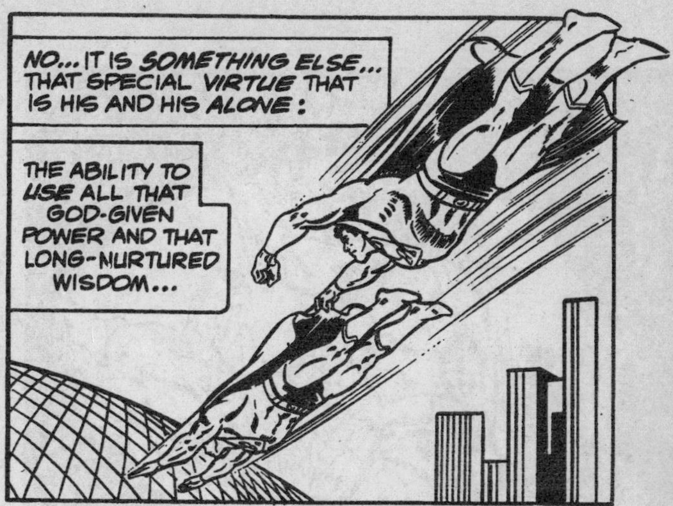
NO... IT IS SOMETHING ELSE... THAT SPECIAL VIRTUE THAT IS HIS AND HIS ALONE:
THE ABILITY TO USE ALL THAT GOD-GIVEN POWER AND THAT LONG-NURTURED WISDOM...

...IN THE NAME OF KINDNESS... ETHICS... MORALITY--THE THING MEN CALL "GOOD"...

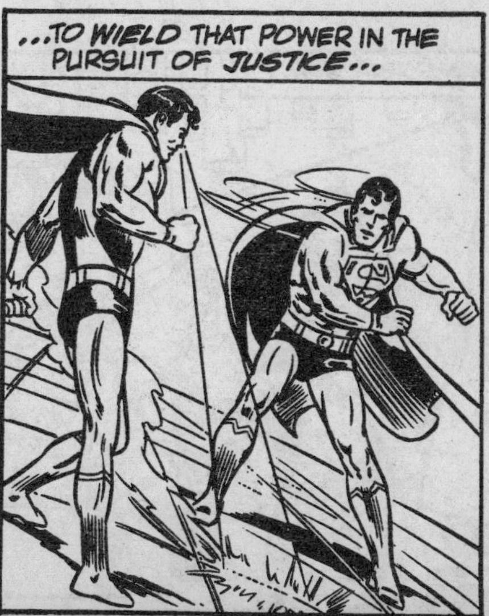
...TO WIELD THAT POWER IN THE PURSUIT OF JUSTICE...

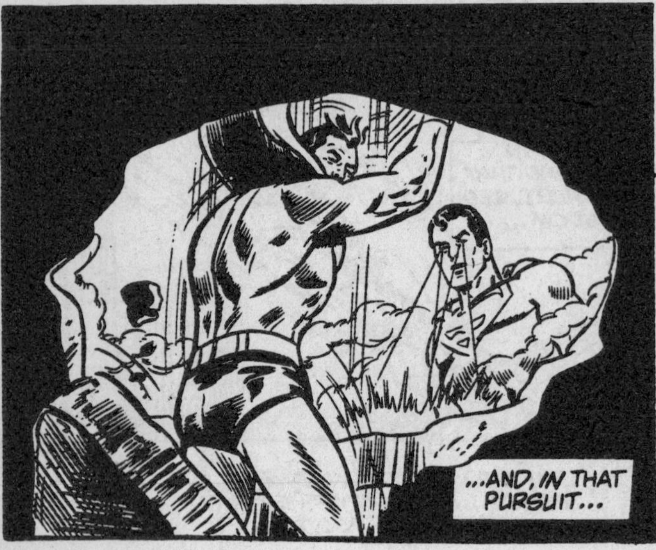
...AND, IN THAT PURSUIT...

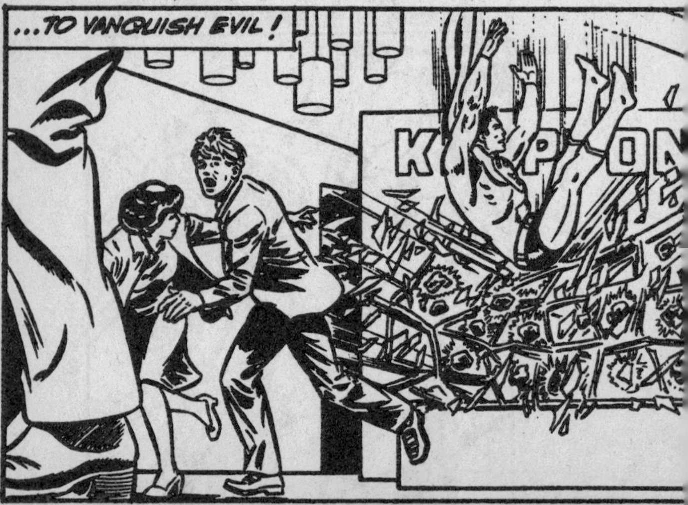
...TO VANQUISH EVIL!

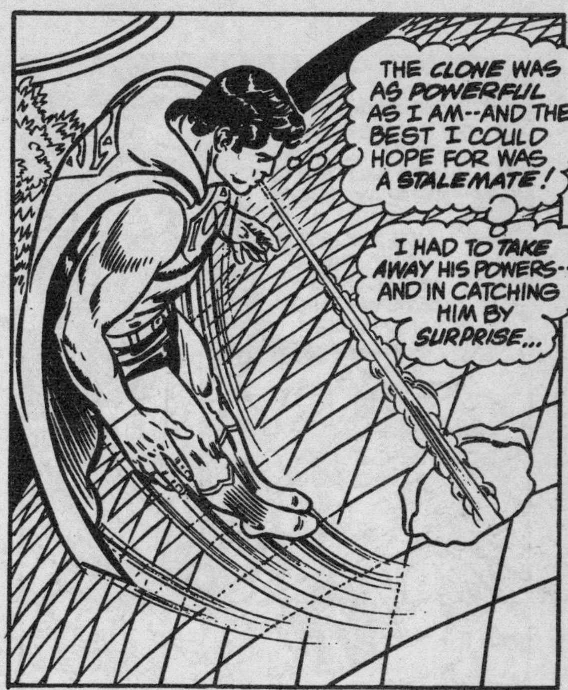
THE CLONE WAS AS POWERFUL AS I AM--AND THE BEST I COULD HOPE FOR WAS A STALEMATE!
I HAD TO TAKE AWAY HIS POWERS--AND IN CATCHING HIM BY SURPRISE...

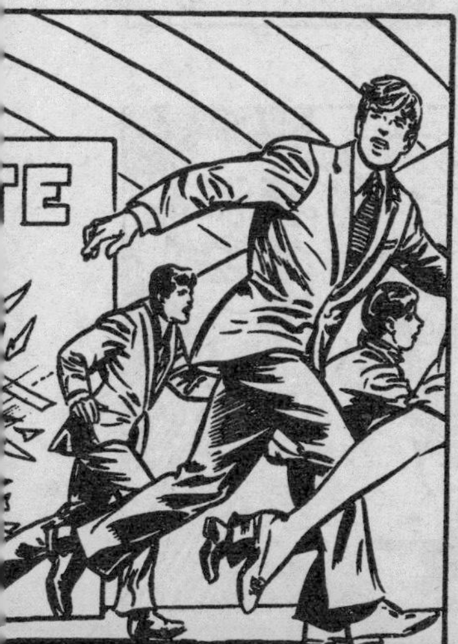

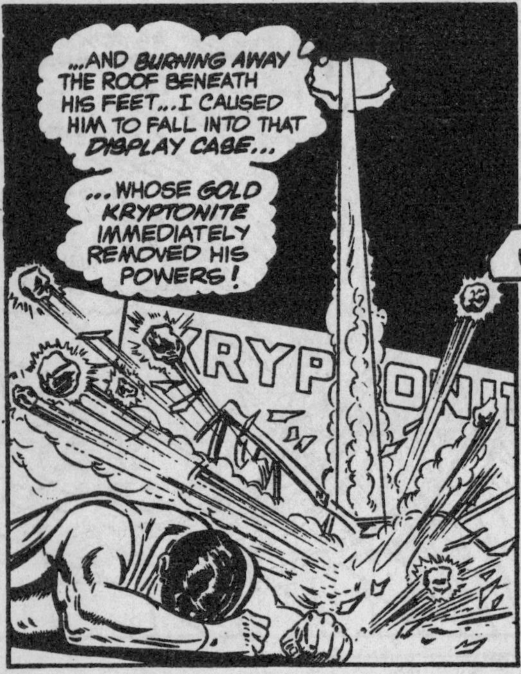
...AND BURNING AWAY THE ROOF BENEATH HIS FEET...I CAUSED HIM TO FALL INTO THAT DISPLAY CASE...
...WHOSE GOLD KRYPTONITE IMMEDIATELY REMOVED HIS POWERS!
KRYP ONIT

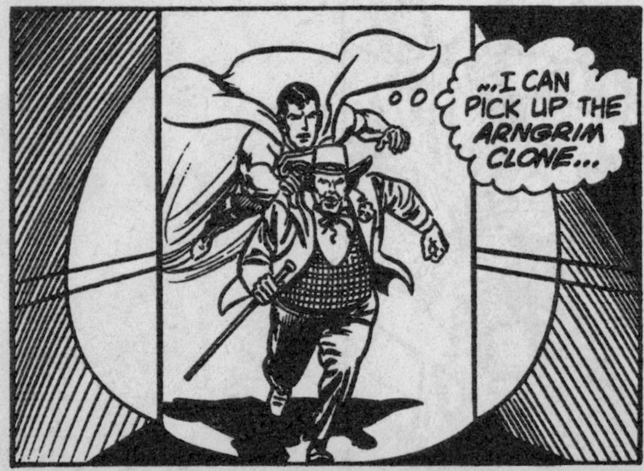
...I CAN PICK UP THE ARNGRIM CLONE...

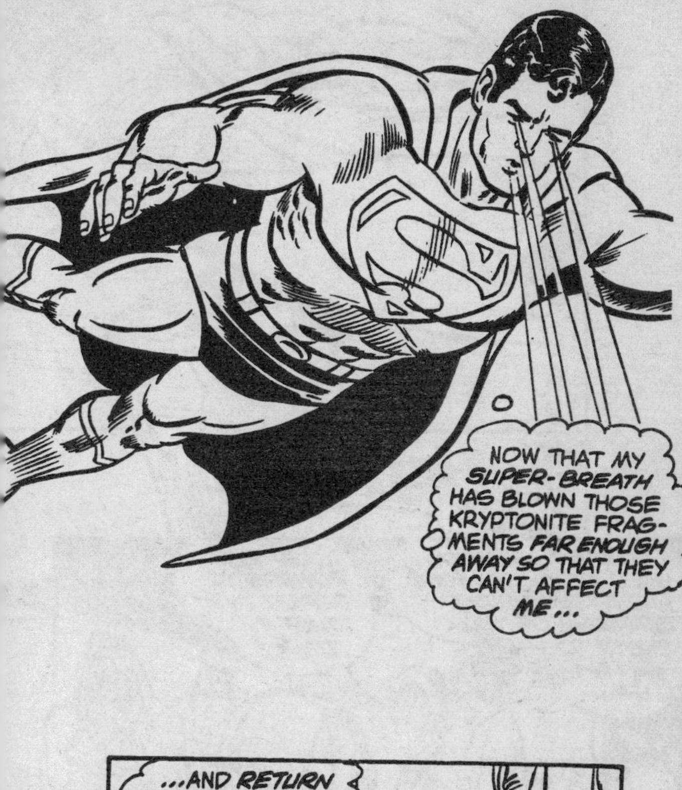
NOW THAT MY SUPER-BREATH HAS BLOWN THOSE KRYPTONITE FRAG-MENTS FAR ENOUGH AWAY SO THAT THEY CAN'T AFFECT ME...

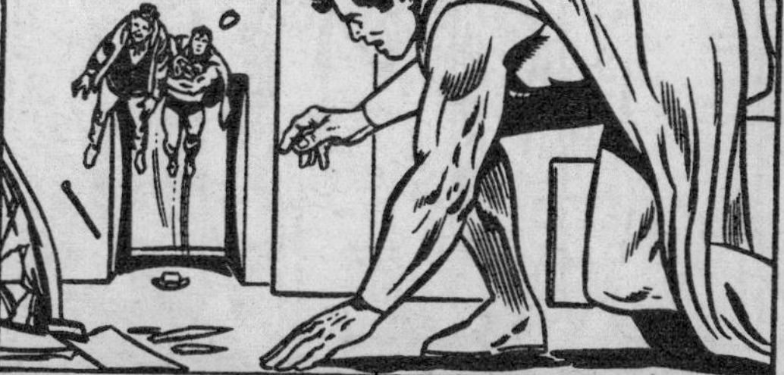
...AND RETURN TO THE SCENE OF THE FRACAS!

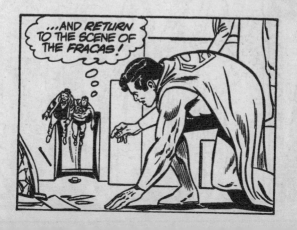

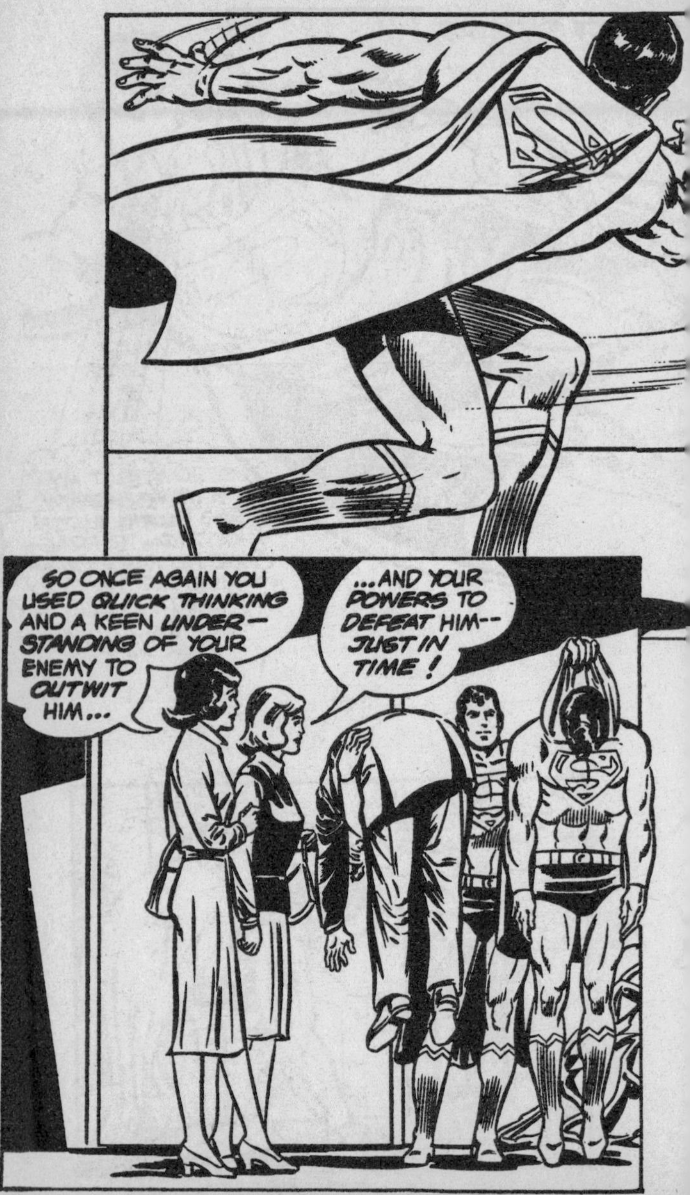
SO ONCE AGAIN YOU USED QUICK THINKING AND A KEEN UNDER-STANDING OF YOUR ENEMY TO OUTWIT HIM...
...AND YOUR POWERS TO DEFEAT HIM--JUST IN TIME!

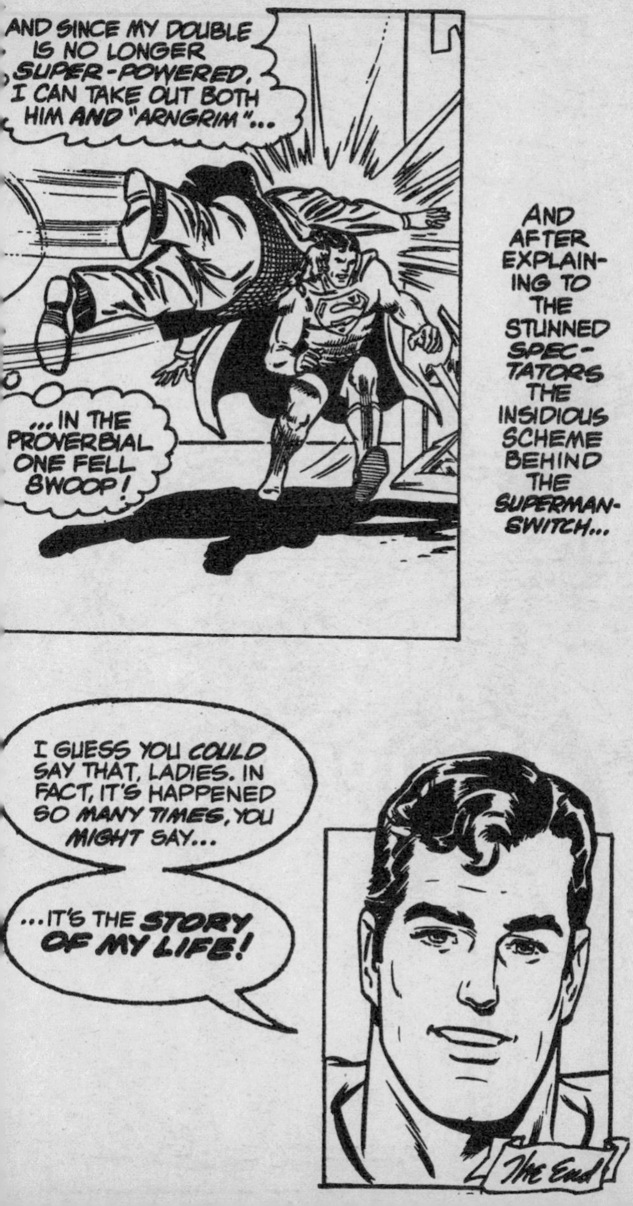
AND SINCE MY DOUBLE IS NO LONGER SUPER-POWERED, I CAN TAKE OUT BOTH HIM AND "ARNGRIM"...
...IN THE PROVERBIAL ONE FELL SWOOP!
AND AFTER EXPLAINING TO THE STUNNED SPECTATORS THE INSIDIOUS SCHEME BEHIND THE SUPERMAN-SWITCH...
I GUESS YOU COULD SAY THAT, LADIES. IN FACT, IT'S HAPPENED SO MANY TIMES, YOU MIGHT SAY...
...IT'S THE STORY OF MY LIFE!
The End

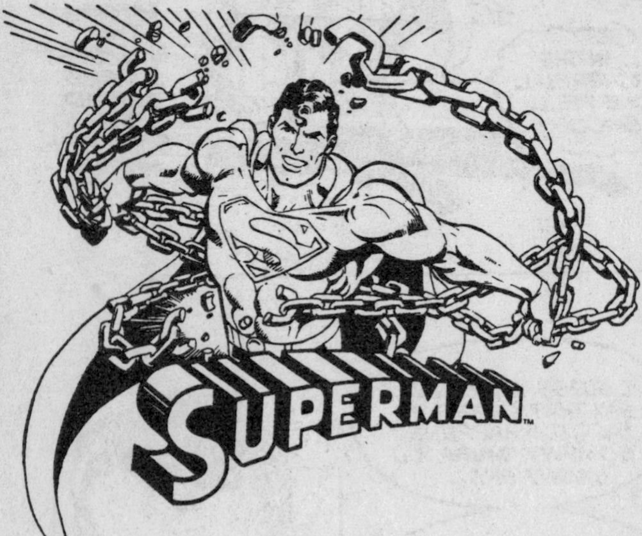
SUPERMAN™